AGENTS AND VOICES

AGENTS AND VOICES

A PANORAMA OF MEDIA EDUCATION IN BRAZIL, PORTUGAL AND SPAIN

Ed. Ilana Eleá

The International Clearinghouse on
CHILDREN, YOUTH & MEDIA
at NORDICOM, University of Gothenburg

Agents and Voices

A Panorama of Media Education in Brazil, Portugal and Spain

Editor: Ilana Eleá

This book is the English version of the 2014 yearbook *Agentes e Vozes: Um Panorama da Mídia-Educação no Brasil, Portugal e Espanha*, published by the International Clearinghouse on Children, Youth and Media at Nordicom, University of Gothenburg.

ISBN 978-91-87957-06-2

Published by:
The International Clearinghouse on Children, Youth and Media

Nordicom
University of Gothenburg
Box 713
SE 405 30 Göteborg
Sweden

Cover by: Karin Persson

Printed by: Taberg Media Group AB, Taberg, Sweden, 2015

MILJÖMÄRKT

3041 0271

Contents

PORTUGAL

Children, Youth and Media

Media Education: Public Policies, Curricular Proposals and Teacher Training

An Overview of Practices in Portugal

Preface

The anthology *Agents and Voices: a Panorama of Media Education in Brazil, Portugal and Spain* aims to contribute to strengthening international networks, the visibility of current research, and the exchange of experience regarding strategies and challenges, while promoting the field in each context.

Agents and Voices is the English version of the 2014 yearbook *Agentes e Vozes: Um Panorama da Mídia-Educação no Brasil, Portugal e Espanha*, published in Portuguese and Spanish by the International Clearinghouse on Children, Youth and Media at Nordicom, University of Gothenburg.

It is important to note that *Agentes e Vozes* was the first time the Clearinghouse had organized a publication in the languages of its authors, Portuguese and Spanish, the official languages of more than 30 countries in Latin America, Africa and Europe. This has long been a wish of the Clearinghouse.

By publishing the book in English as well, we aim to facilitate the spread of information and the partnership among countries, reaching an even wider, intercontinental audience of interlocutors.

Göteborg, August 2015

Ilana Eleá
Scientific Coordinator
The International Clearinghouse on Children, Youth and Media
Nordicom, University of Gothenburg

Introduction

Ilana Eleá

The anthology "Agents and voices: a panorama of media education in Brazil, Portugal and Spain" aims to contribute to strengthening international networks, the visibility of current research, and the exchange of experience regarding strategies and challenges, while promoting the field in each respective context.

To facilitate the spread of information and the partnership among these countries, it is important to note that this is the first time the International Clearinghouse on Children, Youth and Media has organized a publication in the language spoken by its authors, Portuguese and Spanish, the official languages of more than 30 countries located in Latin America, Africa and Europe. This has long been a wish of the Clearinghouse.

Despite having different cultural, economic and educational realities, Brazil, Portugal and Spain share common aspects in the field of media education encompassed by this anthology. The importance of using, analysing, and producing media with an educational outlook has been bravely defended by social movements since the dictatorship periods in these three countries, with a great upheaval of actions aiming at freedom of expression, youth protagonism and the exercise of citizenship. The works of Paulo Freire and Célestin Freinet are often referred to as sources of inspiration.

Since the sixties, Europe, the US, and Canada have been deemed pioneers in bringing together education and media. The first official declaration on behalf of media education was signed by UNESCO in 1982 in Grünwald, West Germany. Since then, alongside developments in the US, Europe has been focusing on a theoretical and practical systematization of this field. This includes curricular experimentation, investments in research, publications, and national associations, especially in France and the UK.

In Brazil, although "media education" was in practice before this term was established, it was only after the year 2000 – which saw the 4th World Summit on Media for Children and Adolescents supported by UNESCO in Rio de Janeiro, Brazil – that the need for a liaison among researchers, media educators, producers and teachers in the field of media education gained new expression and magnitude. The works of David Buckingham, and the formative exchange and development of joint research with Pier Cesare Rivoltella from the Catholic University of the Sacred Heart in Milan, played an important role in bringing together Brazilian and European universities. Monica Fantin's chapter in this anthology is devoted to mapping these intersections.

This book offers an understanding of how isolated investments on behalf of "digital inclusion" in schools have been a generic axis shared by public policy managers in Brazil, Portugal and Spain. Some researchers point to some uncertainty regarding how "digital inclusion" has been planned and implemented at the policy level. According to worldwide efforts made to promote media education (Grünwald Declaration, 1982; Vienna Conference, 1999; Alexandria Proclamation, 2005; Paris Agenda, 2007; MILID Network, 2011; Paris Declaration, 2014), the focus on the instrumental use of media in schools would be considered below the standards of the expected education level for children and youngsters today.

After all, there can be no "digital inclusion" disconnected from a comprehensive political project that invests in the education of teachers (as well as journalists, media professionals, and librarians) – a project that allows improvement in school curricula so that there is room for media education to flow. There is also little evidence that providing schools with computers, tablets and Internet is sufficient, especially if the critical analysis and the creative and collaborative production by children and youngsters using media are not integrated into these actions.

Conceptual compass

In 2011, UNESCO – the institution responsible for the official and worldwide spread of the term "media education" since the seventies – made an important change. Due to technological advances in telecommunications, and the intense proliferation of information being created, accessed and shared daily by children and youth, the challenge of searching, selecting and evaluating the relevance and reliability of this information became the premise used to synch the current demands of contemporary society. The concept currently proposed by UNESCO is *Media and Information Literacy.*

> On the one hand, information literacy emphasizes the importance of access to information and the evaluation and ethical use of such information. On the other hand, media literacy emphasizes the ability to understand media functions, evaluate how those functions are performed and to rationally engage with

media for self-expression. The MIL Curriculum and Competency Framework for Teachers incorporates both ideas. (UNESCO, 2011, p.18)

The document is timely, and deserves careful reading. The new term is not only rhetorical, a package that can be easily promoted and shared. It is also a consequence of the need to modernize pedagogical approaches. Media and information are inseparable fields of study, platforms for analysing the world and areas of participation, literacy and citizenship.

For now, although the authors of this anthology may use different terminologies such as media education, education for the media, media literacy, media competence and educommunication, the general interest seems to be common and there are, thus, more convergences than divergences in this field today.

The reader may be wondering: with so many terms used in Brazil, Portugal and Spain to define what "educate with", "educate for" and "educate through" media might mean (Rivoltella, 2002), why does this anthology prioritize the concept of media education over others? This question encompasses the curiosity and perhaps the astonishment of those who encounter a set of concepts, translations and ideas that at first seem very similar. It is no wonder that this multiplicity of terms may require a short clarification at the beginning of a conversation (or in the introduction of a book).

David Buckingham's (2003) attempt to draw a distinction around these terms is still current, and can be used as a reference in this conceptual entanglement: while media literacy, media and information literacy and their respective translations can be translated into the kind of literacy expected at the present time, i.e. knowledge and competence to be constructed, media education refers to the essential process of teaching and learning necessary for such literacy. In the absence of a definitive term that can be translated from English to Portuguese and Spanish, here we use the concept of media education, hoping that the reader is aware of its implicit subtleties.

Inspiring partnerships

This book both celebrates and seeks to intensify a growing exchange between researchers through conferences and events, in integrated research projects, and in support for writing letters and declarations for Media Education. In Brazil, *Universidade Federal do Triângulo Mineiro* (the Federal University of Triângulo Mineiro), UNESCO's partner, has translated its new curriculum for the education of teachers and integrated it into its licentiate courses.

Regarding the education of professionals in social communications, the group coordinated by Ismar Soares in Brazil has been recognized for its expertise and projects in Educommunication – a field that inspires a new licentiate course for students from ECA-USP and UFCG. At PUC-Rio, the newly launched undergraduate course Production and Management in Media Education coordinated by Rosalia Duarte stands out for its pioneering structure.

In September 2014, the cross-institutional project Media Competencies in Brazilian and Euro-American scenarios, coordinated by Universidade Federal de Juiz de Fora (in partnership with other Brazilian universities and Universidade de Huelva, Spain), was launched during the First International Symposium for Media Literacy. Headquartered in the same institution are the popular Comunicar group and journal. The European and American inter-university research network ALFAMED, led by Ignácio Aguaded, investigates media competencies for citizenship in Spain, Portugal, Italy, Argentina, Chile, Colombia, Ecuador, Venezuela, Bolivia, Mexico, and Brazil.

The Cabinet of Communication and Education at the Universidad Autônoma de Barcelona, with its 20-year-old Master's program in communication and education, has made a great contribution in the European Union, especially thanks to the active leadership of José Manuel Pérez Tornero. Lastly, the European Media Literacy Observatory and EMEDUS projects deserve special attention.

In academia, Portugal and Brazil continuously cooperate in the field of media education in many settings, with a great flow of exchange students at the doctoral level and research cooperation. In his article, Manuel Pinto narrates the singularity and autonomous nature of GILM ("Informal Group about Media Literacy"). Active since 2009 in Portugal, the organization is responsible for a number of partnerships, initiatives and programmes, such as the annual event "Seven Days with Media". The Portuguese section ends with the Simone Pretella's careful study of cross-generational dialogues (the generation of children and their grandparents) interwoven with media-educational tips as a relevant case for social inclusion.

In the Brazilian section, Adriana Fresquet also touches on themes regarding social inclusion, where she invites hospitalized, sight- and hearing-impaired children to attend film workshops. By combining media production *by* children and youth with quality benchmarks in media production *for* all children and youth, this becomes a key to guaranteeing the expression of citizenship and inclusion. This kind of inclusion should be one that reflects the dignity of each individual child and adult, that celebrates and values all kinds of diversity free from stereotypes, and that nourishes and reflects positive aspects of local cultures and traditions (Kolucki & Lemish, 2011).

In addition, researchers in Brazil, Portugal and Spain have been exchanging experiences and mutually benefitting from a programme of international cooperation promoted by the London School of Economics (LSE). Through the project EU Kids Online, a common agenda of investigation has been created to learn how children and youth use the Internet and, specifically, the risks and opportunities experienced by different age groups in their online browsing experiences.

The project currently has 150 European researchers in 33 countries, including Brazil since 2012 (thanks to CETIC.br, linked to the Brazilian Internet Steering Committee). In this anthology, Cristina Ponte, coordinator of the research team for EU Kids Online in Portugal, conducts an interesting appraisal of the project *E-escolinhas*, a public initiative in this country.

In "Agents and Voices", authors comment on the extent to which the impact of the results of media use can influence the welcoming of media education into homes, schools and universities as well as teacher and journalist training courses. It also reveals how these results contribute to social movements, the way research with children and cyberculture is conducted and, lastly, how we can meet the supply based on the needs of the highly media-centred society we live in today. In addition, this anthology offers enthusiastic accounts of experiences with alternative ways of working in the classroom, the education of teachers and advertising professionals, and social projects that have media-based practices as their core activity.

It is important to point out that detailed mappings of the role of media education in Brazil have not yet been made, as opposed to Portugal and Spain, which have benefitted from the efforts of the European Union and the United Nations Alliance of Civilizations. Different large-scale programmes and studies have been conducted in Europe, such as *Current Trends and Approaches to Media Literacy* (2007), a *Study on Assessment Criteria for Media Literacy Levels* (2009), and *Film Literacy* (2012). In this book, the articles of Aguaded & Delgado (Spain) and Reia-Baptista (Portugal) comment on such initiatives, which we hope will encourage new possibilities for partnerships that from this point on include Brazil and other countries in Latin America.

The book and its structure

This collection brings together 29 articles divided into three parts concerning the production of each country being examined. In the first part, "Children, youth and media", research results regarding children and youth are presented from the viewpoint of cultural practices mediated by the convergence of media, new literacies and education. How has the everyday immersion of boys and girls in the digital media culture, characterized by the interactive and convergent use of media and the creation of content, been challenging the processes and content of school curricula?

In the second part, "Media education: public policies, curricular proposals and teacher training", the spotlight is placed on how governments and authorities have been dealing with investments in media education, projects, partnerships between academic research, and the everyday life of the schools and on-the-job teacher training.

The third part offers a "An overview of practices" of projects developed by different social agents, contexts and audiences. These include formal and non-formal educational projects that combine efforts to evaluate the access value among children and youth; the ethical use and the development of analytical abilities regarding information technologies; the study and assessment of media and their impact on the democratic discourse, pedagogical dynamics and social engagement; and the creative production of content in participative environments.

The book offers special ingredients and is meant to celebrate diversity, all the while considering that its purpose was neither to exhaust the topic nor to achieve a total representation of the field. In reading this anthology, the reader will find not only contextual diversity but also diversity in terms of methodological approaches (quantitative and qualitative research, philosophical essays, testimonials), diversity of social agents involved (children, youngsters, teaching and advertising students, Amerindians, Afro-Descendants, integration relations, social movements) and diversity of media (photography, printed and online newspapers, radio, cinema, games, computers, Internet and advertising).

To orient the reader in this landscape, we decided that the opening article for each country in the section "An overview of practices" should generally mention how media education has taken different forms in several implemented initiatives (In Brazil, Lyana de Andrade; in Portugal, Ana Jorge, Luís Pereira and Conceição Costa; and in Spain, Rosa Garcia-Ruiz and Vicént Perez).

Thank You and an invitation

The final words in this introduction should be a thank you note. It has been a great honour to have taken on the scientific coordination of the International Clearinghouse on Children, Youth and Media in February 2014, starting with "Agents and Voices" as my first publication as an editor. I would like to thank Ulla Carlsson, the brilliant researcher in charge of Nordicom for so many years, for trusting me. I also thank Catharina Bucht for her extraordinary support in this debut. And to each and every author of this book, I would like to say *muchas gracias* and *muito obrigada*.

Media and Information Literacy (MIL) is one of the most crucial fields today. Alton Grizzle, co-manager of UNESCO's global actions on MIL, highlights this and adds: "MIL is necessary for everyone to achieve intercultural dialogue and global citizenship in a digital world. MIL for all is possible. MIL for all is a must. We should reject the idea that it cannot be done. It is not too expensive. Literacy cannot be priced. The challenge before us is to keep pressing and pushing until change comes."

We expect this book to be far-reaching among researchers, teachers, licentiates, graduates, social agents, formulators and managers. There are important initiatives described in the book, and a number of others being implemented around the world. Narratives, bonds, links, networks and connections are necessary. Get connected, get involved. We have selected examples of praiseworthy agents and voices, with the potential to support the formulation of public policies focusing on the insertion and use of media in education, be it formal or informal. This 2014 yearbook gathers initiatives and puts them in dialogue, with the intention of being a source of inspiration and an invitation to hear the various voices and learn about the creation of new networks.

I would like to take this opportunity to extend an invitation. If you are not yet a member of the International Clearinghouse global network[1], visit our web site and sign up. It is a pleasure to share information about what is going on and what is being published, wherever you are in the world, to promote research on children, youth, media and media education. Welcome!

Note
1. http://www.nordicom.gu.se/en//clearinghouse/clearinghouse-network

References
Buckingham, D. (2003). *Media education: Literacy, learning and contemporary culture*. Cambridge, UK: Polity Press.
Grizzle, A. (2014). MIL, Intercultural dialogue and global citizenship. In S.H. Culver & P. Kerr (Eds.), *Global citizenship in a digital world*, (MILID Yearbook 2014) (pp.17-26). University of Gothenburg: The International Clearinghouse on Children, Youth and Media/Nordicom.
Kolucki, B., & Lemish, D. (2011). *Communicating with children: principles and practices to nurture, inspire, excite, educate and heal*. New York: UNICEF. http://www.unicef.org/cbsc/files/CwC_Web(2).pdf
Rivoltella, P. C. (2001). *Media Education: modelli, esperienze, profilo disciplinare*. Roma: Carocci.
UNESCO (2011). *Media and Information Literacy: curriculum for teachers*. Paris: UNESCO.

BRAZIL

Children, Youth and Media

Children Making Media in School

Challenges to Authorship and Participation

Gilka Girardello

I begin by recalling a Brazilian film about the power of children who express themselves through the media at school: "*O fim do recreio*" [The End of Recess] (2011).[1] In this short fictional work, a conservative politician proposes doing away with recess at schools, saying that playing is a waste of time. Two boys, upset with the idea, find an old movie camera abandoned in the school storage room and record the joyful games in the schoolyard and statements of children defending recess. School administrators discover the non-authorized use of the camera and the boys are almost punished, but the eloquence of the recorded scenes convinces the teachers to change their minds: the video made by the children circulates nationally, and the case ends with the defeat of the politician's preposterous idea. The film was awarded by children's juries at a number of Brazilian children's film festivals, indicating that many young people felt represented by the film's defense of children's right to use the media for their ethical, aesthetic and political expression.

The role of children as producers of media texts is evidently central to understanding contemporary childhood. The intensity with which they dedicate themselves to the creation and publication of photos, videos, blogs, *memes* and other textual genres using digital equipment is now commonplace, even in the daily lives of a large portion of Brazilian society. This situation raises new challenges for educators who are concerned with guaranteeing the authorship and participation of children in schools. This article discusses some of these challenges, and is inspired by recent Brazilian experiences and the ideas of authors who have contributed to the debate about about this issue in our country.

The importance of children's participation is a theme found in academic debate in Brazil, from the time of studies with children's groups conducted by Florestan Fernandes in the 1940s (Fernandes, 2004) up until the contemporary New Childhood Studies, particularly the Sociology of Childhood. The role of cultural action and social practice in education defended by the work of Paulo Freire since the 1960s, and his idea that literacy is not reduced to reading but also requires *um dizer* e *um fazer* [a saying and doing] about the world (Freire, 1975), continues to reverberate in discourses and cultural practices, even if not always explicitly. Since the Constitution of 1988, which marked the end of the dictatorial cycle, the principal documents of educational policy have included the idea that children's participation is necessary for an education that considers citizenship.

These ideas stimulated a large number of valuable projects in schools and communities throughout the country, although in many contexts they have still not been able to be implemented and generate educational actions that are sensitive to the potential of childhood. One of the most important limits to complete participation of children in schools, as identified by Quinteiro (2000), is the fact that they often have their condition as children – being active and creative – suffocated by their condition as students, being targets of teaching.

In terms of the participation of children in media production in schools, the main theoretical inspirations in Brazil are, in addition to the epistemology of Paulo Freire, the proposal of communication and graphic expression workshops in the work of Celestin Freinet (Freinet, 1974) as well as the pedagogy of communication of Francisco Gutierrez (Gutierrez, 1978), which have planted seeds since the 1970s. Later, the contributions of cultural studies came to be articulated in the debate, including the Latin American cultural studies line and that of European media education, which have emphasized the importance of the creative practice of children allied to a critical reading of the media. As Isabel Orofino affirmed, "if we are to have schools equipped with the new information technologies, they should be used to support the voices of students and not as resources for training for the labor market" (Orofino, 2005, pp. 124-125). As a result of this theoretical-political-epistemological caldron and a greater access to technologies, the past 20 years have witnessed an intense proliferation of projects in schools and communities, and of academic studies focused on the action of children in the production of texts in different media and languages. This is a propitious moment to conduct a review.

Authorship is a key issue in contemporary cultural theories, which since the mid-20th century have radically questioned who an author is and the authorial role of the reader-receiver. The semiotic pulverization and the dilution of borders between production and reception that mark digital culture heighten the problem, raising the question of the political character of issues such as copyrights and the creative dynamics of media mixings, with intense and polemic repercussions for education. The Bakhtinian concept of dialogism helps us understand *authorship* as a practice of textual construction in dialog with the world, in which the subject takes responsibility for his or her thoughts, feelings and actions: "the architectural activity of authorship, which is the construction of a text, is parallel to the activity of human existence, which is the construction of a self" (Clark & Holquist, 2008, p. 90). Along with this critical and reflexive dimension of narrative authorship, the value of its poetic dimension is also considered – in the sense of the inventive creation present in the term *poiesis.*

When one thinks of the promotion of authorship in the case of children, a *ludic concept of authorship* becomes indispensable, which is clearly evident in the most interesting works of media creation in schools. Another aspect of authorship, relevant in the contexts of social inequality and cultural diversity found in Brazilian schools, is its relationship with memory, identity and the local knowledge of different groups. In these cases, the interaction between individual creation, cultural appropriation and social sharing is vital, because authorship is closely related to the sharing of stories and to their power to create communities in the classroom, in projects in which social and cultural differences are not confused with prejudice. Digital culture also favors a *collaborative concept of authorship,* in which a child's willingness to become part of a collective democratic process – suggesting ideas for a script, taking pictures, shaping a doll for animation – is as (or more) important as having his or her name signed alone on the final result.

The importance of children's production through the media is defended by educational documents and projects throughout the country. On the federal level, for example, the participation of students in the production of school newspapers and radio, comic books, photography and video is foreseen by the largest program of the Ministry of Education, aimed at schools in a situation of social and educational vulnerability.[2] A representative example of the production of radio and video by children and youth in public schools are the projects conducted since 2001 in the São Paulo public schools, based on the *educom-munication* references developed at the Universidade de São Paulo that seek "the promotion of a children-youth protagonism through audiovisual production" and the "democratic production of communication in school space".[3] Various media-education studies reaffirm the importance that "experiences in the field of science, art, culture and communication [can] be constructed as opportunities for authorship" (Fantin, 2012, p. 63).

In this scenario, I highlight some of the challenges to the promotion of authorship and the full participation of children in their use of media in schools. I present them here as contributions to a dialog, and not, certainly, as prescriptive indications.

1) *How can children's authorship be guaranteed while simultaneously insuring a project's technical and aesthetic qualities?*

Many teachers are hesitant to leave decisions up to children, because they believe that the final product will not have the desired aesthetic quality. For this reason, children's "participation" winds up being limited to following instructions and the simple operational execution of individual steps of the processes. The debate over what is more important – the quality of the process or of the product – goes far back in education, particularly art education. Concerning pedagogical work with media, it appears to be meaningless to separate these two dimensions: the quality of the product also reflects that of the process (its challenging and democratic character, the intensity of the aesthetic involvement of children, etc.) and vice versa.

Even when working with very young children, it is possible to find ways to validate their perspective and at the same time conduct the technical and aesthetic mediations needed to translate this perspective into the chosen language. One example of this is the *shared camera* strategy that anthropologist Rita Oenning da Silva used in the production of videos with children at a pre-kindergarten in Rio de Janeiro. Here is how she describes these moments:

> That day, we filmed the activities in the park. Four children constantly accompanied the filming, helping to guide the camera. When we separated from the group because we had already filmed a lot (...) [a four-year old girl] came up to the camera and playfully placed her eye very close to the camera lens. Observing her image in the LED screen, which at the time was facing her, she said: "What big eyes you have..." and then, changing her tone of voice, responded: "The better to see you with... (Silva, 2013, p. 5)

Then, the girl narrated a very personal version of *Little Red Riding Hood* in which the authorship was present both in her oral and gestural performance, and in the technical interaction she established with the camera. The child was an agent of the framing; she grasped the microphone, and was also the creator of the story narrated and of the entire expressive scene recorded on video. The intimacy of the relationship with the adult and the affectionate physical proximity between the two, who handled the equipment together in a delicate four–handed dance, is evident upon watching the video.[4]

Interactions that involve complicity, play and partnership between educators and children are vital for the complete exercise of children's authorship. This was a demand made by the children themselves at the closing session of the Fourth World Summit of Media for Children and Adolescents, held in 2004 in Rio de Janeiro, which was a landmark for this field of studies in Brazil. Marisha Shakil, 15, from Kuala Lumpur regarding the event's children and youth forum, said:

> We the youth of the world, have a voice. Please adults, give us the right to use this voice. We know that we still need you to guide us. If you give a piece of paper to a child, she will make a beautiful drawing. With your help, this drawing becomes transformed into something richer. But, please, work with us, not for us. (Girardello, 2004)

In the complicit interplay between adults and children that is established in a sensitive creative process, when it is the adult who is behind the lens, the challenge is to see *with* the children, not only *for* them. This is perceived, for example, in the poetic quality of the camera work in the award-winning film *Sementes do Nosso Quintal* [Seeds in our Backyard] (directed by Fernanda Heinz Figueiredo, 2013), realized among the children at a pre-kindergarten school in the city of São Paulo, and in the short film *Disque-Quilombola* (directed by David Reeks, 2012), filmed with children living in a quilombola village in Espírito Santo state.[5] This is a documentary in which children from two distant communities, who belong to the same ethnic minority, speak to each other in a traditional game of telephone. The director and screenwriter explain that the tin-can "telephone" was to have appeared in only one scene of the film, but that the game "took on considerable strength among the children, so at the end of the recordings, when we saw the images, we realized that we had in our hands the film given to us by the children themselves."[6] The time and space, which guaranteed the playful participation of the children, from the attentive eye and compliance of the adult, can at times be the key to the expressive force of the final product.

2) *How to choose and explore the themes, balancing the interests of children with curricular demands?*

This is another delicate balancing act. On the one hand, the production of videos and blogs can make the approximation to curricular content more interesting, and this is good. If, however, the only opportunity children have to produce media in school is when they address class content in a narrow sense, there is a risk of falling into a utilitarianism that impoverishes the critical and creative value of the experiences, and therefore their media-educational value.

In the many dozens of videos produced by children at Brazilian schools that I have had the opportunity to examine in the past five years, particularly as a member of the team of curators of children's films for a project by the Ministry of Culture[7], some themes are recurrent: the illustration of popular traditional cantigas [songs] or contemporary Brazilian songs; the memory of the community (presented in profiles of residents, statements, narratives); and transversal curricular themes, such as environmentalism, *bullying*, consumerism, the rights of children and violence against children, as well as issues related to health, gender, sexuality, diversity and difference. All these themes have generated projects of great ethical and aesthetic strength. But one challenge that the examination of the video archives suggests is the care to avoid a certain "ventriloquist effect," which occurs when the children's scripts and performances artificially echo the clichés of the major media made by adults. One example of this is the normative or paternalistic tone of advertising discourse, which also often reverberates in the children's projects ("don't pollute the environment," "let's respect animals!").

An authorship more open to the singularity of children's voices requires the expansion of their cultural experiences and repertoires, as well as the transversal presences of media education in schools, in a special dialog with the arts and literature. There is a consensus among Brazilian media-education researchers that children's expression by means of media languages is necessary for their cultural literacy and their education in a broad sense, and that they cannot be limited to technical instrumental learning in computer classes or technology workshops.

At the same time, we know it is important to avoid an *a priori* rejection of the playful re-elaboration that children make of hegemonic cultural conventions. Imitation, parody and the multiple possibilities of a re-reading and mixing of themes and formats that children encounter on TV, the Internet, in the movies and on the radio can also be spaces for expressive exploration. As David Buckingham and colleagues observed two decades ago, we should not neglect "the complexity of students' uses of dominant forms, and the positive functions it might serve, not least [...] in enabling them to 'learn the languages' of the media" (Buckingham, Grahame & Sefton-Green, 1995, p. 215).

3) How to integrate children's participation in media education in schools with a valorization of popular cultures?

Various recent studies in Brazil investigate how to address the differences in abilities and interests among children, guaranteeing everyone's participation in projects. In the media-education field, one example is Kreuch's (2008) analysis of the students' participation in the creation of institutional websites for schools, observing that this is limited to the execution of technical tasks. Children know how to criticize the content and the processes of the websites, but have difficulty proposing alternatives, which the author attributes to the limited experience with participation they are offered at home and in school.

An inspiration for dealing with these challenges may be found in the rituals and mechanisms of the popular culture itself, in relation to participation and transmission. This is what we see, for example in the study by Gonçalves (2006) about the participation of children in the *boi-de-mamão*, a traditional popular dramatic dance from Santa Catarina state. How is it that children learn to sing and dance this ritual? The answer is: by seeing, singing, dancing and playing at the community festivals since they learned to walk, the younger children learn from the older participants, who serve as guides and references. The collective construction of the process allows each child to come close and get involved with that aspect of the process that attracts them most at the time, encompassing an entire educational curriculum. This is what also takes place in experiences like that of the Fundação Casa Grande, in Brazil's northeastern Sertão region, one of the educational-cultural projects in Brazil most highly recognized as fertile territory for children's media production. In the small city of Nova Olinda, boys and girls pass through different workshops as they grow up, depending on their interests and tastes: they make radio programs; direct videos; and edit newspapers, websites and comic books, in an intimate and long-lasting exercise of popular communication about living in the community.

In the scenario of Brazil's great cultural diversity, many forms of traditional expression have been able to revitalize themselves based on arrangements that include the digital technologies, which can be sources of methodological inspiration for work in schools. After all, "the school should also be a center that radiates popular culture, making it available to the community, not for its consumption, but for recreating it" (Freire, 1987, p. 16). A trend is currently visible in the country concerning the valorization of Brazilian popular culture, in a tense (and often productive) dialog with the flows of the cultural industries. This can be seen, for example, in the multitudes of youths who flock to the classes-spectacles of veteran artist and researcher of Brazilian traditions Ariano Suassuna; or in the vibrant methodological production of the digital culture groups associated with the Points of Culture network, created in the first decades of this century by the Ministry of Culture, based on thousands of local initiatives throughout the country. The approximation of these groups with schools and the promotion of students' agency of are part of the conceptual parameters prepared collectively by the participants in the network:

> The emphasis given to have digital culture and open software occupy spaces in schools created the opportunity to transform students from mere users into curious and questioning researchers. This...favors a process of empowerment of the participants to support the appropriation of technology through reflection, from the construction of subjectivities, capable of going beyond a merely instrumentalizing process (Rangel & Labrea, 2009, pp.55-56).

The tie between education and culture strengthens both. Constantina Xavier Filha gives an example of this, reporting on an animation workshop with children at a public school in Campo Grande, in which the group decided to invent the history of a princess who lived in the Pantanal region: "Although we lived close to this ecosystem and the theme is part of the curriculum, many children represented it differently from reality: landscapes containing apple trees, or with animals such as giraffes, elephants, bears" (Xavier Filha, 2013, p. 5), which gave space to a relevant pedagogical-cultural work.

The environment created by the collective work of audiovisual production can thus be a stimulus not only to authorial creation but also to critical school learning. This is yet another argument for an investment in the intimate and intense relationship between the school and its cultural surroundings, by means of media education that is organically united to the artistic vitality of the local culture. The acquisition of a liberated command in new literacies does not take place in isolation from the other languages and forms of artistic expression, or while locked up in disciplinary and architectural spaces dedicated to machines and their technical-instrumental use.

To the contrary, the challenges raised, based on Brazilian experiences, reinforce the idea that participatory creation by children, making use of the media, is a potentially powerful phenomenon for literacy as a form of reading and writing about the world. The creative vitality of children's daily life and of the culture of communities must continue to gain space, so that they also express themselves through the use of media in schools, based on an emphasis on collaborative participation and solidary forms of authorship.

Notes

1. Directed by Vinícius Mazzon and Nélio Spréa. http://youtu.be/t0s1mGQxhAI
2. The program *Mais Educação*, by the Ministry of Education, which sought to reach six million students in 2014.
3. http://portalsme.prefeitura.sp.gov.br/Projetos/ondas/Anonimo/nasondasdovideo.aspx
4. "A incrível história da Vovozinha e o Lobo Mau". Directed by Rita de Cácia Oenning da Silva. http://www.youtube.com/watch?v=dWEUdlO4iPQ
5. A quilombo is a current remnant of a settlement created in the 19th century by runaway or former slaves.
6. Reeks, D. & Meirelles, R. (s/d). Conversas na lata e a mágica do barbante [online interview]. http://www.disquequilombola.com.br/bastidores/telefone-de-lata/
7. *Programadora Brasil* is a project by the National Audiovisual Secretariat of the Ministry of Culture. It provides access to Brazilian films for non-commercial exhibition spaces such as film clubs, schools and universities throughout the country.

References

Buckingham, D., Grahame, J., & Sefton-Green, J. (1995). *Making Media: practical production in media education*. London: The English and Media Center.

Clark, K., & Holquist, M. (2008). *Mikhail Bakhtin*. São Paulo: Perspectiva.

Fantin, M. (2007). Mídia-Educação e Cinema na Escola. *Teias*, 15/16, 1-13.

Fantin, M. (2012). Mídia-educação no currículo e na formação inicial de professores. In M. Fantin & P.C Rivoltella (Orgs.), *Cultura Digital e Escola: pesquisa e formação de professores* (pp. 57- 92). Campinas: Papirus.

Fernandes, F. (2004) *Folclore e mudança social na cidade de São Paulo*. São Paulo: Martins Fontes.

Freinet, C. (1974). *O jornal escolar*. Lisboa: Editorial Estampa.

Freire, P. (2011). *Educação como prática de liberdade* (34th ed.). Rio de Janeiro: Paz e Terra.

Freire, P. (1975). *Pedagogia do Oprimido*. Rio de Janeiro: Paz e Terra.

Girardello, G. (2004). As crianças tomam a palavra. *Observatório da Imprensa*. http://www.obser-vatoriodaimprensa.com.br/news/view/as_criancas_tomam_a_palavra

Gonçalves, R. M. (2006). *Educação Popular e Boi-de-Mamão: diálogos brincantes*. Tese de doutorado, Departamento de Educação, UFSC, Florianópolis.

Gutierrez, F. (1978). *Linguagem total: uma pedagogia dos meios de comunicação*. São Paulo: Summus.

Kreuch, R. (2008). *A participação das crianças nos websites das escolas municipais de Florianópolis*. Dissertação de Mestrado, Departamento de Educação, UFSC, Florianópolis.

Orofino, M. I. (2005). *Mídias e mediação escolar: pedagogia dos meios, participação e visibilidade*. São Paulo: Cortez/ Instituto Paulo Freire.

Quinteiro, J. (2000). *Infância e Escola*: uma relação marcada por preconceitos. Tese de doutorado, Departamento de Educação, UNICAMP, Campinas.

Rangel, A.M.C., & Labrea, V.V. (Orgs.). (2009). *Seminário Internacional do Programa Cultura Viva: novos mapas conceituais*. Pirenópolis: Ministério da Cultura.

Silva, R. C. O. (2013). Quem conta um conto aumenta muito mais que um ponto: narrativa, produção de si e gênero na produção fílmica com crianças. X *Simpósio Internacional Fazendo Gênero*. Florianópolis, 2013.

Xavier Filha, C. (2013). Produção de filme de animação com e para crianças. *Simpósio Internacional Fazendo Gênero*. Florianópolis, 2013.

Narratives as a Basis for Enhancing the Skill of Analysing and Producing Digital Media Content

Rosalia Duarte, Rita Migliora & Maria Cristina Carvalho

The avalanche of information and the reconfiguration of time and space caused by the Internet, coupled with economic and cultural globalization, has created a need to reassess notions concerning what and how youths must learn to secure an active and responsible role in society. This dialogue should also encompass what form of education best ensures that future generations obtain the necessary skills and competencies to live and work in a highly mediatized society. Some scholars operating at the intersection of culture, media and education (Ferrão Tavares, 2010; Livingstone, 2011; Kellner & Share, 2007; Lima & Brown, 2007; Buckingham, 2008) assert that digital literacy is a prerequisite for accomplishing the aforementioned objectives, since it promotes an autonomic and critical analysis of the world. Buckingham (2008) argues that the knowledge and skills required to facilitate digital literacy should be taught specifically, since they are not constructed based solely upon the use of digital devices, although this is a contributing factor. A common quality amongst these authors is their criticism of the largely unexploited use of media in schools.

The Research Group in Education and Media has addressed this concern as part of its on-going studies. Our focus is to understand how youths acquire and construct the necessary skills to use tools and digital content in the acquisition of formal (scientific and academic) knowledge, and how these skills can be promoted and developed in schools. This interest guided the development of a study entitled Juventude e Mídia (GRUPEM, 2012; Migliora, 2013), and the project discussed herein, which focused on digital literacy amongst students attempting to obtain their primary school teaching certificate (Duarte Ribeiro, Garcez & Migliora, 2014).

Juventude e Mídia[1] sought to determine which factors influenced the educational skill (i.e., autonomous and creative use of digital technologies) of ninth-grade students of the network of municipal public schools in the city of Rio de Janeiro. The results revealed that computer use at home, more so than in school, exhibited a significantly positive impact on youths' overall aptitudes, including their educational abilities. However, less than 4% of the study's participants indicated that they regularly used Information and Communications Technologies (ICT) at school. Most schools surveyed had few computers available for student use, and often lacked a reliable Internet connection. Research conducted by the Internet Steering Committee of Brazil (TIC Educação, 2010; 2012; 2013[2]) indicated that while an increased number of students were using the Internet at school, teachers rarely mediated and instead favoured traditional lectures and printed materials.

These findings led us to develop an intervention project utilizing the efforts of students attending a state-sponsored teacher-training school in Rio de Janeiro, who were qualified to teach primary school. The programme's main objective was to create, test, and evaluate both the ninth-grade students' and their instructors' learning and teaching strategies, respectively, to determine which were the most effective in promoting the use of digital media in the acquisition and transmission of scholastic knowledge. The implementation of this programme entailed weekly digital literacy workshops, spanning ten months[3]. The researchers hypothesized that the development of such literacy requires teacher mediation, especially concerning the proper treatment of information (reliability assessment, searching, selection, organisation, synthesis, and sharing) and the production and analysis of narratives in different languages – both essential skills for the independent and critical use of information technology.

Workshops involving collaborative activities between researchers, monitors, teachers, and students with progressive levels of complexity (oral reports related to school life, later, producing, and editing written and audio-visual materials) were a key component of the study's methodology. These workshops encompassed searching, selecting, and analysing information in addition to producing and analysing written, spoken, audio-visual, and photographic content. Empirical evidence in support of the subsequent analyses and conclusions drawn from the project's results included written and audio-visual records of each workshop.

Studies conducted by members of the research group (Sacramento, 2008; Santiago, 2010; Garcez, 2011) and other scholars (Silverstone, 2002; Jenkins, 2008; Livingstone, 2009) indicated that the ability to analyse, understand, and produce narratives using different languages and media is necessary for digital literacy. Student and teacher participation in activities and their subsequent effect on each respective format, coupled with the documentation of each experience, played an important role in enhancing participants' ability to critically analyse media texts and, above all, produce educational content using various languages and media. The present article reflects upon this process.

Study background

The programme was implemented at a public secondary vocational school in the southern section of the city of Rio de Janeiro, which mainly provides training for and certification of prospective primary school teachers. The researchers selected this location in hopes of widening its potential impact by targeting future teachers, who will subsequently influence the spread of digital literacy, even at the earliest stages of education. The programme's participants included 13 students (ten girls, three boys) and three teachers, while eight members of the Research Group in Education and Media and two undergraduate pedagogical researchers assisted in the project's development.

Twenty-one digital media literacy workshops were held, in addition to four cultural activities located outside the school grounds. These activities included two separate film screenings and discussions for students and teachers alike, a guided tour of the Niteroi Museum of Contemporary Art, and a visit to a photography exhibition at the Paço Imperial in Rio de Janeiro. These events supplemented the workshops and enriched the school routine while expanding the students' cultural repertoire, from both an aesthetic and a technical perspective.

The school activities prioritized the adoption of an active learning methodology, which encourages learners to approach the responsibility of knowledge acquisition in an autonomous and interactive manner, while participating in the planning and implementation of activities in a continuous peer partnership. The theoretical-methodological perspective endorsed by Activity Theory (Davidov, 1988; Sforni, 2007) was used as a reference point, which maintains that school education should focus on stimulating learners' intellectual autonomies and promoting an awareness of each action and operation that the individual performs related to knowledge acquisition. From this perspective, a teacher does not discursively dispense content or teach how something is done, but rather creates appropriate and challenging conditions for the learning process to occur, based on the need and initiative of the learner, who subsequently transposes abstract ideas into concrete concepts (Sforni, 2007, p. 40).

The authors created problematic scenarios designed to challenge students' pre-existing knowledge regarding the everyday use of ICT, proposing tasks whose solutions required expanding upon previously acquired skills, in addition to acquiring new ones, both individually and collectively. This approach to teaching considers group work a prerequisite for conducting proposed activities, not merely a possibility.

Workshops were recorded in both written and visual form (using still photography and video) by all participants, including students, monitors, researchers, and teachers. A Facebook[4] group was established for the project, where participants were able to record and exchange their ideas and opinions.

The study was initiated by constructing and consolidating skills related to accessing and managing information available on the Internet, such as searching, analysing, organizing, synthesizing, sharing, and assessing reliability – abilities the researchers believe are rarely acquired without direct mediation from someone who already possesses them. Research conducted by Stewart and Bravo (2013) among Jamaican college students attending an education course revealed that 46% of the participants had serious difficulty completing tasks effectively because they were unable to locate and select the information necessary for the tasks' execution. Thus, accessing and processing information transmitted via the Internet was the foundation for a teaching process in which previously mastered skills served as a basis for future skills.

The table below summarizes the activities performed in the digital media literacy workshops.

Skills	Description	Proposed Activities
Gaming	Ability to search for solutions to problems in one's surroundings	Creation and evaluation of avatars and problem-solving
Performance	Ability to adopt alternative identities for improvisation and discovery	Fan fiction production[5] in pairs involving the creation of a fictitious author. This includes describing the author's social background, demographic characteristics, personality traits, interests, values, and social life. These pairs must then present their authors to the group, and justify their decisions. Afterwards, the group selects an author and develops the story and its characters
Appropriation	Ability to collect a significantly large sample and remix media content	Developing a screenplay and storyboard and recording and editing audio-visual materials; assembling and editing sound and audio-visual materials by remixing others
Multitasking	Ability to map an environment and shift the focus to important details as needed	Finding solutions for simultaneously proposed problems, participating in integrated activities, and parallel demands related to different types of productions such as fan fiction, audio and video, and remixing music
Distributed cognition	Ability to interact meaningfully with tools designed to expand mental abilities	Learning concepts by analysing media content using theoretical categories, narratives about oneself, and the constitutive elements of different languages
Collective intelligence	Ability to share knowledge and compare findings and information with others who share common goals	Searching, organizing, and presenting content in its default format and orally within a pre-set time period; team activities that distribute roles and tasks
Judgement	Ability to evaluate the reliability and credibility of different information sources	Discussion of a controversial subject based on information published on the Internet, news analysis, and development of criteria for reliability assessment
Navigation of different media	Ability to follow the flow of stories and information in various modalities	Discussion of a controversial subject by searching media for information and positions
Networking	Ability to search, synthesize, and disseminate information	Preparing for the various activities by searching and synthesizing new information; organization, presentation, and dissemination of the work performed

Negotiation	Ability to transition between various communities while exhibiting discernment and respecting differing perspectives, in addition to understanding and following alternative rules	Contributing to the project's Facebook group and other Internet environments, participating in formal and informal conversations online, and producing reports and personal materials using different media

Source: Duarte, Ribeiro, Garcez, & Migliora, 2014.

Narratives as a key component of the development of digital literacy

The hypothesis that the public's understanding of the world in mediatized societies depends on society's ability to understand media's textual strategies led the authors to adopt a systematic approach in which narratives (oral, written, and audio-visual) formed the main axis of the project's digital literacy workshops. Our aim was to establish appropriate conditions for expanding participants' ability to critically analyse real or fictional narratives available in different forms and media, including newspapers and magazine articles and fictional printed and audio-visual materials (such as books, comics, song lyrics, online fan fiction, films, television programmes, and Internet videos) to determine students' narrative competence with different media.

The collective creation of stories in different forms (oral, written, aural, and audio-visual) during the workshop allowed narrators to present elements from their personal lives, which promoted group cohesion and participants' exchange and expansion of knowledge regarding each language. This process led the authors to propose problem situations favourable to the establishment of an increasingly close relationship between narratives and experiences (Benjamin, 1994). According to Walter Benjamin, the narrative is an art inextricably linked to the teller's life; as an experience not passed on to an audience in the form of mere information, it 'immerses the thing in the life of the narrator so as later to take it out of him' (p. 205).

Benjamin (1994) indicates that the public is poor at analysing stories, even though every morning it receives news from around the world. He further questions what the value of the world's cultural heritage would be if experience no longer connected it to us. Moreover, he reasserts his belief that people's ability to report experiences – to narrate, recall, and search in the whole for fragments of uniqueness – is a condition for the continuity and transmission of culture.

The narrative activities began with a proposal to create stories orally using images from magazines and the Internet, which were then printed and glued to pieces of cardboard. Fifteen students and three teachers were present at this workshop. The group was invited to sit on the floor in a circle, and pictures were placed in the circle's centre. Next, each person chose a picture and, based on the selected image, created a story and told it to the group.

The task began with a teacher selecting an image and telling a story; the next teacher opted to continue the story, and attempted to maintain some neutrality as well as impersonality. One student asked if her story should be related to the teachers' and, upon learning that this was unnecessary, she recalled an important life experience. Henceforth, other students began relating the images to personal events with varying degrees of emotional involvement, and the narratives became increasingly interconnected with their experiences. Thus, what was initially portrayed as fictional 'storytelling' was gradually transformed into the participants' personal narratives, which in this context served to develop certain aspects of their life stories.

Although the original proposal did not require participants to present a personal or factual account, the group somehow subverted its original purpose, and thus qualitatively altered the process. Given that the last years of secondary school are integrated with vocational qualifications, the young students had reached a juncture where it was necessary to choose and define aspects related to their careers; perhaps this is why they felt compelled to develop their personal stories, and subsequently continue constructing their trajectory. For Josso (2007), self-related narratives determine the extent to which social and cultural changes affect an individual, as they are related to the contextual transformations of one's professional and social life. Narratives also allow actors to access their experiences and existential concerns to resynthesize them.

The next task was to use the same images as themes to collectively construct an oral story based upon that of the previous speaker. Initially, the group was reluctant to accept this proposal, claiming that the resultant story 'would have neither rhyme nor reason'. While constructing the narrative, however, the advantages and possibilities of integrating different images, characters, and situations in a unique fictional universe became apparent to them. The collective story and its embedded personal experiences began to resemble science fiction, and featured time travel, monsters, villains, romance, and heroes, with the possibility of an entirely open ending. Students were surprised and at the same time satisfied with the result. As noted by Benjamin (1994, p. 201), the narrator uses the account of his or her own experience in combination with the accounts of others, subsequently incorporating both into newly narrated materials.

The students' unwavering eagerness to create oral narratives initially seemed paradoxical to the researchers, considering the youths' appreciation and interest in sophisticated technological devices. However, since this was a digital literacy workshop, the students did not expect a non-technological activity to be so interesting and satisfying. This may have been caused by a need to share experiences, which is a commonality amongst generations. Jost (2011) indicates that the behaviours promoted by new media are often rehashed versions of old ones, which have been consolidated throughout human history. In the context described here, combined with the fascinating new possibilities in communication that digital technology offers, the group likely found it pleasurable to narrate and have their narrations heard and understood by others.

The oral narrative workshops were a watershed in the project, from which student production was qualitatively different, from both our perspective and their own; the impact of this activity was reflected, to some extent, in each task and project that followed. The analysis of audio-visual materials, the production of a video based on a short story (to enter a publisher-sponsored contest), and the creation of characters and chapters for a work of online fan fiction displayed the students' increased ability to understand, comprehend, and create stories.

When planning the activities to be undertaken by the group, the authors requested that the project's undergraduate researchers produce individual reports concerning all meetings and activities. These reports also served as a means for producing narratives, as demonstrated in the following excerpt:

> We learned to read and tell stories ... [and] we realized that it is possible to share our ideas in many different ways, whether through conversation or in writing. We also realized that presenting our ideas to all the people around us so that they can understand and share them is difficult, and that it is important to have a very well developed and summarized script that presents important information and some fun facts. (Rafael, 16 years, December 2013)

Therefore, an analysis of these reports causes us to assume that the task of creating narratives impacted workshop participants' writing skills, and was progressively becoming a space for the students to reflect upon their experiences.

The researchers cannot claim that the workshop activities led to the perceived changes in students and teachers' positioning towards the use of digital technologies. However, we believe that the workshops provided opportunities to gain some essential skills that can facilitate an autonomous and creative relationship with these devices. These skills include the ability to question the credibility of information sources, to form personal criteria for reliability assessment, and to narrate and analyse narratives produced by others, using different media and languages. From our point of view, the obtainment and refinement of these abilities is necessary for the acquisition of additional skills in the teaching-learning process designed for the expansion and validation of learners' relationships with digital media.

Conclusion

Activity Theory asserts that psychichological growth entails the continuous development of cognitive structures in an upward spiral of complexity toward the full mastery of higher mental operations (abstraction, reflection, analysis, synthesis, and logical reasoning). This process is the result of organisms interacting with their physical and social environments with the assistance of agents, tools, and signs (Sforni, 2007). Development occurs as subjects encounter situations that require the performance of new operations in conjunction with the proper instruments to execute said action(s) upon an object, and necessitates mediation (ibid., p. 40).

During this mediation, the cognitive operations children are expected to develop are carried out by the Other: a more experienced person who has previously mastered them. In this scenario, the operations might be developed intrapsychicly by individuals through internalization, or the 'internal reconstruction of a foreign operation' (ibid, p. 38). Thus, education and development are connected social processes.

These assumptions are also valid for the learning relationships established through the use of ICT. In this context, there are undeniably some learning processes unmediated by more experienced individuals, since technologies can be inherent instruments of thought capable of increasing their user's level of development. However, the signs, symbols, languages, and mental operations accompanying the use of these instruments are not spontaneously appropriated by the user, but are rather socially transmitted; their appropriation occurs during interactions with people who have previously internalized them.

For Ferrão Tavares (2010), the ability of the Internet to facilitate journeys in and out of oneself, home, or classroom provides a broader, more productive, and educationally fruitful experience when accompanied by navigation guides. According to Tavares, to effectively promote the construction of new learning processes, schools and teachers must undertake the preparation of these guides. One might liken the project presented in this paper, its narrative activities, and its expansion of one's ability to process information available online to a map, which guides future teachers' interactions with digital technologies.

Notes

1. www.grupem.pro.br
2. http://www.cetic.br/educacao/
3. Project funded by the Fundação de Amparo à Pesquisa do Estado do Rio de Janeiro and the Conselho Nacional de Desenvolvimento Científico e Tecnológico.
4. The use of social networking proved to be quite fruitful, allowing the researchers to evaluate whether certain actions were successes or failures, thus increasing team spirit from a non-hierarchical work perspective.
5. Fan fiction is a genre of web stories, written in chapters, and designed specifically for online consumption; its authors and readers are primarily fans of comic books, films, and soap opera characters, upon which they create new stories. See Santiago (2010) for more information about this subject.

References

Benjamin, W. (1994). O narrador. Considerações sobre a obra de Nikolai Leskov. In W. Benjamin. *Magia e Técnica, Arte e Política. Obras Escolhidas I* (pp.199-220). São Paulo: Brasiliense.

Buckingham, D. (2008). Defining Digital Literacy. In C. Lankshear & M. Knobel (Orgs.), *Digital literacies: concepts, policies and pratices* (pp.73-90). New York: Peter Lang Publishing.

Davidov, V. (1988). *La enseñanza escolar y el desarollo psíquico*. Moscou: Editorial Progresso.

Duarte, R., Ribeiro, A., Garcez, A., & Migliora, R. (2014). Parceria universidade/escola na criação de metodologias didáticas para o desenvolvimento de habilidades de uso de mídias digitais. In R.R. Pereira (Org.), *Universidade e Escola: práticas em diálogo*. RJ: FAPERJ (no prelo).

Ferrão Tavares, C. (2010). Viajar para aprender: implicações e potencialidades das TIC no desenvolvimento da literacia. *Exedra Journal*, 9, 69-84. http://dialnet.unirioja.es/descarga/articulo/3398946.pdf

Garcez, A. (2011). *Animar, se divertir e aprender: as relações de crianças com programas especialmente recomendados*. Dissertação de Mestrado, Departamento de Educação, Pontifícia Universidade Católica do Rio de Janeiro, Rio de Janeiro.

GRUPEM (2012). Juventude e mídia, (Relatório de Pesquisa), Rio de Janeiro, RJ, Departamento de Educação, PUC-Rio. www.grupem.pro.br

Jenkins, H. (2008). *Cultura da Convergência*. São Paulo: Aleph.

Jost, F. (2011). Novos comportamentos para antigas mídias ou antigos comportamentos para novas mídias? *Revista Matrizes*, 4 (2), 93-109.

Josso, M. C. (2007). A transformação de si a partir de histórias de vida. *Revista Educação*, 3 (63), 413-438.

Kellner, D. & Share, J. (2007). Critical media literacy, democracy, and the reconstruction of education. In D. Macedo, & S.R. Steinberg (Eds.), *Media literacy: a reader* (pp. 3-23). New York: Peter Lang Publishing.

Lima, C. O. & Brown, S. W. (2007). Global citizenship and new literacies providing new ways for social Inclusion. *Psicologia Escolar e Educacional*, 11 (1), 22-45.

Livingstone, S. (2009). *Children and the Internet*. Cambridge: Polity Press.

Livingstone, S. (2011). Internet literacy: a negociação dos jovens com as novas oportunidades online. *Revista Matrizes*, 4(2), 11-42.

Migliora, R. (2013*). Jovens da rede pública municipal de ensino do Rio de Janeiro: modos de uso e habilidades no computador e na Internet*. Tese de Doutorado, Departamento de Educação, Pontifícia Universidade Católica do Rio de Janeiro, Rio de Janeiro.

Sacramento, W. (2008). *Experiência televisiva como mediadora da relação de crianças com o cinema*. Dissertação de Mestrado, Departamento de Educação, Pontifícia Universidade Católica do Rio de Janeiro, Rio de Janeiro.

Santiago, I. E. (2010). *A escrita de nativos digitais*. Tese de Doutorado, Departamento de Educação, Pontifícia Universidade Católica do Rio de Janeiro, Rio de Janeiro.

Silverstone, R. (2002). *Por que estudar a mídia?* São Paulo: Edições Loyola.

Sforni, M. S. F. (2007). *Aprendizagem conceitual e organização do ensino:*contribuições da Teoria da Aprendizagem. Araraquara: Junqueira e Marin.

Stewart, P. & Bravo, O. (2013). Media and Information Literacy and Intercultural Dialogue at the University of the West Indies. In U. Carlsson, S. H. Culver (Eds.), *Media and Informational Literacy and Intercultural Dialogue* (pp.25-35). http://www.nordicom.gu.se/sites/default/files/publikationer-hela-pdf/media_and_information_literacy_and_intercultural_dialogue.pdf

TIC EDUCAÇÃO. Comitê Gestor da Internet do Brasil (2010, 2011, 2012, 2013). *Pesquisa sobre o uso das tecnologias de informação nas escolas brasileiras*. http://www.cetic.br

Research with Children in Cyberculture

Ethical, Theoretical, and Methodological Challenges

Rita Marisa Ribes Pereira & Nélia Mara Rezende Macedo

This study discusses, from a philosophical standpoint, the various challenges faced when constructing research methodologies to assess the effects of cyberculture on children. What does this research include? What are the conventional methodologies available? What other forms of research need to be invented? On what basis is it possible to construct ethical guiding principles for research with children in today's cyberculture? These questions have become central to the research group which, since its creation in 2005, has been studying contemporary childhood experiences, particularly those related to the media.

Conducting research on contemporary issues involves constructing a position in relation to these issues. This implies remaining truthful to what belongs to the time and to various perceptions of this time. On the other hand, it involves refraining from a certain adherence in order to avoid passing judgement. Hence, it is important to examine not only what is visible but also what, in its obscurity, is presented as an issue. This is, therefore, a pioneer project by the research group, which improves creation in research. However, there also exists a kind of helplessness, since canonical theories and methodologies have already proved to be insufficient in meeting the demands which the process of research requires. In this study, we debate this process, understanding that it is a reflection on processes of knowledge production in the field of humanities and social sciences, with particular attention to research in which the participants are children.

As an ethical principle, we have assumed that research with children – more than an option for having children as interlocutors in the fieldwork – calls into question the social positions held by researchers and children in the socialized production of knowledge and language (Pereira, 2013). This principle is based on Mikhail Bakhtin's (2003, 2010) language philosophy. For Bakhtin, the production of human sciences is responsive, accepting and dialogical by nature.

Research, which is the product of language, evokes 'the other'; it addresses the other and is the subject of all decisions throughout the language process – be it drawing up a problem concerning theoretical affiliations, the delimitation of the field, the development of methodological strategies, the analysis of options, or the circulation of research texts.

Language plays a central role in the production of knowledge, as conceived by Bakhtin (ibid.), and is of fundamental importance to what we propose in this study. 'Research with children in cyberculture' automatically assumes a dialogic encounter between researchers (adults) and children, both of whom occupy a unique place in this type of research. In this space, researchers and children can comment on each other in relation to the theme under discussion, in this case cyberculture. Cyberculture is understood as the *contemporary culture structured by the use of digital technologies in the realms of the cyberspace network and in cities* (Santos, 2011). The dialogue which arises from this encounter cannot be reduced to a simple protocol of questions and answers. Instead, it brings into play complex forms of communication wherein subjects speak out politically about the topic under discussion, discuss what they think of themselves and each other, and talk about any expectations they have of each other.

Therefore, we reiterate that the term 'research with children' involves far more than just having children as partners in conducting fieldwork. The term encompasses the construction of an ethic that, from its inception, becomes part of the research question. It forces us to enunciate, in the smallest decisions throughout the process, what we understand by the term 'childhood', what we think about children, and what our expectations are from them. Based on this understanding, we have developed a guiding ethical principle which we researched with children, in order to arrive at shared directions for contemporary culture. Therefore, we cannot renounce the children's voice and what only they, who hold the position, can enunciate. By the same token, we, as researchers, cannot avoid assuming responsibility for the social, cultural, and ideological place we occupy in this dialogue. This place, under all circumstances, is neutral.

It was through our dialogue with children that we developed an experiment that presented itself 'within a network' and which needed to be investigated 'within a network'. Towards this end, we conducted different studies based on different aspects of online media: sites that children accessed frequently – regardless of whether or not these were produced for them; websites or blogs produced by children; Internet cafés where children browsed; and online[1] social networks that children frequented. All the above areas of study included social games as the main activity that children performed online. In the case of social networking sites, it should be noted that children, in fact, mentioned that their primary motivation for creating profiles was to play games; however, upon entering these sites, they did explore other forms of interaction and communication.

The studies were structured upon two empirical field sources. (1) We mapped our knowledge on the uses children had for the different media to which they had access. This exploratory mapping was conducted in two parts, in 2009 and 2011. Each step involved about a hundred children between the ages of 5 and 9 who were living in the metropolitan region of Rio de Janeiro, Brazil. The children were chosen on the basis of their familiarity with the various researchers involved. (2) The second source consisted of the more specific academic research already conducted in relevant fields of the theses, dissertations, and monographs.

The gap of time between these surveys and the possibility to extrapolate our findings from this study to future research shed light on the fact that within two or four years, the context could be redesigned countless times: the children's 'answers' no longer seemed to fit our questions; therefore, we were forced to find different ways to assess their uses and skills. Meanwhile, the children frequently asked us about our presence on social networking sites like Orkut[2] in Brazil. Between 2004 and 2012[3] Orkut had the largest number of users, including numerous children's profiles. In 2010, the Brazilian government's official statistical research about children and the Internet – ICT Children[4] – revealed that social networking sites, primarily Orkut and Facebook, were the main sites used by children. Thus, national quantitative data combined with our investigations with children gave us reason to rephrase our questions, because experiments with digital media ushered in new forms of sociability and pointed to new possibilities for communication and interaction[5].

To a certain extent, the limitations inherent to our questions, and even some of our approaches and strategies for meeting children, signalled a repositioning of childhood in a culture based on the relationships children forged with new technologies. The emergence of new modes of technical communication and interaction engendered by the liberation of the pole of emission has dramatically changed the communication structure, breaking with traditional forms of message production. Many authors, such as Lemos (2003) and Primo (2008), claim that this transition from the 'all-one' model (wherein companies and economic groups are the only emitters) to the 'all-all' model (wherein any user can be a potential producer of content to be publicized on a large network) forms the framework for the transition from the Web 1.0 phase to the so-called Web 2.0 phase, that is, the current phase of cyberculture. At first, the popularization of the Internet in the last decade of the twentieth century and the phenomenon of globalization guaranteed network access under an instrumental character. Now, however, we are experiencing the possibility of 'any individual, in advance, issuing and receiving real-time information, in different formats and modulations (writing, imagery and sound) to anywhere on the planet' (Lemos, 2003, p. 3).

There arose a new socio-technical environment, marked by the appearance of blogs and new forms of social interaction and networking. The first social network sites, like Orkut, showed some success in Brazil. Our surveys indicated that children participated autonomously and in an authorial form in this new environment. They had now established qualitatively different relationships with digital media experiences compared to those presented to us in our first endeavours to understand how children accessed and used computers and cell phones, for example.

The above information leads us to believe that the Internet is no longer restricted and instrumental in nature, involving the transmission and processing of data. Instead, it is a platform that provides interaction, participation, collaboration, and co-creation among users. It also reformulates the issues that challenged us earlier, making us understand the need for the creation of new research methodologies that allowed not only for the dialogue between the adult researchers and children but also for a dialogue with the particular technical dimension that enters into childhood experiences. How do children inhabit cyberspace? What new social arrangements and interactions are arising in this network? With whom do children communicate? What do they create on the Internet? What do they communicate *online*?

More than a methodological challenge, we had ahead of us an ethical issue that needed discussion because of the reported childhood practices in research, some of which were not recommended, or were even forbidden for children. One such example is children's presence in Internet cafés and their participation in online social networks. However, research indicated that, regardless of whether or not activities were recommended for children, they existed all the same. Therefore, what is the solution?

The literature review we conducted, on the other hand, also indicated that the relationship between the concepts of 'childhood' and 'cyberculture' is indeed problematic. Studies have indicated that cyberculture is the symbiosis between humans and artefacts, the synergy of which, between the technological and social, has altered our ways of seeing and interpreting the world (Lemos, 2003; Macedo, 2014). It has led us to assume that we are in the presence of a new social and cultural order, in which authorship is highlighted from the perspective of the collective and collaborative construction of culture. Research in the field of childhood studies has repeatedly suggested that the child is born into a culture which recreates and reframes the instruments that culture itself allows.

Meanwhile, when the themes of childhood and cyberculture are observed from a relational standpoint, the active attitude which is attributed to a child with regard to his/her actions is treated in relative terms. That child who, in theory, is seen as an active subject who reframes and recreates culture seems to occupy the place of a collaborative social subject experiencing new modes of authorship, subjectivity and sociability in today's cyberculture. Undoubtedly, this quandary lies in the very concept of childhood which is evoked when thinking about children's relationships with culture (Pereira, 2013). It is worth mentioning the political importance of approaches that, in written forms of understanding and narrating, pluralize the experience of childhood: 'childhood', 'the children'. However, it is still prudent to question the hegemonic, modern idea of childhood, which is structured around the pillars of fragility and unawareness of the child, leading to the construction of a pedagogy centred on protecting and preparing for the future. These are the pillars which are evoked when the social history of childhood is discussed; just as, not coincidentally, when placed under suspicion they encourage narratives about a supposed 'death of childhood', as proclaimed by Neil Postman (1999). This death of childhood is also referred to in relative terms by David Buckingham (2007).

The most important aspect under discussion, in our view, is formulating a position with regard to the social place that the child occupies in the production and circulation of culture at the present time. In addition, we also highlight the role played by adults in this culture and their relationship with children. In our view, adults – among them, researchers of the concept of childhood – have studied children's practices imposed or ratified by the adults, which are, rightfully so, considered 'appropriate' to childhood (Pereira, 2003). We also believe that adults avoid positioning themselves in relation to infant practices that they have discredited in the past, or in relation to practices of which they are unaware. It is as though, by not taking part in them, they reassert their inappropriateness. The consequence is that there is greater visibility of children's scientific practices, circumscribed by mediation/recommendation of the adult; on the other hand, though, there are many practices which remain invisible, despite the significance they may have for children. What are the limits of truth that are sought and effectively produced in this condition? What does it mean, actually, for a child to be an interlocutor? To what extent are children's practices and discourses recognized by researchers?

To answer these questions, we must recognize the limitations and biases which are visible at present. We must also determine, intermittently, what remains unclear and requires a stance. Finding this stance extends beyond the scope of research; it can be described by the ethical principle mentioned by Bakhtin (2010, p. 17): 'thinking is a responsive act for which there is no alibi'. The impossibility of an alibi reaffirms the place of authorship that all research evokes to a greater or lesser degree, and highlights the question 'What should I do?' as the founder of an ethic, given that assuming a stance cannot be avoided, whatever it may be. Meanwhile, this inquiry of philosophical nature has increasingly given rise to the pragmatic question 'What can I do?' The answer to this question appears to have already been prescribed by conventional protocol and judicial limits. What is at stake between these two questions is a complex negotiation between subject and standard in the constitution of social life; as a result, it becomes important to research. Bornheim (1989) argues that historically, this relationship has changed; he emphasizes its polarized and antithetical character. Sometimes the norm overlaps the subject or, in reverse, the subjects are placed in a position of insurrection to the norms. This tension between subject and standard tends to increase in times of crisis, be it in political or epistemological terms, since the very notion of crisis implies putting time itself – and its ways of searching – on trial (Bornhcim, 1992; Pereira, n.d.).

We have sought to engage with current standards without losing sight of the fact that the concept of the subject it assumes needs to be updated, considering the contemporary nature of cyberculture. Cyberculture, which encompasses the synergy between the technological and the social, and entails possibilities for the collaborative production of culture, introduces a crisis in that it forces us into new ways of living and interpreting the world, different from those that have thus far been established. It necessitates a review of the relationship between subjects and current regulations which are once again called into question. For us as researchers, this 'crisis' has emerged most visibly in our dialogue with children. They showed persistent interest in social networks in the following situations: when we were invited to 'play with them' instead of interrogating them from the sidelines of their experience, in Internet cafés or private spaces in which the children were studied in the presence of the connected computer. These childish enunciations destroyed our most basic questions with regard to ascertaining whether the children had skills in computer use. Such questions were often an attempt to reaffirm our role as protectors. An experience of hori-zontality in relation to culture proved to be decisive for us to start considering online research as a methodology to be questioned. What was the step forward? Could we experiment with settings, the standards of which are neither trusted by nor appropriate for children? Could we follow, from the sidelines, a dialogue that had already revealed itself to be artificial?

One of our experiments was to test, on a trial basis, children's online play as well as to communicate with them online using the tools and languages avail-able on social networks. To accomplish this, we had to become users of online networks, an effective part of a contemporary social phenomenon in which we are immersed today. It seemed more appropriate to investigate 'the inside' by living in their own language context. By the same token, we formed groups of child contacts based on their familiarity with the researchers. By way of a pres-entation protocol of research and dialogue with parents or those responsible, we followed the patterns of websites directed at children[7].

We realize that every methodological choice is combined with the ethical principles that draw on the conceptions of science, truth and, especially, child-hood. We opted to conduct the dialogue with children unconditionally, that is, without prejudging whether or not these practices were appropriate for them.

It is important to point out that, far from neglecting our responsibility towards the children, this was an effort to develop another concept of responsibility that is consolidated on the 'inside' and is based on otherness and dialogue. In this sense, the phenomena to be investigated can be thought of as a form of education using media. Through this investigation, our research questions will be examined and viewed from the perspectives of the participants, including the children. We would like to share, *online*, the research question itself and, along with it, question, ponder, compare and rethink. From this perspective, research with children in today's cyberculture involves finding a meeting point with children without compromising the socio-technical dimensions that configure contemporary relations with digital media.

Notes

1. The studies in question are as follows: Freire (2012), Macedo (2014), Mendes (2013), Macedo (2012). Available at www.gpicc.pro.br
2. Orkut is a social networking site affiliated with Google. It was created in January 2004.
3. More details at http://pt.wikipedia.org/wiki/Orkut
4. This survey was conducted by the Centre for Research on Information Technology and Communication. The agency conducts studies that are offered as a reference for the elaboration of public policies that guarantee Information and Communication Technologies (ICT) access to the Brazilian population as well as to monitor and evaluate the socioeconomic impact of ICTs. The report of the ICT Kids 2010 research, as well as other editions (2009 and 2012), are available at www.cetic.br
5. One of the major challenges in this scenario is that until 2010, Orkut and Facebook recommended their use for individuals aged 18 years or older. Later, this was changed to 13 years. Despite their own recommendations, these sites offer games and language features—inspired by movies and products—aimed at small children; this leads us to question the interest of these sites in dialoguing with children and covertly attracting them.
6. In Brazil, LAN houses are prohibited to children under the age of 12 if they are unaccompanied by their parents.
7. The details of these studies are available at www.gpicc.pro.br

References

Agambem, G. (2009). O que é o contemporâneo. In G. Agambem, *O que é o contemporâneo? E outros ensaios* (V. N. Honesko, Trad.). Chapecó, Santa Catarina: Argos.

Bakhtin, M. (2003). *Estética da Criação Verbal*. São Paulo: Martins Fontes.

Bakhtin, M. (2010). *Para uma filosofia do ato*. São Carlos: Pedro & João Editores.

Bornheim, G. (1992). O sujeito e a norma. In A. Novaes (Org.), *Ética* (pp. 247-260). São Paulo: Companhia das Letras, 1992.

Lemos, A. (2003). Cibercultura: alguns pontos para compreender a nossa época. In A. Lemos & P. Cunha (Orgs.), *Olhares sobre a cibercultura* (pp. 11-23). Porto Alegre: Sulina.

Macedo, N. M. R. (2014). *"Você tem face?" Sobre Crianças e Redes Sociais Online*. Tese de doutorado, Universidade do Estado do Rio de Janeiro, Rio de Janeiro, RJ, Brasil.

Pereira, R. R. (2012). A pesquisa com crianças. In R. R.Pereira & N. M. Macedo (Orgs.), *Infância em pesquisa*. Rio de Janeiro: NAU Editora.

Pereira, R. R. (2013). Entre o (en)canto e o silêncio das sereias: sobre o (não)lugar da criança na cibercultura. *Childhood & Philosophy*, 9 (18), 319-343.

Pereira, R. R. (n.d.). Precisamos conversar! Questões para pensar a pesquisa com crianças na ciber-cultura. In M. Reis & L. Gomes (Orgs.), *Infância, sociologia e sociedade*. São Paulo: Attas.

Primo, A. (2008). Fases do desenvolvimento tecnológico e suas implicações nas formas de ser, con-hecer, comunicar e produzir em sociedade. In N. de L. Pretto & S. A. Da Silveira (Orgs.), *Além das redes de colaboração: internet, diversidade cultura e tecnologias de poder*. Salvador: EDUFBA.

Santos, E. (2008). *Cibercultura: o que muda na educação*. Programa Salto para o Futuro. http://tvbrasil.org.br/fotos/salto/series/212448cibercultura.pdf

Media Education: Public Policies, Curricular Proposals and Teacher Training

Contexts, Perspectives and Challenges for Media Education in Brazil

Monica Fantin

Historic and conceptual context of media education: trajectory, letters and definitions

Internationally, media education has been understood as a field of knowledge and intervention; as educational praxis with methodological and didactic aspects; and as an instance for theoretical reflection about this praxis (with objectives, methodologies and evaluation) in a context in schools and beyond (Rivoltella, 2002). Media-education intervention always involves a praxis, the activity and the theoretical reflection that guides and sustains this praxis, which construct the context of media education based on perspectives: those that are *institutional* and supported by relevant official documents, those of a *social nature* and/or inspired by a social movement or networks of international cooperation, and *theoretical* ones based on conceptual models and methodologies (Rivoltella, 2012).

In the Brazilian context, these perspectives reveal themselves in the tensions and/or overlap between the practical and reflexive dimensions of media education, because media education is often practiced without being denominated as such.[1]This is because in Brazil, and perhaps throughout Latin America, certain social needs require actions in which media-educational experiences are invented and created without the required reflection and theorization.

Recently, the richness of media-education practices began to gain more recognition because of Brazil's unique and diverse culture[2] in interlocution with international experiences (Girardello & Orofino, 2012). In this process, it is relevant to highlight dialogs between Brazilian and foreign researchers (Bevort & Belloni, 2009) and research in partnerships that are the fruit of institutional contracts and cooperation agreements between Brazilian and foreign universities (Fantin & Rivoltella 2012), which play an important role in the growing visibility of media education in the Brazilian and international scenario.

Thus, media-educational experiences construct proposals that are constantly re-elaborated in official documents, organized movements, academic events and encounters that promote and publicize ideas, thus consolidating practices and contributing to the construction of this field in our country.

The pioneering Grünwald Declaration (1982) and the *Carta de Bellaria* [The Bellaria Letter, 2005] were documents that guided the construction of later letters in Brazil: the *Carta do Rio* [The Rio de Janeiro Letter, 2004], written at the Rio Summit on Youth, Media and Children, and the *Carta de Florianópolis para a Mídia Educação* [The Florianópolis Media Education Letter, 2006], produced at the first Seminar of Media-Education Research, conducted at the Federal University at Santa Catarina (UFSC), in Florianópolis.

In this most recent letter, media education is presented as "an interdisciplinary field that is under construction at the border between education, communication, culture and art, and which is dedicated to reflection, research and intervention for the critical and creative appropriation of the media and the construction of citizenship." Its presence in education was understood "as part of the educational system, in the activity of media producers, in the communication companies, and in the civil society organizations (...) as an instrument in the defense of civil rights and the construction of citizenship" (Girardello & Fantin, 2009, pp. 161-162).

Other challenges to media education are reconsidered in the *Alexandria Proclamation on Informational Literacy and Lifelong Learning* (2005), the Paris Agenda: 12 Recommendations for Media Education (2007) and the European Community Recommendation for Media Literacy in the Digital Era (2009), as well as other documents now being drafted.[3] We also mention the *Standards of Competence in ICT for Teachers*, a document on the use of the technologies in education (UNESCO, 2008) and *The Media and Information Literacy Curriculum for teachers* (UNESCO, 2013), important guidelines for policies and strategies concerning the new demands of media education.

Nevertheless, recognizing the specificities of the countries in which different agencies promote specialized media-education regulation programs, and despite the initiatives of Brazilian letters, the strength of these documents as generators of public policy is still far from being consolidated in our country (Zanchetta, 2009). Although these debates and studies promoted by UNESCO and some international agencies have little or no official participation from Brazil (Belloni, 2012), we cannot fail to mention them, both for their importance and because they indicate trends and serve as inspiration for future practices and conceptual redefinitions.

The multiple nature of the concept and its articulations and movements define media education over the years as a methodological and epistemological reflection onthe praxis of educating for, with and through the media (Rivoltella, 2002). As a field still under epistemological and methodological construction, media education constitutes a space of theoretical reflection on cultural practices as well as educational ones, through a transformative perspective that emphasizes reapproximating culture, education and citizenship. With this in mind, we list the three threads that form the weave of media education: culture (considering the expansion and diversity of cultural repertories), criticism (analysis, reflection and evaluation) and creation (expression, communication and construction of knowledge). To these three words, which begin with the letter "C"[4], we have added the C of citizenship to establish the "4 Cs" of media education – culture, criticism, creation and citizenship – in an analogy to the "3 Ps" of the rights of children in relation to media: protection, provision and participation (Fantin, 2006, p. 100). We understand media education as the articulation of the rights of protection, provision and participation, with the right to culture, criticism, creation and citizenship.

New media-education paradigms: themes and trends

To problematize the new modes of seeing, knowing and inhabiting digital culture, thinking of the educational uses of the media and technologies both within and outside the school, in person or through online spaces side-by-side with television screens, movies, computers, videogames, smartphones and tablets is a current requirement of media education that calls for the construction of cultural, technical and social competencies. Highlighting the challenge of participatory culture and of media education in the 21st century, Jenkins (2006) lists a range of abilities[5] that children and youth must develop, and emphasizes the role of schools and community programs in the promotion of these new literacies that change the focus from individual expressions to that of collaborative work in networks.

The convergence of medias, technologies, and language promotes new forms of participation in the culture and designs new trends in the ecological concept of media education (Rivoltella, 2002; Pinto, 2005), which implies the responsible use of all the media – photography, radio, cinema, television, Internet, video-games, smart phones and social networks – without forgetting the dimension of corporality and movement in conjunction with nature (Fantin, 2011). In this changing landscape, the New Media Education appears as a fresh paradigm for responding to the challenges of the centrality of the media, not only in the key factors of media education (representation, language, production and audience) but also as a "new pedagogy" expressed both in the conceptual "correction" of media education in the change of paradigm in the realm of media and cultural studies, and in its definition as "Technologies of the Self" ((Rivoltella, 2006, p. 244; Rivoltella, 2008, p. 227).

This conceptual redefinition promotes the idea that media education becomes a posture of the teacher/educator and of education itself, as Rivoltella affirms.

The great challenge today is to understand media education as education itself, he adds. That is, media education becomes education, not only a field of study and intervention but a media-educational position, an asset of each one.

The challenges and redefinitions translate how the concept of media education expresses the challenges of each historic moment. Today, it should consider the central role that the medias and technologies occupy in contemporary life and the new theoretical methodological challenges placed before media education (Buckingham, 2006), because their dynamic nature "reflects the connection between children, youth and the communication media – during their leisure time and in educational institutions – and because it develops at the tense border between media-education practices, empiric knowledge and theories" (Tufte & Christensen, 2009, p. 102).

In this way, in addition to the constant and recurring themes in the media-education tradition, it is important to incorporate other emerging issues and understand the media beyond the instrumental sense, affirming them as culture and working with the sense of multiliteracies and formal-informal learnings in the different spaces of culture (Fantin, 2013). The new forms of interaction with technologies in the context of digital culture mentioned above are discussed in the concepts of multiliteracies (Cope & Kalantzis, 2000; Fantin, 2011b), media literacy (Buckingham, 2006), new media literacy (Jenkins, 2006), informational literacy (Rivoltella, 2008) and new literacies (Lankshear & Knobel, 2011).

Media education in the curriculum and education

Although the borders of media education are fluid, to guarantee epistemological legitimacy in various contexts it must be present in the curriculum and in the teaching systems. In various countries, the curricular insertion of media education appears in various forms: as an *autonomous discipline,* with a *transversal character,* as *integrated education* and through *mixed models* (Fantin 2012, 2012a). The presence of associations and research centers linked to universities performs an important role, considering a certain epistemological resistance of the school system and of poorly conceived or episodic laws (Rivoltella, 2002).

The various disciplinary positions of media education and the curriculum models present in different countries suggest positive and negative aspects, strengths, fragilities, risks and potential. To make the best choice, it is necessary to consider criteria such as didactic relevance, interdisciplinary/transversal articulation, programmatic-curricular organicity and their operationalization at different levels of teaching.

In Brazil, despite recent strong investment in the introduction of ICTs in schools, public policyfor teacher education and the curricular insertion of media education leaves much to be desired. Although education for the media has been mentioned in the Law of Guidelines and Bases (1996), the National Curricular Parameters (1997), the National Curricular Guidelines for Schools of Pedagogy (2006) and the National Education Plan (2011),[6] there is still no specific national policy for the sector. In sum, when they are not absent from the debate, the proposals concerning this issue have proved ineffective given the challenge mentioned.

The fact that it does not "officially" exist as a mandatory class or transversal theme means that media education continues to be regarded only as a pedagogical resource and not as an object of study that is articulated with other fields of knowledge. This is reflected in delays, in comparison to other countries where media education is more consolidated[7] and in the distancing between the current curriculum and the emerging questions of contemporary culture.

Nevertheless, despite the insignificant presence of classes on media and technologies in most teacher education courses in Brazil, a mapping of an introduction of the issue of media education in pedagogy programs at recognized Brazilian universities reveals some encouraging data (Fantin, 2012). The theme of media education is contemplated as a mandatory course in a large portion of these teacher education programs, with different emphases and terminologies, and also as an optional elective andor isolated offer.

Through a qualitative survey on the presence of media education in the curriculum of the pedagogy courses in Brazil (Fantin, 2012; Fantin, 2012a), we investigated 38 federal universities there that offer the course[8] and 11 state and private universities[9] analyzing information from their respective sites. The criteria for the choice of state and private universities were based on these institutions contributions to the field of Brazilian education in general, and to research in communication and education in particular.

Among the federal universities, of the 38 courses studied only 12 make no reference or do not have any class related to the issue of media education. In the curricula of the other universities, all have at least one course related to media education.

We found that, at the largest Brazilian universities, the issue of media education is usually included as a mandatory course,[10] an elective or optional class,[11]an isolated offering,[12] or a thematic seminar,[13] with different emphases, approaches and terminologies. The class programs are diversified, and express the theoretical affiliations of the courses or research groups at the institutions. Their approaches range in emphasis: from theoretical and conceptual; to operative and instrumental; to taking a pragmatic approach to the pedagogical and social implications of the uses of technologies in education.

Although the names and emphases of the courses vary in the curricula, and even if all do not provide detailed course descriptions, at the federal universities 70% of these courses emphasize ICT and education while 30% highlight "Education, Communication and Media", a proportion that at the other universities is about 50% for each emphasis.

The investigated sample suggests that, despite an apparent change in direction, the presence of a course linked to media education still appears to be marked by instrumental aspects. If, on the one hand, this has been a historic trend of the discipline of *Educational Technology* in the curriculum and the different theoretical-methodological affiliations of the field research group at each university and their territories, on the other hand it reveals that the media-education approach still needs to be consolidated in the teacher education courses.

We know that the curricular insertion of media education in initial teacher education is sufficient to handle all the teachings necessary regarding the demands mentioned, but its absence aggravates this situation even more, leading teachers to fill in the gaps in other ways, for instance through personal effort, specialization courses, permanent education, etc. (Fantin & Rivoltella, 2012).

This questioning of the curriculum model, education focused on courses and other transversal possibilities, leads us to ask: To what degree does the insertion of media education in teacher education and schools point to another perspective for curriculum organization? We still do not have an answer to this, so the question remains open.

In countries like Brazil, where media education has still not been guaranteed in the school curriculum or in initial teacher education, it is worth asking what model would be best suited to consolidate it in education. Regardless of the various possibilities, it is important to keep in mind that media education is more than a need, and is now a required condition for allowing students to attain belonging as well as instrumental and cultural citizenship. For this reason, being included in the curriculum can signify the digital, social and cultural inclusion of teachers and students; in this sense, we still have much to be consolidated.

Some challenges of media education in public policy

In addition to the challenges indicated in this article, we cannot fail to mention the need for a media-education perspective in the different federal government programs involving science, technology, education and communication in general, particularly those concerning the insertion of ICT in education and schools: the National Program of Computers in Education (ProInfo), the Broadband in Schools Program (PNBL), One Computer per Student(ProUCA), and others undertaken in Brazilin recent years.[14]

Given the absence of the principles that are dear to media education in the official documents of these programs, we note only the rhetoric of the salvationist discourse of digital-technological inclusion in the schools, as if this is sufficient to assure the citizenship and learning of children and youth. But this political-

-instrumental emphasis is not unique to the Brazilian programs, as we can see from research in other countries (Sancho, 2013).

The discontinuity and lack of a critical and more impartial perspective about what was and is being realized, has usually caused the political and economic interests of each government to prevail over those of education and culture, which is revealed in the inefficiency of the types of education proposed, the weak involvement of teachers, and the absence of dialog with academic research. This absence is translated into the reproduction of mistakes already identified in previous programs, such as the ProUCA, in which inadequate teacher preparation, the low quality of the equipment, non existent maintenance, and the precarious connection speed in the schools compromised the principles of the program and the 1:1 model, problems now being repeated in the program involving the use of tablets in schools (Fantin, 2013).

Statements by teachers and students support what various studies have found regarding the insertion of technology in schools, in which the strongly instrumental character is not enough to trigger innovative processes that transform the pedagogical practice, thus requiring other concepts and proposals. A possible contribution would be the presence of the foundations of media education, above all in relation to an educational policy that allows a critical eye and instrumentalizes students and teachers for other uses of technologies in and outside schools, because these questions transcend subjects, instances and school spaces (Quartiero, Bonilla & Fantin, 2012).

As seen, there are many challenges to the consolidation of media education in the various scenarios of Brazilian education. This paper sought to reflect on some aspects – notto compare Brazil with other contexts, but above all to reveal contrasts and places of critical construction of a unique history that is still being shaped in various Brazilian landscapes and situations, and in the challenges on the horizon before us.

Notes

1. Since the 1930s there have been experiences in Brazil that fit our understanding of media education; but since they were not defined as such, and in the absence of a more systematized reflection onthe field, they were not always considered to be part of it. For example, educators and filmmakers who in the 1930s published analyses and comments about films in specialized magazines highlighted the links between cinema and education, and affirmed the viability of this "resource" in Brazilian schools. At the time, different proposals for "educational cinema" were implemented in the context of educational reforms that took place in various Brazilian states, and the creation of the National Institute of Educational Cinema (INCE) in 1937 stimulated the production of more than 400 documentaries for educational purposes (Fantin, 2011, p. 117).

2. The diversity of Brazilian culture is characterized by a plurality of cultural and ethnic matrixes of whites, indigenous and blacks composed by the colonizers, African slaves, the indigenous peoples and European, Asian and other immigrants; see Ribeiro (1995). And among the singularities, although not exclusive to Brazil, one is expressed in the media monopoly, above all by a single media company that concentrates power and which for more than 30 years has

thrived through "benefits" legitimated by its approximation with different governments; see Guareschi (1981).

3. See the Carta de Ponta Grossa de Mídia e Educação (2013) [The Media and Education Letter from Ponta Grossa], a document that is still open to contributions. https://secure.avaaz.org/po/petition/Apoie_a_Carta_de_Ponta_Grossa_e_Midia_e_Educacao/?launch

4. The "3 Cs"– culture, criticism and creation – as essential aspects of media education suggested by Bazalgette (2005). Media Education in Inghilterra: incontro con Cary Bazalgette nel suo ufficio. *Boletim InterMED*, 10 (3), Roma.

5. Play; Performance; Simulation, Appropriation; Multitasking; Distributed cognition; Collective Intelligence; Judgment; Transmedia navigation; Networking; Negoatiation, Visualization.

6. The National Education Plan (PNE) 2011 -2010 was sent to the national congress in 2010. As of January 2014 it had not been approved.

7. Countries in which the ITCs are an integral part of the elementary and high schools and a priority in university courses, particularly in Pedagogy; see Fantin, 2012a.

8. UFAC;UFAM;UFPR;UFRR; UFPA; UFMT; UFMS; UFG; UFT; UFMA; UFPI; UFC; UFP; UFRN; UFPE; UFSE; EFAL; UFBA; UFES; UFES; UNB; UFRJ; UFF; UNIRIO; UFRRJ; UFMG; UFJF; UFOP; UFU; UFV; UFLA; UFESP; UFSCAR; UFPR; UFSC; UFRGS; UFFS; UFPEL; UFSM.

9. USP; UNICAMP; PUC-SP; PUC-GO; UNEB; UERJ; PUC-RIO; PUC-MG; PUC-PR; PUC-RS; UNISINUS.

10. Examples: Medias, Digital Technologies and Education (UFRGS), Education and Contemporary Technologies (UFBA), Education and Communication (UFSC), Information and Communication Technologies Applied to Education (UFSM), Online Education: reflections and practices (UFJF), Digital Technologies and Education (UFFS), Education, Communication and Medias (UFG), Media and Education: a contemporary debate (USP), Education and Technologies (Unicamp), Media, Technologies and Education (PUC-Rio), New Technologies in Different Pedagogical Spaces (PUC-SP).

11. Media and Education: a Contemporary Debate (USP). Available at http://www4.fe.usp.br/graduacao/institucional/curriculo/pedagogia; Communication, Education and Multimedias. Available at http://sistemas3.usp.br/jupiterweb/obterDisciplina?sgldis=EDM0324&codcur=480 12&codhab=203

12. Digital Technologies, Youth and School (UFMG). Available at https://colgrad.ufmg.br/pedagogia/pedagogia/Home/Solicitacoes-Academicas

13. Education and Communication Technology and Education and Anthropology and Media (UNEB). Available at http://www.uneb.br/salvador/dedc/pedagogia/ementario/

14. Available at http://inclusaodigital.gov.br/programas

References

Belloni, M. L. (2012). Mídia-educação: contextos, histórias e interrogações. In M. Fantin & P. C. Rivotlella (Eds.), *Escola e cultura digital* (pp. 31-56). Campinas: Papirus.

Bazalgette, C. (2005). Media Education in Inghilterra: incontro con Cary Bazalgette nel suo ufficio. *Boletim InterMED*, 10 (3), 2-4.

Bevort, E., & Belloni, M. L. (2009). Mídia-Educação: conceitos, história e perspectivas. *Educação e Sociedade*, 30 (109), 1081-1102.

Buckingham, D. (2006). La media education nell'era della tecnologia digitale. In M. Morcellini & P. C. Rivoltella (Eds.), *La sapienza do comunicare*: dieci anni dei media education in Italia ed Europa (pp.111-122). Trento:Erickson.

Girardello, G., & Fantin, M. (Orgs.) (2009). Carta de Florianópolis para a Mídia-Educação. In G. Girardello & M. Fantin, *Práticas culturais e consumo de mídias entre crianças*. Florianópolis: UFSC/CED/NUP.

Cope, B. & Kalantzis, M. (Eds.) (2000). *Multiliteracies: literacy learning and the design of social futures*. New York: Routledge.

Fantin, M. (2006). *Mídia-Educação: conceitos, experiências, diálogos Brasil-Itália*. Florianópolis: Cidade Futura.

Fantin, M. (2011). *Crianças, Cinema e Educação: além do arco-íris*. São Paulo: Annablume, 2011.

Fantin, M. (2011a). Mídia-educação: aspectos históricos e teórico-metodológicos. *Olhar de professor*. UEPG, 114(1), 27-40.

Fantin, M. (2011b). Beyond Babel: multiliteracies in digital culture. *International Journal of Digital Literacy and Digital Competence*, 2 (1), 1-6.

Fantin, M. (2012). Mídia-educação no ensino e o currículo como prática cultural. *Currículo sem Fronteiras*, 12 (2), 437-452.

Fantin, M. (2012a). Mídia-educação no currículo e na formação inicial de professores. In M. Fantin & P. C. Rivoltella (Orgs.), *Escola e cultura digital: pesquisa e formação de professores* (pp. 57-92). Campinas: Papirus.

Fantin, M. (2013). Novos e velhos problemas no contexto do PROUCA: fronteiras entre BA e SC. Trabalho encomendado GT16 da *36ª Reunião Anual da ANPED*.

Fantin, M., & Rivoltella, P. C. (2012). Cultura digital e formação de professores: usos da mídia, práticas culturais e desafios educativos. In M. Fantin & P. C. Rivoltella (Orgs.), *Escola e cultura digital* (pp. 309-346). Campinas: Papirus.

Girardello, G., & Orofino, M. I. (2012). Crianças, cultura e participação: um olhar sobre a mídia-educação no Brasil. *Comunicação, mídia e consumo*. 9, (25), 73-90.

Guareschi, P. (1981). *Comunicação & poder: a presença e o papel dos meios de comunicação de massa estrangeiros na América Latina*. Petrópolis: Vozes.

Jenkins, H. (2006). *Confronting the Challenges of Participatory Culture:Media Education for the 21st Century*. MacArthur Foundation.

Lankshear, C., & Knobel, M. (2011). *Nuevos Alfabetismos*. (3º ed.) Madrid: Morata.

Pinto, M. (2005). A busca da comunicação na sociedade multi-ecrãs: perspectiva ecológica. *Comunicar*, 25, 259-64.

Quartiero, E.; Bonilla, M. H., & Fantin, M. (2012). Políticas para la inclusión de las TIC ne las escuelas públicas brasileñas: contexto y programas. *Campus Virtuales*, 1 (1), 115-26.

Ribeiro, D. (1995).*O povo brasileiro: a formação e o sentido do Brasil*. São Paulo: Companhia das Letras.

Rivoltella, P.C. (2002). *Media Education: modelli, esperienze, profilo disciplinare*. Roma: Carocci.

Rivoltella, P. C. (2006). *Screen Generatio:gli adolescenti e le prospettive dell´educazione nell´età dei media digitale*. Milano: Vita e Pensiero.

Rivoltella, P. C. (2008). From Media Education to Digital Literacy: A Paradigm Change? In P. C. Rivoltella, *Digital literacy: tools and Methodologies for Information Society* (pp. 217-229).New York: IGI Publishing.

Rivoltella, P. C. (2012). Retrospectivas e tendencias da pesquisa em mídia-educação no contexto internacional. In M. Fantin & P. C. Rivoltella, P.C. (Orgs.), *Escola e cultura digital* (pp. 17-29). Campinas: Papirus.

Sancho, J. (2013). La fugacidad de las políticas y la inércia de las practicas. II Seminário Aulas Conectadas. Florianópolis, UDESC.

Tufte, B. & Christensen, O. (2009). Mídia-Educação: entre a teoria e prática. *Perspectiva*, 27 (1), 97-118.

UNESCO (2008). *Padrões de competência em TIC para professores*. Brasília, UNESCO.

UNESCO (2013). Alfabetização midiática e informacional: Currículo para formação de professores. Brasília: UNESCO, UFTM. http://unesdoc.unesco.org/images/0022/002204/220418por.pdf

Zanchetta, J. J. (2009). Educação para a Mídia: propostas européias e realidade brasileira. *Educação e Sociedade*, 30 (109), 1103-1122.

Media Education in Teacher Training

The Experience of the Federal University of Triângulo Mineiro Based on a UNESCO Proposal

Alexandra Bujokas de Siqueira

Despite not being truly new, media-education teacher training has gained new footing in Brazil with relatively recent events. In 2009, the first National Conference on Communication (CONFECOM) mobilized sectors of the organized civil society to debate communication policies and their relation to citizenship. The experience chosen to be reported in this paper was the State Conference on Communication (CONECOM-MG), which was held in the state of Minas Gerais. One of the conference's main proposals for the national round was the incorporation of media outlets as part of the curriculum in Brazilian schools, hand in hand with training actions aimed at educators. Presented to the national conference by Work Group 12 within Theme 3 (Citizenship: Rights and Duties), the proposal was not approved (Secom & FGV, 2010). However, while the federal scenario did not see the theme as important, there seems to be a demand for it in the state of Minas Gerais.

Three years after CONFECOM was staged, the Minas Gerais State Education Secretariat launched the programme *Reinventando o Ensino Médio* (Reinventing Secondary School). This programme has the aim of reformulating this education level, reordering the curriculum and fostering the implementation of innovative pedagogical practices, focused on creativity and autonomy 'for concluding or continuing to study, or for preparing for the work market' (Minas Gerais State Education Secretariat, 2012, electronic document). The programme prioritized 18 areas, one being Applied Communication, which has the aim of providing 'capacity-building on different media types, with the objective of developing communication and social interaction skills' (Minas Gerais State Education Secretariat, 2012, electronic document).

Aware of these demands, the Federal University of Triângulo Mineiro (UFTM) has been promoting media education through the curriculum used in formal courses, or research and extension projects. Actions became more consistent in

2010, when a partnership between the university and UNESCO's Communication and Information Sector was established to publish a Brazilian Portuguese version of the book 'Media and Informational Literacy – Curriculum for Teachers' (UNESCO, 2013), as well as conduct a test with the proposal.

For just over four years UFTM, through the Distance Learning and Education Centre with Communication and Information Technologies (CEAD), has been offering regular courses on the critical use of media. In addition, it implemented the Media-Education Laboratory, which offers short courses to basic education students and teachers, as well as developing research that has resulted in media-education teaching materials and methodologies[1]. The theoretical-methodological foundations and some results of this experience will be presented below.

Coordinating a proposal

Teacher training courses at the Federal University of Triângulo Mineiro were designed in the scope of actions of the Support Programme for the Restructuring and Expansion of Federal Universities (REUNI)[2]. Launched in 2009, the courses had the aim of offering a curriculum that addressed innovative content and practices. The components were organized in three sets: common basic training, specific course training[3] and pedagogical training. Common basic training, offered in the first two years of the course together with specific training components, includes the theme of Multiple Languages, organized in three disciplines: Reading and Writing, Scientific Methodology and Communication, Education and Technology. The last of these, a 30-hour course, has focused since its beginning on education for the media.

Organized in four topics (digital technologies and contemporary culture; analysis of media texts; media education's key concepts and methodologies; content production and remix), this course has the goal of developing skills for accessing, understanding and critically using digital media in educational actions. Therefore, lessons follow a specific path.

Everything starts with the study of a recent controversy involving media culture. Controversial issues have been addressed, such as the Ministry of Education's anti-homophobia kit[4], vetoed by President Dilma Rousseff, as well as the 'Hope Teaches' campaign, featuring Gisele Bündchen, which led to a formal complaint by the Special Secretariat for Women's Policies to the Advertising Self-regulatory Body (CONAR)[5]. The goal of this unit is to look at how various people interpret messages in differing manners, how diverse actors try to impose their point of view, and how educators may proceed to trigger questioning without imposing correct readings.

The expectation is that students will develop a better understanding of the power relations that shape media culture (Hesmondhalgh, 2006): the concentration of 'old' types of media in the hands of just a few groups gives these actors more power to strengthen their values and points of view, while the emergence of new types of media potentially undermines historically established power structures, as non-professionals may become content producers and reach a large audience. However, citizens have to be educated to learn to exercise this power. The school plays an important role in this scenario, and the so-called 'media-education' area may provide a foundation for critical and innovative work on media.

The second topic (analysis of media texts) is based on the presupposition that the contemporary school has changed from a place where knowledge is transferred to one where analysis and reasoning take places (Cope & Kalantzis, 2000). Analysing the media, its languages and representations seems to be a legitimate task for education provided in schools and, thus, student teachers start to get to know and practice methods for disassembling messages, taking evidence into consideration and summarizing informed opinions. In practical terms, one may start from something popular and apparently inoffensive, like the advert *Caçadores de Neuras* (Raiders of Concern) produced for a kitchen cleaning product[6]. Aired exclusively on the Internet, the video shows the opposite of a macho man, who does not let his wife cook or clean, which could suggest a female representation in the marriage, with the woman having a job and the husband looking after the home. By taking apart the audiovisual narrative, identifying change processes, describing the characters and their roles in history, as well as mapping values associated with each of them, other possibilities come to light. In *Caçadores de Neuras*, the woman's role is to obey her husband: eating the dinner he has made for her (the word dinner is presented together with a gesture suggesting sexual intercourse) and not doing any housework, because heavy work is something for men to do. When a pair of scientists are shown in the narrative, presenting the macho man character with the kitchen cleaning product, he changes his mind and calls his wife over to discuss his rights. The division of roles between the couple should be reviewed because this is what he wants, in the same way that the wife did not work in the kitchen because he did not want her to.

The representations in the advert were later compared with data from the study 'Violence against Women: femicides in Brazil'[7], conducted by the Institute for Applied Economic Research (IPEA), which compared data on the death of women in relation to domestic violence for the periods 2001 to 2006 and 2007 to 2011. The goal of the study was to assess the impact of the so-called Maria da Penha Bill, passed to inhibit and prevent domestic and family violence against women. According to the study, the bill has not reduced the number of deaths as expected, and such crimes continue to be committed mainly by partners or ex-partners, in situations in which family abuse and sexual violence have been identified, or when women find themselves with less power or fewer resources than the man.

The conclusion is that it is obviously not possible to establish a cause-and-effect relation between the advert and the data collected by the study. However, legitimate reflection is possible in relation to the representations contributed by the advert to play down how serious issues are perceived, like violence against women.

According to Cortés (2005), the way the media present information (a cleaning product for a modern couple), organize ideas (inverted sexism), disseminate values (played-down and even funny sexual violence), provide modes of behaviour and reinforce expectations (the persistent obedience by women in relation to men's wishes) is how media teach us, even if it is not the intention of communication professionals. And users learn, regardless of whether they are aware of this. From the author's perspective, means of communication may act as non-school, informal and omnipresent pedagogical materials. Education would gain relevance if it knew how to critically take ownership of these materials.

Therefore, in the third stage of the discipline   Communication, Education and Technology   the task is learning to transform symbolically powerful controversies and disputes, in media terms, into educational activities. Guided by four key concepts (language, audience, media and representation institutions), student teachers explore national and international pedagogical materials that have the media as their object of study. They get to know the background of media education in Brazil and the world, and discuss UNESCO's proposal, summarized in the document 'Media and Informational Literacy – Curriculum for Teachers' (UNESCO, 2013) which, as they are informed on their first day, is what the subject they are studying is based on. Students are guided to identify how the materials and experiences trigger skills inherent to the critical use of media, like those mentioned in the International Clearinghouse on Children, Youth and Media:

1. dealing with all means of communication, including the printed word and graphic representation, sound, still and moving pictures, aired on any type of technology;

2. understanding the context of media communication in the society where one lives and how its means of communication operate;

3. acquiring skills in using the media to communicate with others;

4. critically interpreting media texts, identifying sources, their cultural, political, social and commercial interests;

5. selecting the appropriate means through which to communicate their own messages and reaching their target audience;

6. achieving access to media support, for receiving and producing. (Vienna Conference, 1999)

The fourth and final topic (content production and remix) focuses on the use of multimedia applications for producing messages. At this stage, students are already familiar with political issues implied by the media, possess language foundations, and know structuring concepts and essential methodologies for the area; it is now time to get their hands dirty. In each semester, the last four lessons are allocated to the production of content that solves so-called communication problems. In order for the production not to run the risk of celebrating the student's wishes, but rather teach a bit about media (Buckingham, 2003), pupils should solve a language issue, producing something using that language. For instance, a photographic essay is produced using connotation processes (Barthes, 1990), as an induction of senses for objects, recording the same scene with and without photogenia (such as using light sources, exposure and framing techniques) or inserting texts in the photo that change its original meaning. These essays are posted on Flickr[8] and organized into exhibitions, with legends, arguing why a certain photo represents a certain connotation process[9].

In previous semesters, after studying the foundations of comic strip language (Eisner, 1999), students have produced stories using the application Strip Generator[10], building narratives with beginning, middle and end, protagonists and antagonists, expressing ideals with the use of 'iconic metaphors' (Eco, 2008). In addition, radio reports have been produced about local public education and cultural services available for young people, using the free software Audacity[11], and then shared on Sound Cloud[12]. Furthermore, infographics have been produced of previously chosen texts using the application Piktochart[13].

Production activities have shown to be a productive moment to summarize the path through which the discipline develops. By producing content, students see in practice how to reproduce codes, conventions and stereotyped media representations, without being aware they are doing this. And alternative proposals are very difficult to create.

Dialogue at the international level

The previous section attempted to show that, although UFTM initiatives are focused exclusively on teacher training, we are not working from the perspective of the use of ICTs in education. Our starting point is the idea that education for the media is a basic citizen right in any country in the world, as through this people can exercise their freedom of expression. Obviously, there has to be some sort of education that prepares citizens to seek, receive and transmit information and ideas through any means. In fact, school education should play a central role in this endeavour.

By bringing the demand for studying media culture into the school, it could be said that young people have wide knowledge of media, which is the fruit of their constant interaction with this scope of culture from a very early age. However, they probably do not have the skills to identify, analyse and reflect on the processes they use to assign meaning to media messages, considering social context characteristics and where they are generated. Furthermore, being aware of individual ownership processes, in dialogue with social processes, is the most fundamental definition one may have of the critical reading of the media, which has been built here conversing with two theories that complement each other: coding and decoding in the perspective of Cultural Studies (Hall & Whannel, 1964; Hall, 2003) and the Mediation Theory, from the Latin American perspective (Martín-Barbero, 2004).

In both cases, the authors consider that different types of media provide young people with conflicting information and ideas about the society in which they live. Therefore, it is up to the student, guided by the teacher, to test these descriptions and interpretations of reality, comparing mass culture products with their own experiences.

The theoretical perspective of the British cultural studies, in dialogue with the mediation theory, seems to find practical recognition in UNESCO's recommendations. Guided by the International Programme for the Development of Communication (IPDC), the organization has outlined the Media Development Indicators (UNESCO, 2010), which help to identify and assess the quality of actions in the area of communication in each country. The indicators take into consideration five categories[14], which are divided into a set of more specific general indicators. Their significant number implies the promotion of education for the media.

Category 4 of the indicators guides the analysis of the professional capacity-building on offer and institutions that support freedom of expression, pluralism and diversity. Indeed, two indicators of this category are of interest: professional capacity-building on offer, and academic courses on media practices.

In this context, promoting freedom of expression, pluralism and diversity requires the empowerment of the greatest number of social actors as possible, so they may act as content producers. There is no reason to exclude the school audience (students and teachers). Therefore, the systemic view of a country's communication structure shows us ways through which we may develop education for media actions. According to this perspective, new ways of teaching technical, aesthetic, cultural and political issues at the same time need to be found. This is what has been happening within the scope of another UNESCO programme, part of the wider-reaching IPDC: Media and Information Literacy. This initiative was mainly developed between 2008 and 2010, culminating with the publishing of the English version of the curriculum model mentioned earlier.

Firstly, a group of experts met in Paris to discuss the foundations of a reference curriculum for teacher training. The work was published in a report (UNESCO, 2008) outlining the basic themes and skills that characterize a capable educator in the use of different types of media. The themes were divided into two groups: topics for the media literacy training of teachers, and topics to teach teachers how to teach media. The 2008 report resulted in the document Media and Information Literacy Curriculum for Teachers. The curriculum proposal is made up of two parts. The first describes seven basic skills to access, assess, use and produce content using media, and how to integrate these skills into teacher training curricula. In addition, ten pedagogical practices that facilitate the teaching and learning of these skills are provided. The second part brings together 11 modules summarizing relevant concepts to guide the study of media, such as freedom of expression, ethics and media accountability, audiences, advertising, news production systems, language and representation.

The tests carried out at UFTM follow the steps recommended by the curriculum matrix itself (UNESCO, 2013, p. 53): teachers and students interested in the theme made a full review of the proposal; then, actions in course, to which the proposal could be incorporated, were identified. Finally, the more relevant modules were selected, taking into consideration time available as well as human and technological resources. The discipline Communication, Education and Technology is the main result.

The experience indicates that the media-education proposal is a practical and achievable way to train this audience intellectually and pedagogically, in tune with the school's contemporary demands. Data collected continuously from the work of student teachers, assessment questionnaires answered at the end of each semester, and spontaneous thoughts provided in day-to-day activities show that students regard media education mainly as a viable proposal to promote innovation in teaching and learning practices. It incorporates critical stances vis-à-vis the media, which at the end of the day has a ubiquitous influence on their lives, as well as the lives of their students.

Possibly the greatest hurdle for the materialization of the proposal is the school structure. As soon as trainees find themselves in the classroom as interns, or take part in teaching initiation programmes[15], they question whether media education is viable, as a result of crowded rooms, overworked teachers – who have to work in two or three schools to make ends meet – and a lack of equipment, access to the Internet and technical support personnel. Therefore, implementing a national media-education policy remains a probable utopia. Sooner or later, Brazil will have to become part of the international movement.

Notes

1. Courses are offered within the scope of the permanent extension programme *Redeci – Engajando jovens atráves da mídia-educação* (Engaging young people through media education). www.uftm.edu.br/redeci
2. The REUNI, established by Decree No. 6,096 from 24 April 2007, as part of the National Education Development Plan (PDE) actions, provides for an increase in vacancies in graduate courses, a greater number of night courses on offer, the promotion of pedagogical innovations, and a combating of drop-out rates: http://reuni.mec.gov.br/
3. Six teacher training courses are offered: Biological Sciences, Physics, Geography, History, Mathematics and Chemistry.
4. Made up of three videos and a guide for teachers, the material addressed transsexuality, bisexuality and female homosexuality. According to the press at the time, after a great deal of pressure from evangelical parliamentarians at the National Congress, President Dilma Rousseff vetoed the material's distribution. As soon as the controversy was published, videos made available on YouTube reached over 200,000 views, triggering posts and other videos providing contrary positions, and ensuring a heated and at times rude debate.
5. Broadcast in 2011, the campaign of the female underwear brand 'Hope' brought model Gisele Bündchen showing the best way of breaking bad news to husbands. First, she was shown fully clothed and the visual graphics said that something was wrong. Then, when she was dressed only in her underwear and gave him the same news, the strategy was considered correct. A narrator suggested: "You, Brazilian woman, use your charm". SPM received complaints through its ombudsman office and forwarded a formal complaint to CONAR, requesting that the airing of the advert be suspended. The allegation was that it reinforced the stereotype of the woman as her husband's sex object, and efforts to dismantle sexist practices and thoughts were ignored. CONAR did not rule in favour of the complaint, and the campaign continued to be aired.
6. http://www.youtube.com/watch?v=KTRRzuOUZiU
7. http://goo.gl/oByBXs
8. www.flickr.com
9. A more detailed report of this activity and students' Flickr page addresses can be found at http://wp.me/p1oN8X-5J
10. www.stripgenerator.com
11. http://audacity.sourceforge.net/
12. https://soundcloud.com/
13. http://piktochart.com/
14. 1. A system of regulation conducive to freedom of expression, pluralism and diversity of the media; 2. Plurality and diversity of media, a level economic playing field and transparency of ownership; 3. Media as a platform for democratic discourse; 4. Professional capacity building and supporting institutions that underpin freedom of expression, pluralism and diversity; 5. Infrastructural capacity is sufficient to support independent and pluralistic media.
15. Created by the Ministry of Education in 2009, the Teaching Initiation Programme (PIBID) provides student teachers grants, as long as they take part in teaching initiation projects developed by higher education institutions in partnership with public basic education schools.

References

Barthes, R. (1990). *O óbvio e o obtuso: ensaios sobre fotografia, cinema, pintura, teatro e música.* Rio de Janeiro: Nova Fronteira.

BRASIL. Ministério da Educação (2000). *Parâmetros Curriculares Nacionais (Ensino Médio): Parte II – Códigos, Linguagens e suas Tecnologias.* Brasília: MEC.

Buckingham, D. (2003). *Media education literacy, learning and contemporary culture.* Cambridge: Polity Press.

Cortés, C. E. (2005). How the media teach. In G. Schwarz & P. Brown (Eds.), *Media literacy: transforming curriculum and teaching* (104th Yearbook of the National Society for the Study of Education). Malden: Blackwell.

Cope, B. Kalantzis, M. (2000). *Multiliteracies – Literacy learning and the design of social futures.* Londres: Routledge.

Eco, U. (2008). *Apocalípticos e integrados* (6a ed.). São Paulo: Perspectiva.

Eisner, W. (1999). *Quadrinhos de arte sequencial.* São Paulo: Martins Fontes.

Hall, S. (2003). *Da diáspora.* Belo Horizonte: Editora UFMG.

Hall, S., & Whannel, P. (1964). *The popular arts.* Londres: Hutchinson Educational.

Hesmondhalgh, D. (Ed.) (2006). *Media production* (Volume 3). Berkshire: Open University Press.

Martin-Barbero, J. (2004). *Ofício de cartógrafo.* São Paulo: Loyola.

Secretaria Estadual de Educação (2013). *Reinventando o Ensino Médio.* http://goo.gl/iC6JTI

Secretaria de Comunicação da Presidência da República – SECOM (2010). *Caderno da 1ª Conferência Nacional de Comunicação.* Brasília: SECOM/FGV.

UNESCO (2010). *Indicadores de desenvolvimento de mídia – Marco para avaliação do desenvolvimento dos meios de comunicação.* Brasília: UNESCO.

UNESCO (2013). *Alfabetização midiática e informacional – Currículo para formação de professores.* Brasília/Uberaba: UNESCO/CEAD-UFTM.

Vienna Conference (1999). *Recommendations addressed to UNESCO adopted by the Vienna Conference "Educating for the Media and the Digital Age"*, 18-20 April 1999. http://www.nordicom. gu.se/sv/unga-och-medier/recommendations-addressed-unesco-media-education

An Overview of Practices in Brazil

Media, Reflection and Action

An Overview of Media-Education Activities in Formal and Informal Contexts of Brazilian Education

Lyana Thédiga de Miranda

Experiences in Media and Education in Brazil: a Brief Overview

Since the 1960s, various efforts have been made to understand the practical and theoretical possibilities that embrace the relationship between communication and education in Brazil. A variety of terminologies, such as *media education, education for the medias, educommunication* and others, compose a frame of reference that characterizes actions of education, interventions and studies located at this interface. In common, the critical, creative and participatory approach in the relationship of children, youth and adults with the media and communication technologies.

Based on a historic course of action and reflections in this field still under construction (Fantin, 2006; Belloni, 2009, 2012; Girardello & Orofino, 2012; Soares, 2013), this paper presents a scenario of the relationship between education and communication as it is presented in Brazil today. With a descriptive character, yet simultaneously objective, the text presents key points that encompass themes about media-education practices[1] found in formal and informal education, in a didactic manner and without the pretension of encompassing the entire field. The issues covered include: *legislation and public policy; civil society organizations, infancy and consumption practices; curriculum and* finally, *academic research.*

Legislation and public policy

There have been various attempts to develop public policy in the two fields focused on here. In the realm of communication, there have been efforts to implement a national communication policy capable of regulating the various forms of media and the companies involved (radio and TV broadcasters, print media, and the Internet), over which there is still little regulation in the country,[2] as well as social communication as a whole. In education, a National Education Plan (PNE) is being deliberated by congress. This is a set of articles, goals and strategies, to be complied with within the next ten years, which emphasizes the eradication of illiteracy and the universalization of schooling – from nurseries to public universities – and is a historic demand concerning Brazilian education.

The intersection between education and communication takes place through inter-ministerial programs (Quartiero, Bonilla & Fantin, 2012) concerning the adoption of communication technologies, particularly in schools, in an effort to "modernize" classrooms. Among the government programs, we can mention the Broadband in Schools Program (PBLE),[3] the One Computer per Student program[4] and its continuation with the adoption of tablets,[5] in addition to others, such as the National Education Technology Program (ProInfo),[6] which has been in place the longest. Nevertheless, because of the fragmented nature of the laws and actions, there is a contrast between the measures for access to digital technologies and the realizations that adopt an integral vision of media technology, culminating in the incapacity to establish a set of planned policies for the field.

Civil society organizations

In the context of the pulverization of public policy for the sector in Brazil, civil society entities conduct initiatives that involve media education. They are highlighted by the configuration of networks, collectives and publications, such as the work undertaken by the Association planetapontocom [planet dot com][7] and its publication revistapontocom.[8] These agents come together with the objective of strengthening and giving visibility and vitality to the projects in the formal realm of education.

The Network of Communication, Education and Participation (Rede CEP) brings together a group of non-governmental organizations (NGOs) spread throughout Brazil, and is dedicated to projects, methodologies and publications – such as the guide *Mudando sua Escola, Mudando sua Comunidade, Melhorando o Mundo!* [Changing Your School, Changing your Community, Improving the World!] (Rede CEP 2010) – which strives to be a base for the implementation of public policy in the field. The network is currently organized in a collective administration, composed of: Ciranda – Central de Notícias dos Direitos da Infância e Adolescência [The Children's Circle – Center of News of the Rights of Children and Adolescents] (Curitiba-PR)[9]; Cidade Escola Aprendiz [City School Apprentice] (São Paulo-SP)[10]; Cipó – Comunicação Interativa [Vine – Interactive Communication] (Salvador-BA)[11]; Comunicação e Cultura [Communication and Culture] (Fortaleza-CE)[12]; MOC – Movimento de Organização Comunitária [Movement of Community Organization] (Feira de Santana-BA)[13]; Oficina de Imagens

[Image Workshop] (Belo Horizonte-MG)[14]; Portal Bem TV [The Good TV Portal] (Rio de Janeiro-RJ)[15]; CECIP – Centro de Criação de Imagem Popular [Center for Creation of Popular Image] (Rio de Janeiro-RJ)[16]; Saúde e Alegria [Health and Joy] Núcleo de Educação e Comunicação e Educação da Escola de Comunicações e Artes da Universidade de São Paulo [Education and Communication Center of the School of Communication and the Arts of the University of São Paulo (SP).[17]

With the objective of subsidizing the school activities, Rede CEP provided assistance to the *Programa Mais Educação* [More Education Program][18] of the Ministry of Education (MEC), and prepared a manual based on the experiences encountered – which assists in the actions involving communication and the uses of media. With the same goal, the Rede Nacional de Adolescentes e Jovens Comunicador@s (RENAJOC) [National Network of Communicating Adolescents and Youth][19] created the guide *Mais Educomunicação* [More Educommunication] (RENAJOC, 2012), [20] which encourages youth to produce media content, applying this initiative in school environments. These projects are supported by the concept of *Educomunicação,* which guides actions, programs and communicational products to promote educational media practices and education for citizenship (Soares, 2013).

Media Education Lab[21] (MEL) is a Brazilian initiative that aims to strengthen media education in the country. It is a social enterprise that believes in the power of the network to connect hundreds of students, teachers, companies, government and social organizations to transform education in a creative way. MEL works with this theme based on two different strategies. On the one hand, it develops projects with students and teachers in schools involving the analysis, comprehension, production and publication of different media products. Students can produce media content ranging from a movie or blog to a magazine or radio program. To date, thousands of students from different states in the country have created more than 50 different products. On the other hand, MEL also plays an important role in advocacy.

Childhood and consumer practices

Involved with the rights of communication allied to those of childhood, institutions such as the National Agency for the Rights of Childhood (ANDI)[22] and the Instituto Alana[23] promote campaigns, provide incentives for the creation of contents suitable for different age groups, guide the posture of news professionals – monitoring their production and supporting the debate about the need for public policy in this area – in addition to conducting research and study about issues involving the children and youth public and media.

The need for legislation on advertising and consumption by children, which still has no official regulation in Brazil, is being deliberated within various legislative spheres in the form of proposed law 5921/2001, which seeks to regulate advertising aimed at this public. To support the debate, the Brazilian Association of Advertising Agencies (ABAP) created the campaign *We are All Responsible*,[24] which provides videos and booklets that propose an informative and educational dialog on the issue. The debate has also touched the academic sphere, where research groups are working with the issue. The complex discussion is still far from achieving consensus among educators, professionals and educational and communication researchers.

By public initiative, the Indicative Classification of the Ministry of Justice, based on the Statute of the Child and Adolescent (ECA), provides guidelines for audiovisual works (TV programs, movies, video/DVD, electronic games, theater and music) by age group (10, 12, 14, 16 and 18), to be indicated at the beginning of each (Secretaria Nacional de Justiça, 2012). The Indicative Classification is based on a concept of shared responsibility between producers, exhibiters, government and the audience, with the participation of all of society.

Curriculum

It is possible to identify educational actions with the media being conducted in daily school activities, but without the systematization that would be possible if they were found in specific courses with planned curricula. With a lack of organic policies and curricular references, the identification of the media-educational activities is conducted in surveys and scientific studies that portray these experiences, in an interaction between the academy and the school.

These studies are characterized by efforts to map academic research, like the critical survey conducted in 83 public and private elementary schools in Florianópolis (SC) to identify the activities with, about, and/or through the media conducted at the schools (Pereira, 2008). Media-educational activities are also conducted in workshops such as the Projeto Redeci[25] in Minas Gerais, which strives to develop abilities and promote reflection by allowing public school students to create productions in various media. The importance of the workshops is found, above all, in a publication produced by the project, which supports theoretical discussion and pedagogical practice (Siqueira & Carvalho, 2013; Siqueira & Cerigatto, 2012).

In the survey conducted within the study Cultura digital e Escola [Digital Culture and the School] (Fantin & Rivoltella, 2012), the issue was identified in required, elective and optional courses in the curricula of various universities with a range of titles and course descriptions, although with a more instrumental bias, marked by the use and appropriation of tools and technologies.

It is worth emphasizing the implementation of the recently created teacher certification courses in Educommunication at the School of Communications and Arts at the University of São Paulo (ECA/USP), and the bachelor's course in Communication with certification in Educommunication at the Federal University at Campina Grande (UFCG/PB) (Soares, 2013). While these programs promote the education of professionals trained to conduct educommunicative practices in schools, creating a new field of action, those that present the media-education theme in early teacher education seek to train all future teachers, so that they will be media educators in their daily educational practices.

Without explicit alignment with the perspectives presented, since 2008 the Accreditation Course in Cinema and Audiovisual[26] at the Federal Fluminense University (UFF) accredits teachers to work in this field, and is supported by the institution's traditional Cinema School.

Another successful experience is Idade Mídia[27], created in 2001. Developed by the founder of Media Education Lab (Le Voci Sayad, 2012), the program is administered in Colégio Bandeirantes, in São Paulo. Students have created magazines, movies, apps, sites, TEDs and other communication products in this MIL experience. Four universities in Brazil use this model as an MIL case.

Academic research

The research groups linked to universities in different regions of the country combine various experiences that congregate the interaction of education and communication in themes such as cinema, culture, the body and human movement, sports, childhood, television, advertising and consumption, digital culture and others. Groups that stand out include: Núcleo Infância, Comunicação Cultura e Arte [The Center for Childhood, Communication Culture and Art] (NICA/UFSC)[28]; Grupo de Pesquisa Infância e Cultura Contemporânea[29] [The Childhood and Contemporary Culture Research Group] (GPIC/ProPEd/UERJ); Grupo de Estudos e Pesquisas em Infância e Mídia [The Childhood and Media Research and Study Group] (GEPIM/UEL)[30]; Grupo de Pesquisa da Relação Infância, Adolescência e Mídia [The Research Group on the Relationship between Childhood, Adolescence and the Media] (GRIM/UFC)[31]; Educamídia (UNB)[32]; Laboratório e Observatório da Mídia Esportiva [The Sports Media Laboratory and Observatory] (Labomídia/UFSC)[33]; Núcleo de Estudos sobre Mídia, Educação e Subjetividades [Center for Studies of Media Education and Subjectivities] (Nemes/ UFRGS)[34]; Grupo de Pesquisa, Educação e Mídia [Group of Research, Education and Media] (Grupem/PUC-RJ)[35]; Cinenarrativas[36] (UNIRIO), Mídias, Educação, Cultura e Novas Cidadanias [Medias, Education, Culture and New Citizenships] (UFTM/ Unesp/ Uniube)[37]; Grupo de Pesquisa em Educação, Comunicação e Tecnologias [Research Group in Education, Communication and Technologies](GEC/UFBA)[38]; Departamento de Comunicações e Artes da ECA/USP[39] [Department of Communications and Arts of ECA/USP; Rede Kino,[40] and others based at Brazilian universities.[41]

The diversity of the groups supports discussions and experience socialized in the Research and Working Groups of events such as that of the National Association of Graduate Studies and Research in Education (Anped)[42], the Brazilian Congress of Communication Sciences (Intercom) ,[43] and the Colloquium of Research in Education and Media (Colóquio de Pesquisas em Educação e Mídia)[44].

Tendencies: in search of new profiles

In addition to the endeavors mentioned, the articulation with the digital media has presented new challenges to education that stimulate participation and production in a critical, creative and responsible manner. The trends that align media and education definitively approximate this relationship to other fields such as culture, art and, more recently, digital culture.

Projects that seek collective financing on the web,[45] online pages created intuitively, news published at a distance with a click – without the intermediary of large media outlets, producers, organizations, editors or even the education media – point to a new perspective that reveals the education-communication interface, a route marked by diversity, engagement, collaboration and belonging. Nevertheless, the path to follow continues to be in question.

This overview of the media-education activities in Brazil reveals how the variety and inter-combination of concepts and programs, and their influences in macro and micro contexts, seek to consolidate a position of citizenship. This practice is not always consecrated, but particular nuances are being created that generate specific dynamics and results, as demonstrated by the texts below. These are reports in which it is possible to find an intertwining of the *sensitive perspective of young people* with cultural diversity – *the white, black and indigenous* from which we are composed – and ally them to different *points of seeing and hearing*.

Notes

1. We refer to actions/reflections that are located at the interface of education-communication as *media-educative practices* merely to maintain textual coherence, while recognizing the polyphony that this term presents.
2. Regulation of radio and telecommunications broadcasters in Brazil was promulgated in the 1960s, when the country was under a dictatorship. Today, proposals such as the Civil Mark for the Internet (PL 2126/2011), which would provide guarantees, rights and responsibilities for users, are being deliberated in the federal congress.
3. http://portal.mec.gov.br/index.php?option=com_content&view=article&id=15808:programa-banda-larga-nas-escolas&catid=193:seed-educacao-a-distancia
4. http://www.uca.gov.br/institucional/
5. http://www.fnde.gov.br/portaldecompras/index.php/produtos/tablet-educacional
6. http://portal.mec.gov.br/index.php?Itemid=462
7. http://planetapontocom.org.br/institucional/
8. http://www.revistapontocom.org.br/

9. http://ciranda.org.br/
10. http://cidadeescolaaprendiz.org.br/
11. http://www.cipo.org.br/portal/
12. http://www.comcultura.org.br/
13. http://www.moc.org.br/
14. http://www.oficinadeimagens.com.br/home/
15. http://www.bemtv.org.br/portal/
16. http://www.cecip.org.br/
17. http://www.usp.br/nce/?wcp=/quemparticipa/lista,5,15,16
18. portal.mec.gov.br/index.php?option=com_content&view=article&id=16690&Itemid=1115
19. renajoc.org.br/
20. Mais Educomunicação is a project undertaken in partnership with the NGO Viração Educomunicação (www.viracao.org) and the Instituto C&A (www.institutocea.org.br).
21. http://mediaeducationlab.com.br
22. www.andi.org.br/
23. http://alana.org.br/
24. http://www.somostodosresponsaveis.com.br/
25. http://www.uftm.edu.br/redeci/
26. http://www.uff.br/iacs/site/grad_cinema_audio_lic.html
27. http://idademidia.colband.blog.br
28. www.nica.ufsc.br/
29. www.gpicc.pro.br
30. http://www.uel.br/ceca/spg/pages/comunicacao/comunicacao-popular.php
31. www.grim.ufc.br/
32. http://www.educamidia.unb.br
33. labomidia.ufsc.br
34. www.ufrgs.br/nemes/
35. grupem.pro.br/
36. http://cinenarrativas.blogspot.se
37. http://midedcult.wordpress.com/quem-somos/
38. www.gec.faced.ufba.br/twiki/bin/view/GEC
39. www.cca.eca.usp.br/educom
40. redekino.com.br
41. The groups work with different understandings of the relationship between education and communication.
42. www.anped.org.br/
43. www.portalintercom.org.br/index.php
44. http://4cepem.wix.com/4cepem
45. Highlighted by the production of the video Guarani Kaiowa (catarse.me/pt/kaiowa), by the Video in the Reserves project (www.videonasaldeias.org.br/2009/), and the documentary Quando sinto que já sei [When I Feel that I Already Know] (catarse.me/pt/quandosintoquejasei)

References

Bévort, E., & Belloni, M. L. (2009). Mídia-educação: conceitos, história e perspectivas. *Revista Educação e Sociedade*, (30), 1081-1102.

Belloni, M. L. (2012). Mídia-educação: contextos, histórias, interrogações. In M. Fantin & P. C. Rivoltella (Orgs.), *Cultura digital e escolar: Pesquisa e formação de professores* (pp. 31-56). Campinas, SP: Papirus.

Fantin, M., & Rivoltella, P. C. (Orgs.) (2012). *Cultura digital e escolar: Pesquisa e formação de professores*. Campinas, SP: Papirus.

Fantin, M. (2006). *Mídia-educação: conceitos, experiências, diálogos Brasil-Itália*. Florianópolis, SC: Cidade Futura.

Girardello, G., & Orofino, M. I. (2012). Crianças, cultura e participação: um olhar sobre a mídia-educação no Brasil. *Comunicação, Mídia e Consumo* (9), 73-90.

Le Voci Sayad, A. (2012). *Idade Mídia: a comunicação reiventada na escola*. São Paulo: Editora Aleph.

Pereira, S. C. (2008). *Mídia-educação no contexto escolar: mapeamento crítico dos trabalhos realizados nas escolas do ensino fundamental em Florianópolis*. Dissertação de Mestrado. Departamento de Educação. Universidade Federal de Santa Catarina, Florianópolis.

Projeto de Lei 2126/2011. Estabelece princípios, garantias, direitos e deveres para o uso da Internet no Brasil.

Projeto de Lei 5921/2001. Proíbe a publicidade / propaganda para a venda de produtos infantis.

Quartiero, E., Bonilla, M.H., & Fantin, M. (2012). Políticas para la inclusión de las TIC em las escuelas públicas brasileñas: contexto y programas. *Campus virtuales*, 1 (1), 115-126.

Rede de Comunicação, Educação e Participação (Rede CEP) (2010). *Mudando sua Escola, Mudando sua Comunidade, Melhorando o Mundo! Sistematização da Experiência em Educomunicação*. Retrieved from: http://www.unicef.org/brazil/pt/br_educomunicacao.pdf

Rede Nacional de Adolescentes e Jovens Comunicadores (RENAJOC) (2012). *Guia Mais Educomunicação: Orientações, conceitos e metodologias para subsidiar as ações*. Retrieved from: http://www.institutocea.org.br/midiateca/188/publicacao/guia-mais-educomunicacao.aspx

Secretaria Nacional de Justiça (2012). *Classificação Indicativa – Guia Prático*. Retrieved from: http://portal.mj.gov.br/services/DocumentManagement/FileDownload.EZTSvc.asp?DocumentID=%7B981E1E6C-C5B8-401F-9F34-79D2689B4AED%7D&ServiceInstUID=%7B59D015FA-30D3-48EE-B124-02A314CB7999%7D

Siqueira, A. B. de, & Carvalho, L. C. S. (2013). Experiências de mídia-educação: estudando a fotografia no Ensino Médio. *Pro-Posições*, 24(3), 117-138.

Siqueira, A. B., & Cerigatto, M. P. (2012). Mídia-educação no Ensino Médio: por que e como fazer. *Educar em Revista*, (44), 235-254.

Soares, I. O. (2013). Educomunicação: as múltiplas tradições de um campo emergente de intervenção social na Europa, Estados Unidos e América Latina. In R. G. C. J. Lima & J. M. (Orgs.), *Panorama da comunicação e das telecomunicações no Brasil: 2012/2013* (pp. 169-202). Brasília; Ipea.

The Media in Education

The Strengthening of Identities and Rights

Leunice Martins de Oliveira

The construction of a new society project that acts independently, with willingness and a political conscience, has been a challenge for this new era. Human events we have experienced and witnessed at the beginning of the twenty-first century have shown us that intolerance, racism, and discrimination – i.e., ways of dealing with differences – can lead us to a process of deep dehumanization. Overcoming racism is imperative in our society. It is an ethical assumption and a remarkable political task.

In Brazil, the materialization of a historical claim regarding the black social movement (Rodrigues, 2005) at national and international levels has been accomplished by the federal government's adoption of actions toward achieving the justice for which the movement has been fighting.

After Brazil's participation in the World Conference against Racism, Racial Discrimination, Xenophobia, and Related Intolerance in Durban (South Africa) in 2001, the topic of affirmative action as a necessary policy for reducing inequality and promoting racial equality has become prominent in the Brazilian political agenda.

Affirmative action policies are specific policies that promote equal opportunity and include concrete conditions for participation in society that are aimed at overcoming racism, discrimination, and racial inequality (MEC/SECAD, 2006).

Thus, since 2003, the Brazilian government has been active in this process by promoting debates and taking constructive measures regarding this matter. One of the first concrete actions was the enactment of Federal Law 10.639/03,[1] which established the compulsory teaching of African and African-Brazilian history and culture in primary schools.

By using this legislation to change the national curriculum guidelines and the National Educational Bases and Guidelines Law, information and communication technology has been included in pedagogical practices. This new context has motivated the offer of multimedia products for diverse audiences, and several projects have been created to make African-Brazilian culture visible in the school environment. These anti-racism, public educommunication[2] policies affect the citizenship of all Brazilians.

Educational systems and institutions at different levels have to conform to the demands for educational diversity and inclusion when making decisions and taking initiatives to recognize and value differences through measures consistent with a political educational proposal that outlines education relationships in everyday teaching. This is a political decision with strong pedagogical implications, including implications for teacher training. The strengthening of identities and rights will be implemented to end negative images of black people, with a pedagogical approach to ethno-racial issues in everyday schooling.

Meanwhile, the research group EDUCOM AFRO (*Educommunication and African-Brazilian Cultural Production*), created at the Pontifícia Universidade Católica do Rio Grande do Sul, integrates the theory and practice of education for diversity from an educommunication perspective. The research group supports the academic and continuing education of teachers and social actors as a way of implementing Federal Law 10.639/03.

The research by the Afro-Cultural Production for Children (PACC) initially dealt with Brazilian ethnic, cultural, social, and economic diversity by surveying Afro-cultural production for Brazilian children, highlighting the role of *children's literature* in the emancipation of children, and disclosing stereotypes still present today (Proença Filho, 2004). It established a dialogue with other cultural manifestations intended for children, such as *toys, movies, newspaper inserts, TV listings,* and *Internet websites*. It investigated which Afro-cultural products were being offered to all children in Brazil, considering above all the cultural manifestations with the theme 'Afro-Brazilian history and culture', were intended for children, and were produced based on the Law. We were committed to analysing and reflecting on the content of cultural productions that children acknowledge daily, which end up becoming an important element of their world, which is full of sense and meaning.

It becomes necessary to reflect on the relationship between cultural production and the construction of children's self-image in different educational settings, especially when one considers that the current reality of life for our children is deeply marked by interactive experiences with media. These devices can be used as educational instruments, and might be a powerful educational tool. Age-appropriate, educational television, for instance, could be not only an entertainment device but could also be beneficial to children.

The role of the educator as a mediator of the learning process entails helping children understand and critically interpret the conveyed information in an effort to understand the persuasive intention of the message. Hence, it is important to select topics that are relevant to the formation of individual self-identities, and – to understand that self-identities are not simplistic or static – it is necessary to research more in terms of the experiences children have in everyday reality (Hall, 2000, 2003). These dialectical and multiple processes of self-identity formation are closely linked to how children experience day-to-day routines.

Thus, we have the challenge of constructing a critical and reflective dialogue with children, enabling them to analyse both the way the subjects of their culture are represented by the media and educational materials. This enables students to reach a critical awareness and learn new ways of acting, which contributes to the formation of a new human being who has an attitude, posture, and values that respect differences. In this sense, education is understood here as a process of humanization directed toward a reflection on the human being and an opening of one to the other (Freire, 1996).

Our study deals with the importance of creating a positive identity for black children. This is critically important, considering that these children are dis-criminated against in their routine through pejorative statements, insults, and stereotypes regarding traits of African origin and their social position (they are ranked lower). They are called 'neguinha' (nigger), 'macaca' (monkey), 'beiçuda' (big-lipped), 'cabelo ruim/pixaim/fuá' (bad hair/nappy hair/kinky hair), 'nariz chato' (flat nose), and 'burra' (dumb).

The important action of the Law regarding its own enunciation process will occur through rebuilding the self-esteem of Afro-Brazilian children and the reconfiguration of black identity by emphasizing the creation of proposals for educational activities and reflection on our daily lives focusing on educating people about difference – which also serves as a way to foster a mindset free of prejudices and stereotypes.

In the path of PACC research, the EDUCOM AFRO group has accessed some materials produced for the promotion of "African and Afro-Brazilian culture and history". They have identified the multimedia project *A Cor da Cultura* (The Colour of the Culture) from the channel Futura[3] as an example of the public policy in education and communication promoted by the Ministry of Education as an affirmative action that appreciates Brazilian blackness. The kit for the *A Cor da Cultura* project includes the following products: textbooks called *Saberes e Fazeres* (Knowledge and Practices), divided into volumes called *Modos de Ver* (Ways of Seeing), *Modos de Sentir* (Ways of Feeling), and *Modos de Interagir* (Ways of Interacting); a book called *Memória das Palavras* (Memories of Words), which is a glossary of 206 words of African origin; a CD called *Gonguê: a herança africana que construiu a música brasileira* (Gonguê: African heritage that builds Brazilian music) containing 16 songs/sounds; a board game called *Heróis de Todo o Mundo* (Heroes from All Around the World) featuring trivia about black Brazilian personalities; and lastly, five TV series, divided into *Livros Animados* (Cartoon Books), *Heróis de Todo o Mundo* (Heroes from All Around the World), *Mojubá* (Mojubá), *Nota 10* (Score 10), and the programme *Ação* (Action). The kit is available at www.acordacultura.org.br.[4]

Figure 1. A Cor da Cultura kit

Heróis de todo o mundo   Mojubá   Nota 10

Livros Animados   Ação

Source: A Cor da Cultura website.

In 2010, inspired by the *A Cor da Cultura* project, the EDUCOM AFRO research group created and launched the *RS Negro project: Educating for Diversity*.[5] It is an *educommunicative* multimedia kit that includes a book called *RS Negro: cartografias da produção do conhecimento* (RS Negro: cartographies of knowledge production), a *SOU* video-documentary, a *RS Negro Magazine*, a *RS Negro Posterbook*, a *RS Negro Classes* CD, and a *Negro Grande CD Player* with Afrodescendant musicians from Rio Grande do Sul. The products of the kit can be found at PUCRS's website (http://ebooks.pucrs.br/edipucrs/rsnegro), and they were freely distributed to Rio Grande do Sul's educational network.

Figure 2.   RS NEGRO project kit

Book   Magazine   Movie

CD   Classes

posters

Source: EDUCOM AFRO/PUCRS

Such productions pursue ways of comprehending diversity in education. They expand school contents by contextualizing and integrating the content as a way of propagating themes that are more engaged with plurality.

The material produced in both projects was highly adequate regarding the educative reality that children, youth, adults, and educators must find their own way, being free to create and recreate the suggested activities by adapting and adjusting them to each educational and learning level. This strategy involves them in the dialogue between the school and social movements, cultural groups, and popular organizations. There are no prescribed practices in these projects, but there is a sharing of ideas that can favour the study of African and African-Brazilian culture by understanding that it is in children's realities that they construct themselves as subjects and produce knowledge, which must be respected and taken into account.

We are facing new educational needs, and the media cannot be seen as an educational panacea or as a simple educational device. Based on the contact between education and communication, from an educommunication perspective, a new practice of educative communication is coming to light: a space for the critique of and intervention in the production of knowledge regarding social, racial-ethnic, and cultural diversity.

The development of children's abilities to interpret how language is used is imperative. It is important to identify and discuss power issues inscribed in literary, visual, spoken, and multimodia texts to enable children to understand how and why they have always been represented by stereotyped and stigmatized messages.

This new conceptual basis, from the point of view of educommunication, requires children to be active receptors, becoming more critical and less vulnerable to the messages they receive. It also requires children to become producers of media through the events experienced in educational practice in order to realize the role media and culture can play in their lives.

Notes

1. In 2008 this law was reformed by Law 11.645, which added the teaching of 'Indigenous history and culture'.
2. Educommunication is the act of teaching using mass media and technology. It is the act of reading critically with regard to social facts and the media. The term educommunicator–mediator of processes of alternative journalism and community radio projects–was used by Argentinian journalist Mário Kaplún and has inspired the concept of educommunication as used by Jesus Martin Barbero, John B. Thompson, and Armand Mattelart. Moreover, in Brazil, journalist and professor Ismar de Oliveira Soares is the founder of this type of study, having contributed greatly with the Centre of Communication and Education of the Universidade de São Paulo NCE/USP (Soares, 2000).
3. An educational TV channel with private sector investment that develops social projects aligned with the causes and demands of the lower-income classes.

4. In 2004, the project A Cor da Cultura was conducted in partnership with the Centre for Information and Documentation of the Black Artist of Rio de Janeiro (CIDAN). The federal government, through the Ministry of Education (MEC) and the Special Secretary of Racial Equality Promotion Policies (SEPPIR), partnered with Rede Globo, through the Fundação Roberto Marinho via Futura Channel, to engage in dialogue with the black movement of several Brazilian states. The project was funded by Petrobras.

5. In 2010, the *RS NEGRO* project was conducted in partnership with the Foundation of Education and Culture of the International Sport Club (FECI), the EDUCOM AFRO research group of Faced/PUCRS, the state government (through the Justice and Social Development Secretary of RS (SJDS), together with the Black Community´s Participation and Development Council of the State of Rio Grande do Sul [CODENE]), the Universidade Estadual do Rio Grande do Sul (UERGS), the Historical Archives of Rio Grande do Sul (AHRS), and the gaucho black movement. The project was funded by the Grupo CEEE.

References

BRASIL (2006). Ministério da Educação. Secretaria de Educação Continuada, Alfabetização e Diversidade. MEC/SECAD. *Orientações e Ações para a Educação das Relações Étnico-Raciais.* Brasília, DF.

Freire, P. (1996). *Pedagogia da Autonomia.* Rio de Janeiro: Paz e Terra.

Hall, S. (2000). *A Identidade Cultural na Pós-Modernidade* (T. T. da Silva & G. L. Louro, Trans.). Rio de Janeiro: DP&A.

Hall, S. (2003). *Da Diáspora: identidades e mediações culturais.* Belo Horizonte: Editora UFMG.

Lei Federal 10.639, de 9 de janeiro de 2003 (2003). Altera a Lei nº 9.394, de 20 de dezembro de 1996, que estabelece as diretrizes e bases da educação nacional, para incluir no currículo oficial da Rede de Ensino a obrigatoriedade da temática "História e Cultura Afro-Brasileira", e dá outras providências.

Lei Federal 11.645, de 10 de março de 2008 (2008). Altera a Lei nº 9.394, de 20 de dezembro de 1996, modificada pela Lei nº 10.639, de 9 de janeiro de 2003, que estabelece as diretrizes e bases da educação nacional, para incluir no currículo oficial da rede de ensino a obrigatoriedade da temática "História e Cultura Afro-Brasileira e Indígena".

Machado, S. P. (2010). A cor da cultura: crianças, televisão e negritude na escola. In G. F. da Silva, J. A. dos Santos & L. C. da C. Carneiro (Orgs.), *RS Negro: cartografias sobre a produção do conhecimento* (pp.322-332). Porto Alegre: EDIPUCRS.

Proença Filho, D. (2004). A trajetória do negro na literatura brasileira. *Estudos Avançados, 18*(50), 161-193.

Rodrigues, T. C. (2005). *Movimento Negro no cenário brasileiro: embates e contribuições à política educacional nas décadas de 1980-1990.* Dissertação de mestrado, Universidade Federal de São Carlos, São Carlos, Brasil.

Soares, I. O. (2000). Educomunicação: as perspectivas do reconhecimento de um novo campo de intervenção social: o caso dos Estados Unidos. *EccoS Rev. Cient.,* 2 (2), 61-80.

Film Schools in Rio de Janeiro's Public Education

Adriana Fresquet

In 2012, six film schools were created based on the pilot project Cinema for Learning and Unlearning (Cinema para Aprender e Desaprender, CINEAD) at the Application College of the Federal University of Rio de Janeiro (UFRJ), under the Postgraduate Program in Education Research 'Curriculum and cinematic language in basic education'. The project (Fresquet, 2013a, b) included two municipal schools, two state schools, and two federal schools (specialized in visually impaired and deaf students).

Alain Bergala worked as a consultant during this process to design the training of teachers, inclusion of initial activities, and creation of didactic materials. In building the project, teaching, research, and outreach activities were articulated with the involvement of professors and researchers in education and cinema studies, professionals and technicians, doctoral and master students, and scientific initiation or extension scholarships recipients at the graduate and secondary education levels. Students and teachers from the schools involved also participated, adding new choices and contributing to the production of audio-visual experiments and the school curriculum. In this article, we will present the project, processes and products, didactic materials, and training exercises that comprise our proposed film curriculum for basic education schools.

The CINEAD project, dating back to 2006, emerged as a research and outreach project that sought to investigate childhood/youth in cinema, primarily through the lens of educational psychology. A small group began meeting weekly to organize study and research seminars, which were complemented by the first outreach project, preferentially offered to public school teachers. Each new member and each partnership[1] with new institutions were expanded and reconfigured in format, as can be seen in both the on-going and completed studies[2]. In 2008, we signed an agreement with the Museum of Modern Art (MAM-Rio) and the Application College of the UFRJ. The CAp film school was created for research purposes, but also served as a pilot project for the future creation of new film schools in public schools. In 2009, we strengthened ties with the Martagão Gesteira Institute of Paediatrics and Child Care, the paediatric branch of UFRJ's University Hospital. In 2011, we issued a call for proposals and offered a film course for elementary school teachers; 28 schools submitted proposals and projects for their ideal film school. We selected 15 schools for the training course because, and the course would involve up to 30 participants. We then requested two participants from each school. A particular highlight of the experience was the challenge and delight brought by the participation of the Benjamin Constant Institute (IBC) and the National Institute for Deaf Education (INES).

The selection criteria primarily considered were as follows: the desire expressed in each project that included the commitment of two teachers (or one teacher and another school employee), as well as the school leadership's consent to participate in both the project and training in 2012; images of a screening room (even a simple one that was properly darkened and with acoustic possibilities); and a place to safely store equipment. The school should also promote film club and other audio-visual production activities that reference cinema. The training course had two parts: The first, in January (the only month of vacation for teachers, lasting two weeks) resulted in the selection of finalist schools that would receive temporary and renewable support for equipment and training sessions as well as *in situ* monitoring during the first year. The second part took place during the rest of the year, scheduled every two weeks on Saturdays. The decision criteria considered the distance from the metropolis (Nova Friburgo and Paraíba do Sul), conditions within the city (Vidigal), and the students' diversity (São João de Meriti). We chose two additional schools, INES and IBC, to involve in the collective development of specific procedures for monitoring cinema school projects for the particularity of their students and professors, who are blind or visually impaired and deaf or hard of hearing, respectively.

During the training course, we followed the suggestions of the consultant Alain Bergala, whose experience included the project La Mision (Bergala, 2006), which introduced the arts into public schools in France. Briefly, he suggested that we concentrate our efforts on four exercises that would raise major topics for discussion and oblige us to learn specific issues of language. In addition, he suggested that we work with professors on the issues we wanted them to address with their students afterward, ideally in an autonomous classroom setting.

Thus, the jointly developed exercises were as follows:

1. Lumière Minute: This exercise involves capturing one minute of reality with a fixed camera, without using any camcorder/mobile phone/photographic camera features, similar to the experience of the first cinematographer. The 'filminutes' produced ended up referencing the visions of Louis and

Auguste Lumière. Although a simple contextualizing exercise, it produces expressive visual poetry and requires the three cinematographic gestures of choice, arrangement, and attack (Bergala, 2006, 2013).

2. Filmed/edited: This activity is an experiment referencing the work of the filmmaker Jonas Mekas, in which participants experience filming (editing) using the camera. The process allows for a great deal of freedom, but requires intense care in envisioning the final result, as re-filming or editing after a shoot is not possible. This task thus requires a high level of concentration and organization, making decisions as planned at the beginning, and speed and flexibility in the moment of action. Mistakes should be taken into account in the narrative.

3. Hiding/showing: This exercise is more free-form in nature. It aims at a more subtle challenge of hiding an object or concept in the script, image, or each shot that will be revealed gradually. Thus, it is a way of thinking about a film that avoids equating it with 'sending a message' or 'providing a response to something'; instead, it promotes collective thinking as well as creating curiosity, expectation, and questions that ultimately lead to surprise.

4. Close reading: This exercise draws the viewer extremely close to cinema by creating an intimate relationship between the viewer and a shot from a film. In a pretend scenario in which two people (professors or students) act as director and editor, a first take is played exactly how it is. Then, the shot is replayed as if it were in editing software with the dialogue off; the editor and director let the other viewers see every possible detail, contextualizing the shot as it is advanced in slow motion, reversed, highlighted, etc., making use of whatever tool is necessary to follow the dialogue from cinema experts. At the end the shot is projected again, in silence. As such, viewers experience genuine immersion to deepen their understanding of a shot, which lasts only a few seconds. It is an exercise and effective method for introducing historical and linguistic elements without didactic chronological or grammatical formatting.

These exercises, carried out by the teachers in 2012 and by their students from the schools in 2013, all proved to be cinematographically and pedagogically powerful. Some of them can be watched at the website www.cinead.org. As a reflection of the process of creating the film schools, training teachers, and monitoring their work, we developed a film curriculum for basic education schools that can be viewed on the same site.

Currently, our research focuses on 13 outreach projects: CINEAD University Outreach Course; Schools go to the MAM Cinematheque; CAp Film School of the UFRJ; Cinema at the hospital? (IPPMG/UFRJ); Cinema Schools in the Public

Elementary Schools network; internal support (building the memory of FE/UFRJ events) and consulting activities (public network) in the Laboratory of Cinema and Audio-visual Education; Film Club Education on Screen; Film school at INES; Cinema school at the IBC; Cinema with the 'Female Day-care Workers' at the Women's Reference Centre in Maré; Cinema and aging: imagination traversing memory; PIBID project with History teachers from Rocinha and Tijuca; and the cinema project in the School of Early Childhood Education (UFRJ). Among all these institutes, the most challenging to work with were those that catered to deaf and blind children, whose difference highlights the radical incompleteness of the human condition.

Figure 1. Children from a public school at the Museum of Modern Art's Cinematheque. They watch fragments of films from different time periods and countries projected in the screening room, and then visit the graphic documentation room. The activity is a sensory experience of the materiality of film: light, sound (including isolating each speaker in the screening room), the texture of the big screen or holes in the film, and the cold temperature of film storage vaults.

© CINEAD

With regard to specific teaching activities, special topics were created in UFRJ's Postgraduate Program in Education from 2007 to 2013: Media and Education; Cinema and Education; Curriculum and Cinematic Language in Basic Education; Cinema, Education and Learning; and Pedagogy of Filmmakers. In 2013, the

Figure 2. The first class at the Cinema School at INES. The interpreter makes a C with his hand to symbolize the cinematographer during the projection of films by the Lumière brothers and Georges Méliès. On this day, three new signs in Brazilian Sign Language (Língua Brasileira de Sinais, LIBRAS) had to be created, taking the shape of C for cinematographer, L for Lumière, and M for Méliès.

© CINEAD

Figure 3. Child hospitalized at the Martagão Gesteira Institute of Paediatrics filming a Lumière minute through the window after having watched the Lumières' films *The Bread and the Alley* (Kiarostami, 1970) and *Reisado Miudim* (Cariry, 2008).

© CINEAD

programme incorporated as electives the courses Cinema and Education and Pedagogy of the Image.

The CINEAD film club of the Faculty of Education has gone by different names from 2007 to the present: MAM, CAp of UFRJ and, currently, Education on the Screen. Acquiring films from *Programadora Brasil* represented a forceful way to draw learners closer to Brazilian cinema at both the university and each of the schools, thereby contributing to the continuation of film club activities, including at the paediatric hospital.

Each year in November, we organize an International Meeting on Cinema and Education at UFRJ, together with an Education Department Film Screening at MAM-Rio and a Mirim Screening of Lumière Minutes Event, where the work of students and teachers is projected and discussed by specialists from cinema studies and education, as well as filmmakers. We believe that in this meeting, some curiosities and prospects are discussed and revised. The schools have also participated in various national festivals of significant prominence[3]: Generation Screening at the Rio Festival, Joaquim Venâncio Screening at FIOCRUZ, Little Filmmakers Festival; and Hacelo Corto (UNESCO, UBA), an international festival held in the municipality of Buenos Aires.

We believe that creating an introduction to cinema, both within and outside school, brings specific learning experiences to basic education teachers and students. Through this initiative, we demonstrate that what cannot be seen or known from an individual viewpoint supports/promotes the presence of 'others' for the social construction of knowledge. Cinema, as another 'other', expands our knowledge of the world, time, and ourselves. The possibility of identifying the relationship between us and the 'other', as mediated by the camera, is a spring on which the tension between two states of believing and doubting is activated; cinema employs the pedagogical power of such a tension excellently. In moving between these two poles, which approach in parallel from the reality to materiality and from the imaginary to infinity, teachers and learners can exercise their inventiveness in two of education's fundamental gestures: discovering and inventing the world.

Notes

1. Museum of Modern Art (MAM-Rio); KINO Network: Latin American Education, Cinema and Audio-visual Network; Cinema research project at the State University of Southwest Bahia (UESB); Learning in Higher Education research project (Educational Science, Philosophy and Literature, Universidad Nacional de Cuyo, Argentina); Kumã Laboratory (IACS/UFF); Martagão Gesteira Institute of Paediatrics and Childcare (IPPMG/UFRJ); Institute Benjamin Constant (IBC); National Institute for Deaf Education (INES); Contemporary Image, Text and Education Research groups (Imagem, Texto e Educação Contemporânea, ITEC/FE/UFRJ); Centre for the Research and Study of Aging (Centro de Estudo e Pesquisa do Envelhecimento, CEPE/RJ).
2. Resende (2013), Rebello (2013), Fasanello (2013), Leite (2012), Rodrígues (2012), Pires (2010), Paranhos (2009).

3. http://www.festivaldorio.com.br/br/mostras/mostra-geracao-curtas; http://mostrajoaquimvenan-cio.wordpress.com/contato/; http://www.pequenocineastafest.com.br; http://www.buenosaires.gob.ar/areas/educacion/programas/corto/afiche.php?menu_id=31162

References

Bergala, A. (2006). *L'hipothèse-cinéma. Petit eraité de tansmission du cinèma à l'école et ailleurs.* Paris: Petit Bibliothèque des Cahiers du Cinéma.

Bergala, A. (2013). Escolha/disposição/ataque. In A. M. Fresquet, A. & C. Nanchery, *Abecedário de cinema com Alain Bergala.* Rio de Janeiro: LECAV. [DVD] 36', cor.

Cariry, P. (Diretor). (2008) *Reisado Miudim.* [Curta-metragem], Brasil.

Fasanello, M. T. (2013). *Cinema, literatura oral e pedagogia da criação: reflexos a partir do projeto "A escola vai à Cinemateca do MAM".* Dissertação de mestrado, Departamento de Educação, Universidade Federal do Rio de Janeiro, Rio de Janeiro.

Fresquet, A. (2013). *Cinema e Educação: Reflexões e práticas com professores e estudantes de Educação Básica.* Belo Horizonte: Autêntica, 2013.

Fresquet, A. (Org.) (2013). *Currículo de Cinema para Escolas de Educação Básica.*www.cinead.org

Kiarostami, A. (Diretor). (1970). *O pão e o beco* (Trad. Nanva Koutcheh). [Curta-metragem], Irã.

Leite, G. (2012). *Linguagem cinematográfica no currículo da educação básica: uma experiência de introdução ao cinema na escola.* Dissertação de mestrado, Departamento de Educação, Universidade Federal do Rio de Janeiro, Rio de Janeiro.

Paranhos, E. (2009). *Nós: do-discentes e espect-atores!* Dissertação de mestrado, Departamento de Educação, Universidade Federal do Rio de Janeiro, Rio de Janeiro.

Pires, J. (2010). *Reflexões sobre currículo e linguagem a partir de uma experiência da Escola de Cinema no CAp/UFRJ.* Dissertação de mestrado, Departamento de Educação, Universidade Federal do Rio de Janeiro, Rio de Janeiro.

Rebello, S. T. (2013). *Educação em tela: limites e possibilidades da experiência do cineclube da faculdade de Educação/UFRJ na formação de professores.* Dissertação de mestrado, Departamento de Educação, Universidade Federal do Rio de Janeiro, Rio de Janeiro.

Resende, G. (2013). *Cinema na escola: aprender a construir o ponto de escuta.* Dissertação de mestrado, Departamento de Educação, Universidade Federal do Rio de Janeiro, Rio de Janeiro.

Rodrígues, M. O. (2012). *Autonomia e Criatividade em Escolas Democráticas: outras palavras, outros olhares.* Dissertação de mestrado, Departamento de Educação, Universidade Federal do Rio de Janeiro, Rio de Janeiro.

Indigenous Digital Inclusion

Action through Information

Joana Brandão

In order to understand some of the motivations behind the sites and blogs authored by indigenous people, and how such people use these virtual spaces, we undertook an analysis of the cybermedia borne of them.

Among 74 cybermedia mapped during previous research, we chose to conduct a more in-depth analysis of certain sites, including the Índios *Online* portal (2013), based on the frequency of publication – 3,943 publications between 2005 and 2012. This is indicative of an expansion of indigenous networks connected to the project: at least seven ethnic groups from three states directly connected to the network, and indigenous groups irrespective of their ethnicity (belonging to any part of Brazil) can request a login and password in order to be a contributor.

Originally created in 2004 by the non-governmental organization Thydêwá, today Índios *Online* is an autonomous network in which indigenous people connected to the Internet produce multimedia content of individual and/or collective creation[1] (NGO Thydêwá, 2013).

The field research was conducted in the villages of Água Vermelha, Caramuru and Bahetá (municipalities Pau Brazil and Itaju do Colônia, state of Bahia), and involved questionnaires and face-to-face interviews, in addition to field observations and analysis of the content of the publications. The question that motivated our research was: What are the main features of information provided in indigenous cybermedia?

Distinct cybermedia offered different answers to this question, with some common points or convergences. Political actuation, re-circulation and/or critical reading of the news media and the self-definition of identity stood out in the Índios *Online* (henceforth *IO*) , with some nuances that motivate reflection on the importance and consequences of media literacy and education and participation through citizen media. As the document *Media and Information Literacy and*

Intercultural Dialogue (Carlsson & Culver 2013, p. 13) points out, information and communication technology can collaborate either to generate conflict and reinforce differences on the one hand, or to encourage dialogue, comprehension and respect for differences on the other.

Participation and political mobilization in Índios *Online*

Studying cybermedia authored by indigenous people raises issues derived from the union of two terms which, to many, seem antagonistic: indigenous and technology. But these technologies are used precisely to combat the social exclusion and deprivation of basic rights to which these populations are subjected.

A central theme in the publications of *IO* is social and cultural issues surrounding the life of their communities for centuries, and now also in the "digital age". Of the 78 publications analyzed, most express complaints (19 publications), followed by information on events (17 cultural events and 15 political events), while 13 deal with land disputes.

Most notable is a preponderance of two elements, mobilization and daily life in the villages, which are at 40% and 47%, respectively. It is observed that indigenous rights are highlighted, and that the portal is purportedly used as a tool for political combat by the indigenous people.

The mobilization related to the production of indigenous cybermedia reflects specific purposes of the political and cultural setting of each of these peoples². Some conflicts are related to the merging of the new technology with the existing old ways of political mobilization, better explained as the confluence of indigenous people, the Internet and public communication. Among them, prominent is a generation gap between the youth and the elders regarding the integration, or non-integration, of the Internet with community goals. The intersection of these characteristics is addressed in a meaningful categorization by Renesse (2011).

Two models of political organization of indigenous communication in cybermedia

Renesse (2011, p. 19) recognized two ways in which new information technologies are appropriated by indigenous communities³: one that derives from community goals established in conjunction with the group, and another whereby cybermedia is introduced without defined objectives, such that its goal is not clear to the community.

According to the author, when an inclusion project does not take into account the peculiarities of each indigenous people, and lacks a plan involving community goals, there is a risk of not being fully integrated into that community. Working inefficiently can even lead to the abandonment of the medium (cybermedia) in the future. The existence of a governance plan and clarity of the positive uses of the medium within the community determine the acceptance of this innovation by the leaders and elders in villages. If there is no acceptance of the projects, the gains are few and distrust of traditional leaders arises (Renesse, 2011, pp. 38-39).

One can see that the political mobilization at community level with the use of new technologies by indigenous people involves two worlds: that of an existing political movement, the leaders, usually elders; and the youth, who act more frequently via the Internet. In the Índios *Online* portal, a positive model of interaction and integration of digital technology among indigenous communities has been found. In the following case, the participation in *IO* made the indigenous person approach and come closer to the elders of his village, motivating his participation in the fight for land and indigenous rights:

> From the beginning, the fight for land, demarcation of territory, health, education among the Tupinambás was older population oriented. We still see them as connoisseurs of our experience. But with the arrival of Índios *Online*, I started to get closer to these leaders, who were among those that who fought for territory, and defended the right to health, as well as quality education. Because I needed to do stories about them, I needed to get closer (Tupinambá, 2012).

The indigenous people seek to negotiate with the leaders to demonstrate the importance of cybermedia for their community goals, and support of the elders emerges from the negotiation. Once there is a link between the use of cybermedia with the indigenous cause they defend, a space is opened for acceptance. Although insecurities and differences still persist with respect to the acceptance of the elders (Ramos, 2012), in general, *IO* is used as an ally to achieve the ancient community goals such as recovery and keeping their land, improvements in health, education, and improving living conditions in the village, according to the second model described by Renesse (2011).

The indigenous people themselves testify to the importance of the portal, for instance, during the process of the recovery of land: "Many, many other actions that have been going on concern land recapture, and when we have the conditions to shoot films, or photos, we always post and ask for help, and this help has inevitably come"[4] (Ramos, 2012). There have been times when the leaders and elders themselves have used the portal, such as the denunciation of the transfer of Chief Babau from the prison in Salvador to Rio Grande do Norte, which features a recording of the Cacique Nailton Pataxó Hãhãhãe. Another example is the testimony of Chief Xiquinho in a protest at the Fundação Nacional do Índio (FUNAI) in Brasília.[5]

In a way, the members of *IO* provide the community leaders and elders with authority over publications, thus giving continuity to the political structure existing before the creation of cybermedia in the community. It is a joint effort of old and new political actors to achieve common goals, combining online activism with community mobilization, youth connected to the Internet, and the leaders and elders who direct the political struggles[6].

101

The political struggle also occurs through the self-definition of identity, as opposed to those identities defined by external narratives as a determination of autonomy in this symbolic space. This self-definition confronts a refusal by society to see the indigenous people in the current context, as pointed out by Martin-Barbero (2003, p. 272): "The indigenous people were converted into what is irreconcilable with modernity nowadays, thus deprived of a positive existence."

The desire to perform this self-definition of identity is evident in the testimony of a member of the *IO* network, Fábio Titiá:

> To use this means of communication to spread the story of our people, and demystify (them), change a vision that many people in the society have towards the indigenous. Many people imagine the indigenous to be that person who lives in the forest, isolated, walking barefoot, having low grade housing, without the right to any social/digital inclusion. And, over the Internet, we are making way for a much broader vision concerning these people. Because *IO* shows Brazilian society that the indigenous is a person with a cell phone, even a laptop, and is nonetheless indigenous (Titiá 2012, emphasis added by author).

This demystification is the deconstruction of the ideals conceived by the public, which enables the indigenous to determine their territory; this time not physical, but rather that which is cultural and identity-related. In this space, indigenous people express their own opinion about what is to be indigenous.

Recirculate journalistic cybermedia

The indigenous also claim to seek to fill a gap in the approach taken by traditional journalism about life in the villages and the rights, needs and culture of indigenous people.

The construction of stereotyped reports on the reality of the village and identity of indigenous people is a common plaint in several texts. It is recognized in the testimonies: an opposition "indigenous media versus traditional journalism" that provides cybermedia as an opportunity to juxtapose the discourse of traditional journalism, due in part to the proximity of indigenous authors to reality and daily life in the village.

Among other things, the news coverage on indigenous people is the subject of publication, as in "*Rede Globo* manipulates story against Pataxó Hãhãhãe society"[7]. The text points to the absence of the indigenous perspective in the report by *Jornal Nacional* on the *Rede Globo* channel, and accuses the channel of making false accusations against indigenous people.

When the indigenous people reply to the story, they confirm the existence of an intricate relationship between the media of citizen authorship and that authored by news organizations. The information is being recirculated[8], even if this is done through critics. Indigenous cybermedia are produced by people who consume traditional media, so traditional journalism serves as a source of information for them.

As part of citizen initiatives, the community communication encourages critical reading of the traditional news media since, for the prospect of community communication, the main use of the communication is educational and cultural development and the critical reading of mass media (Peruzzo, 2007, pp. 69-89; Paiva, 2007, p. 144). This is what Isabel Gatti and Raúl Bermúdez (2010, p. 18) call media literacy, and what the United Nations Educational, Scientific and Cultural Organization (UNESCO) defines as media and information literacy (Wilson et al., 2013).

Media literacy, as a solution to the separation between producers and consumers of mass media information, means more than technical skills: "The challenge is not only to know how to read and write, but knowing to steer decisions about which issues are important, what knowledge accounts for and which are the ways of knowing command, authority, and respect" (Jenkins, 2008, p. 342).

Notes

1. Of the three villages surveyed, two contained Points of Presence (POP), with computers connected to the Internet. The POP, financed by the GESAC Program of the Ministry of Communication, aim at the digital inclusion of disadvantaged populations and are made available to the community. In the course of our visit, we witnessed that they were mainly accessed by children and young people. In another village, the chief had a private computer and Internet access, which he used for making publications for the network.

2. The various concepts of "people" presented by Peruzzo (2009) show the variety and complexity of relationships drawn between popular culture and the media, as well as the different ways of approaching the people by these means. With cybermedia authored by the indigenous, a new issue emerges in this context. The ethnic peculiarities of each of these peoples challenges studies of community communication and media communications – only to give rise to theoretical concepts that can envision partnerships, which would be anthropological in nature, as a way to grasp the complexities that manifest themselves in some cases.

3. Eliete Pereira (2012) points out that the first records of participation of the indigenous people of Brazil on the Internet are from 2001. The analyzed data amounted to about 37 sources of cybermedia in the year 2007. The *Sites Indígenas* (online) blog has a list of 57 websites and blogs developed by indigenous people in Brazil. The most recent survey, presented by Renesse, identifies 77 cybermedia authored by the indigenous and/or partners (Renesse 2011, p. 51) and 111 Internet access points in indigenous villages.

4. Some of the first members of the *IO* network participated in photography, video and journalism workshops, organized by the Thydêwá NGO. But these workshops are offered sporadically and do not cover all members of the network, due to the prohibitive costs of transportation of participants and hiring teachers. In general, indigenous respondents also mentioned difficulty in gaining access to equipment such as cameras or recorders; when used, these were borrowed from either NGOs or colleagues.

5. The publications "Cacique Babau da Aldeia Serra do Padeiro é Transferido de penitenciaria sem o conhecimento das Comunidades Indigenas!" ("Cacique Babau from Serra do Padeiro Village is transfered from penitentiary without knowledge of Indigenous Communities!") from April 19, 2010, and "The Protest of Xiquinho" from April 29, 2009. Available at http://www.indiosonline.net

6. The start of the *IO* project occurred in parallel with the deployment of the first Points of Presence (POP) in three indigenous communities. In these communities, the indigenous were learning to use the computer for the first time ever using the *IO* portal. In one of the indigenous communities studied the Internet was available at the school, but this was not the case for those related to this project. GESAC's POP are the primary means of providing the structure of computer and Internet connection to these communities. As these points are opened, as can be expected, they attract a flood of young people and children living in the neighborhood.

7. Available at Índios *Online*, 14th April, 2012. Link: http://www.indiosonline.net/rede-globo-manipula-reportagem-jogando-a-sociedade-contra-os-pataxo-hahahae/

8. As conceived by Zago (2011).

References

Carlsson, U., & Culver, S. H. (Eds) (2013). *Media and Information Literacy and Intercultural Dialogue* (MILID Yearbook 2013*)*. Gothenburg University: Nordicom.

Demo, P. (2001). *Participação é conquista* (2nd ed.). São Paulo: Cortez.

Gatti, I., Bermudéz, R. (2010). Experiencias y reflexiones sobre la comunicación comunitaria en Argentina y América Latina. In G. Cicalese (Ed.), *Comunicación Comunitaria: Apuntes para abordar las dimensiones de la construcción colectiva* (pp. 17-31). Buenos Aires: La Crujia.

Índios Online (2013). Available at www.indiosonline.net

Jenkins, H. (2008). *Cultura da Convergência* (2nd ed.). São Paulo: Aleph.

Lippman, W. (2008). *Opinião Pública*. Petrópolis: Vozes.

Martín-Barbero, J. (2003). *Dos meios* às *mediações: comunicação, cultura e hegemonia* (2nd ed.). Rio de Janeiro: Editora UFRJ.

NGO Thydêwá (2013). Available at http://www.thydewa.org/portfolio/indios-online/

Paiva, R. (2007). Para reinterpretar a comunicação comunitária. In R. Paiva (Ed.), *O retorno da comunidade: Os novos caminhos do social* (pp. 133-148). Rio de Janeiro. Mauad X.

Pereira, E. (2012). *Ciborgues indígen@as.br: a presença nativa no ciberespaço*. São Paulo: Ed. Anablume.

Peruzzo, C. K. (2007). Rádio Comunitária, Educomunicação e Desenvolvimento. In R. Paiva (Ed.), *O retorno da comunidade: Os novos caminhos do social* (pp. 69-94). Rio de Janeiro: Mauad X.

Peruzzo, C. K. (2009). Conceitos de comunicação popular, alternativa e comunitária revisitados e as reelaborações no setor. *Revista ECO-Pós*, 12 (2), 46-61.

Ramos, R. (2012). Interview during field research in the village Bahetá, municipality of Itaju do Colônia from 04th to 11th January, 2012.

Renesse, N. D. (2011). *Perspectivas indígenas sobre e na Internet: ensaio regressivo sobre o uso da comunicação em grupos ameríndios no Brasil*. Master Dissertation, Social Anthropology Department, Universidade de São Paulo, São Paulo.

Sites Indígenas (2014). Available at http://sitesindigenas.blogspot.com.br

Titiá, F. (2012). Interview during field research in the village Água Vermelha, municipality of Pau Brasil, from 04th to 11th January, 2012.

Tupinambá, J. Y. (2012) Interview during field research in the NGO Thydêwá headquarter, municipality of Olivença, Ilhéus.

Wilson, C., Grizzle, A., Tuazon, R., Akyempong, K. & Cheung, C. (2013). *Alfabetização midiática e informacional: Currículo para formação de professores*. Brasília: UNESCO.

Zago, G. S. (2011). *Recirculação jornalística no Twitter: filtro e comentário de notícias por interagentes como uma forma de potencialização da circulação*. Master Dissertation, Communication and Education Department, UFRGS, Rio Grande do Sul.

Collaborative Learning

Challenges and Strategies for Digital Inclusion

Magda Pischetola

Social and collaborative learning: a new paradigm?

In the late 20th and early 21st centuries, social studies popularized the vision of networks as spaces for interaction, communication and social organization (Castells, 1999; Martinho, 2003; Watts, 2003). Thus, with the network metaphor being increasingly applied to all areas of society, new theories of learning and new proposals with respect to the social construction of knowledge began to emerge. Most of them reflect, either implicitly or explicitly, the interest of the authors in socio-constructivist theories, based on the concepts of education as reconstruction of experience and motivation as a driving force of learning (Dewey, 1944). These views consider that content is more easily learned when it holds meaning for the student, because it is based on a foundation of prior knowledge. Learning, therefore, should be considered a social activity that requires the development not only of the individual, but also of the community to which he or she belongs (Vygotsky, 1978).

Advocating that we can only know that which is the product of an active construction on the part of the subject, the foundations of socio-constructivist theories are based on the most recent study of networked learning, which Siemens (2005) calls "connectivism". In this new theory of learning, knowledge construction continues to be considered a social activity, but in a community which is expanded and increasingly overlapping with the "network" (Castells, 1999). With the emergence of the Internet, social relations can dispense with physical and geographical space, communication times contract, and environments for interaction (at a distance) multiply, enabling unpredictable flows of information and collective self-organization (Franco, 2011). According to Siemens (2005), the drastic change in learning in today's world is due to the speed of the generation, processing and storage of knowledge. The period in which knowledge becomes obsolete is contracting at a rate which is inversely proportional to the increase in the capacity to process and store information.

In this new scenario, the connectivist theory suggests that even more important than knowledge itself is the *channel* that leads to it: i.e., the network structure. Given this, one might say that access to information facilitated by digital technologies is the first step in the construction of knowledge (Tomaél, Rosecler & Guerreiro, 2005). However, surveys indicate that virtual networks may also be inconsistent in terms of learning, if used in traditional form for those accessing them, rather than in an innovative manner (Pischetola, 2011; Warschauer, 2006). Thus, in order not to fall into a technological determinism trap (Smith & Marx, 1994), it is crucial to recognize that "it is the social aspect that determines behavior, not technology" (Franco, 2011, p. 9).

The possibility of real learning occurs when information is rooted in interactions between users, being structured around mutual exploration and problem-solving in groups (Williams, 2013).

One computer per student: a case study

The One Computer per Student Program (ProUCA) aims to "be an educational project using technology, digital inclusion and intensification of the commercial production chain in Brazil" (MEC, 2005)[1]. Today the program covers public elementary schools in all the Brazilian states, the result of a public policy that brings together federal, state and local governments, universities, the NTEs (418 Education Technology Support Centres throughout Brazil), schools and businesses (ibid).

A laptop for digital inclusion

The purpose of ProUCA is to "promote educational and social inclusion through the acquisition and distribution of laptops in public schools" (MEC, 2005).

In Brazil, digital inclusion is the focus of public policies at all levels of public administration, as well as initiatives by public, private and non-profit institutions (Bonilla & Pretto, 2011). As some research has indicated in recent years, these approaches for the integration of ICTs in schools seem to affirm that a new technology, by the mere fact of appearing in a school context, will result in digital inclusion, which creates a danger of falling into deterministic interpretations of society (Lemos, 2007; Peixoto, 2009; Pischetola, 2011).

Our proposal is to look at digital inclusion beyond the technical and financial access to the ICTs, and more in the sense of the inclusion of younger citizens in a digital culture, by helping them develop skills in the strategic use of technology (Van Dijk, 2005). This means challenging the idea that digital inclusion is merely an economic or infrastructure problem and trying to consider it from a broader point of view, as a cultural problem (Lemos, 2007; Pischetola, 2012). Seeking to understand a paradigm that seems to answer the needs felt in an educational context, we have tried to relate the concept of social and collaborative learning to the concept of digital inclusion. Two key issues guide our path: (1) Does the introduction of the laptop into the school context generate new forms of collaboration and knowledge sharing? (2) What are the uses/practices that create significant access to the networked society, towards a broader conception of "digital inclusion"?

Methodology and fieldwork

The research used a qualitative approach based on participatory observation of classroom activities, interviews with teachers, and focus groups with students. The fieldwork was conducted throughout the 2012 school year in the states of Santa Catarina[2] and Bahia[3], and involved four schools: two located in capital cities (Florianópolis and Salvador)[4] and two in the interior of the two states (Jaraguá do Sul and Feira de Santana)[5]. The collected data consist of participatory observation in ten classes, 25 interviews with teachers, directors and project coordinators, and ten focus groups with students, one for each class observed.

Main results

(1) Does the introduction of the laptop into the school environment create new forms of collaboration?

Most teachers claimed to have detected a high level of student engagement with the laptop, especially from the point of view of information exchange, interaction in gaming activities, and social communication. The chart below confirms that games and online chat are among the activities students say they prefer.

Figure 1. Laptop-based activities students say they prefer

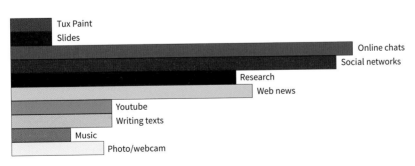

At the same time, the students' performance did not improve significantly in terms of strategic use of the laptop. Many of the teachers interviewed stressed that the new technology brought a lack of attention and distraction to the classroom[6], and that the more obvious learning by the students was primarily related to the development of technical skills (36% of interviewees) and self-guided research (26%). Collaboration was mentioned by a quarter of interviewees, almost always as a synonym for mutual assistance and/or social interaction.

(2) What are the practices that provide significant access to the networked society?

In addition to concerns of an educational nature, in relation to lack of attentiveness created by the laptop in the classroom, teachers pointed out the difficulties relating to the students that arose from the use of the tool. It is understood that on a day-to-day basis technology creates insecurity, leading not only to no didactic innovation, but also to the strengthening of established educational habits. A particularly interesting fact that emerged in the interviews, and which was reinforced in the focus groups, is that the student develops skills that the teacher often does not have. However, at two of the schools surveyed, it was part of the plan for students to contribute to the implementation of the program by working voluntarily as monitors. These are also the schools where the ProUCA project was seen to have had a greater impact in terms of autonomy in access to information and critical, guided use of the tool beyond the gaming and social aspects.

Given this scenario, the results of the research confirm the initial hypothesis that digital inclusion does not depend only on promoting physical access to technological resources, but rather on the quality of this access; i.e., to employ such resources placing value on developing students' skills and the learning opportunities provided by the existing social networks in the school community.

Conclusions

The research shows that the recognition of the digital age as fertile ground for renewing ways of learning also means using technological resources with discretion, to build significant learning methodologies. Successful approaches are mainly those relating to "learning by discovery", whereby the teacher puts him- or herself in a position to guide the students' learning process. That is, it is up to the teacher to direct the students' skills with a learning purpose in mind, with a lack of defined goals being the primary reason for lack of attentiveness. We recognize that creating a learning environment following this approach is much more difficult than planning a series of traditional educational interventions. However, students can be an active part of the construction of a didactic strategy, as long as their skills are understood to be helpful. If the teacher recognizes the importance of literacy acquisition through media (UNESCO, 2013) and understands the classroom as a privileged *locus* for it to happen, learning can become challenging, meaningful and thought-provoking, through collective work dynamics, group discussion, and a spirit of mutual support and cooperation (Behrens, 2012). Once again taking up the socio-constructivist perspective and connectivism, the methodological proposal for future action is to enhance the space for mutual questioning between teacher and student, giving input for critical reflection on teaching practices and, at the same time, giving the student responsibility for the use of technology within the spaces and time frames allocated by the teacher.

Notes

1. The program began in 2006 as part of the international One Laptop per Child program with a pilot implementation at five schools in Brazil. In 2010 there was country-wide adoption of the proposal, which replaces the XO laptop, produced by the CCE/DIGIBRAS/ METASYS Consortium.

2. Located in the center of the southern region of the country, the state of Santa Catarina was largely colonized by European immigrants. With a total population of 6,250,000, thanks to a diversified and industrialized economy it is the sixth richest state in the Federation and one of those mainly responsible for national economic growth. The social indices of the state are among the best in the country: the index of illiteracy for those aged 15 years or older in the state is 4.1% (IBGE, 2010); the index for Internet access (population aged 10 or older) is 69.5% (PNAD, 2008).

3. The population of Bahia is the largest in the Northeast, and the fourth largest in Brazil (IBGE, 2010). According to the latest census data the state has more than 14 million inhabitants, spread among 417 municipalities in the state. With regard to education, the index of illiteracy for those aged 15 years or older in the state is 16.6%. About 32% of the population in this same age group are considered functionally illiterate (IBGE, 2010). The index of Internet access (population aged 10 or older) is 26.9% (PNAD, 2008).

4. Florianópolis is the capital of the state of Santa Catarina and one of Brazil's three "islands capitals". It is known for being the Brazilian capital with the highest Human Development Index, on the order of 0.87 according to the latest report released by the United Nations Development Programme (HDI, 2000). The three pillars that comprise the HDI are health, education and income (UNDP, http://www.pnud.org.br). With 2.7 million inhabitants (IBGE 2010), Salvador is the capital of the state of Bahia and the center of Brazil's Afro-Brazilian culture.

5. The city of Jaraguá do Sul, in the state of Santa Catarina, has one of the highest Human Development Indexes in Brazil, due mainly to a high level of access to education (HDI, 2000). Moreover, economically it is one of the fastest growing cities in the state. Many of the industries present in the territory (Lunender, Menegotti, Bretzke, Argi, Trapp and others) were originally family businesses that over time became large industrial complexes (IBGE, 2010). It was settled by Hungarians, Poles, Italians and Germans. Feira de Santana is the largest city in the hinterland of Northeast Brazil. Thanks to its geographical position, is an important industrial and commercial center. It has a population of 556,642 of highly diverse races, due to the migratory movements from all regions of Brazil (IBGE, 2010). From 2005 until 2012 there was an increase in the crime rate, driven mainly by drug trafficking (Trindade, 2013).

6. The observations confirmed that the children were often involved in entertainment activities, such as online games and chats on social networks, during school hours, usually without the teacher's permission.

References

Behrens, M. (2012). Projetos de aprendizagem colaborativa num paradigma emergente. In J. Moran, J., M. Masetto & M. Behrens (Eds.), *Novas tecnologias e mediação pedagógica* (pp. 73-123). São Paulo: Papirus.

Bonilla, M. H., & Pretto, N. (Eds.) (2011). *Inclusão digital: polêmica contemporânea*. Salvador: Edufba.

Castells, M. (1999). *A sociedade em rede*. São Paulo: Paz e Terra.

Dewey, J. (1944). *Democracy and education*. New York: Free Press.

Franco, A. (2012). A Rede. *Escola de redes,* (vol. I.). São Paulo: Série Fluzz.

IBGE – Instituto Brasileiro de Geografia e Estatística (2010). *Censo demográfico 2010.* http://www.ibge.gov.br/home/

Lemos, A. (2007). *Cidade digital: portais, inclusão e redes no Brasil*. Salvador: Edufba.

Martinho, C. (2003). *Redes. Uma introdução às dinâmicas da conectividade e da auto-organização*. Brasília: WWF.

Ministério da Educação (2005). *Programa Um Computador por Aluno,* http://www.uca.gov.br

Peixoto, J. (2009). Tecnologia na Educação: uma questão de transformação ou de formação? In S. Cecilio & D. M. Falcone Garcia (Eds.), *Formação e profissão docente em tempos digitais* (pp. 217-235). Campinas: Alínea.

Pischetola, M. (2011). *Educazione e divario digitale. Idee per il capacity building*. Milano: Unicopli.

PNAD – Pesquisa Nacional por Amostra de Domicílios (2008). *Acesso a Internet e Posse de Telefone Móvel Celular para Uso Pessoal,* IBGE.

Siemens, G. (2005). Connectivism: A learning theory for the digital age. *International Journal of Instructional Technology and Distance Learning,* 2 (1). http://www.itdl.org/Journal/Jan_05/article01.htm

Smith, M. R., & Marx, L. (1994). *Does technology drive history? The dilemma of technological determinism*. Cambridge MA: MIT Press.

Tomaél, M. I., Rosecler, A. A., & Guerreiro, I. (2005). Das redes sociais à inovação. *Ci. Inf.,* 34 (2), 93-104.

Trindade, A. (2013). Polícia de Feira de Santana registrou 412 homicídios em 2012. *Acorda Cidade,* 02 de Janeiro de 2013.

UNESCO (2013). *Alfabetização midiática e informacional. Currículo para a formação de professores*. Brasília: UNESCO Brasil.

Van Dijk, J. (2005). *The Deepening Divide. Inequality in the Information Society*. London-New Delhi: Sage Publications.

Vygotsky, L. (1978). *Mind in society: The development of higher psychological processes*. Cambridge:Harvard University Press.

Warschauer, M. (2006). *Tecnologia e inclusão social: a exclusão digital em debate*. São Paulo: Senac.

Watts, D. (2003). *Six Degrees: The Science of a Connected Age*. New York: Norton.

Williams, A. (2013). *Projeto de Educação Livre. Reduzindo a falta de habilidades no Brasil: Como uma Educação Livre pode despertar a oportunidade econômica e promover a Inclusão Social?* Brasília: CNI/UNESCO.

PORTUGAL

Children, Youth and Media

Opposite Cultures?

Schools' and Children's Practices with Digital Media

Cristina Ponte & Karita Gonçalves

Since 2007, Portugal has witnessed a rapid diffusion in Internet access among children and young people. This diffusion has largely been encouraged by a national policy presenting technology as a dimension of modernity and development. Running in schools from 2008 to 2011, the programmes *e-Escolas* and *e-Escolinhas*, the latter popularized by the laptop *Magalhães*, sought to provide equipment and Internet access to students and schools. Embraced by families with fewer resources and lower levels of education, these policies of digital inclusion meant a democratization in computer ownership among students. By the end of 2010, over 1,600,000 laptops had been purchased at low cost, including 400,000 *Magalhães*[1].

Confirming families' engagement, in 2010 Portuguese data from the *EU Kids Online* survey (Ponte, Jorge, Simões & Cardoso, 2012) showed that two-thirds of respondents aged 9-16 used their personal laptops to go online, placing them ahead of Nordic countries, where Internet penetration is among the highest in Europe. At home, approximately two-thirds of Portuguese interviewees declared accessing the Internet from their bedrooms, more than the European average (49%). With regard to the engagement of parents in shared activities involving the Internet, the numbers fluctuated significantly according to social background. In middle- to high-income families, the values varied between 52% and 62%. However, among families with lower income this proportion was much lower (28%).

The *EU Kids Online* survey also demonstrated that Portuguese children accessed the Internet from school (72%), public libraries or other public spaces with free Internet access (25%) in greater numbers than their European counterparts (European average 63% and 12% respectively). Likewise, the numbers concerning teacher mediation were above the European average, with 70% of children declaring that their teachers spoke to them about the helped them find materials and complete tasks, in addition to explaining why certain websites are either good or bad. Access to the Internet in public spaces was found to be more pronounced among children and teenagers who did not have Internet access at home, or among those who experienced restrictions on its use at home due to the costs involved. Interviewed children noted that they liked being in these places with friends, and appreciated the opportunity to experience a degree of freedom in internet use they could not enjoy at home or in school (Ponte, 2011).

In an attempt to understand the ways in which digital means challenged educational processes and were incorporated into children's cultures, this text addresses current key features of the digital experience of Portuguese children aged 8 to 12. As seen, these ages benefit from the programme *e-Escolinhas*, which was in place at the time they entered or attended primary school.

Between school and family – Exploring the computer Magalhães

Inspired by the *Classmate* PC from Intel, the laptop *Magalhães* had built-in educational software and Internet access for the first grades of school. The computer was expected to circulate between home and school, since it was intended to foster communication between teachers and families. Like in similar projects elsewhere, in Portugal the initiative was presented as a sign of modernity. As noted, this programme was more centred on the notion of technology as a gateway to become the "citizens of tomorrow" than on the actual needs, skills and digital culture of today's children (Pereira, 2013)[2].

For several lower-income families *Magalhães* was the first computer to enter their household, and it was considered the family computer. By contrast, in households already equipped with computers, *Magalhães* was viewed as the "child's computer". In addition to educational games and Internet access, *Magalhães* was also equipped with a pre-loaded version of Microsoft Office (Word, Power Point and Photo Story) aimed at facilitating the acquisition of skills in the fields of IT and communication, and at supporting the curricular learning process.

In 2009-2010, the first year of the *e-Escolinha* project, the Ministry of Education interviewed approximately 9,000 thousand teachers who were using *Magalhães* in their classrooms. The national survey showed that more than two-thirds of the teachers agreed that using *Magalhães* improved learning and stimulated the children's creativity. Among the educational activities mentioned, most involved resorting to content available online, such as songs, videos and digital libraries. More than half of the teachers admitted only utilizing these resources once a week or less; this low rate of recurrence would decline even further in 2010-2011 (Vieira, Silva, Coelho & Fernandes, 2012). Only one in ten teachers referred to the possibility of using this mobile technology in educational activities, such as taking pictures or creating short movies. Furthermore, experiences with digital networks were virtually ignored by teachers (less than 1% mentioning it), in spite of being one of the activities most cited by children in the *EU Kids Online* survey.

In studies conducted at a regional level, teachers acknowledged the potential of *Magalhães* to enhance learning while simultaneously highlighting a number of factors that inhibited its use. In the predominantly rural district of Bragança, teachers listed some of the main constraints they were faced with. These included: unreliable Internet access in the classroom; lack of personal and educational competence to work with the device; and low level of interest or difficulties revealed by rural families in relation to their children's digital activities (Eiras & Meirinhos, 2012; Esteves, 2012). On the other hand, research carried out in urban centres, where most families had Internet access at home, indicated that *Magalhães* was not widely used as a tool of communication between parents and teachers or in the preparation of school activities by teachers (Silva & Diogo, 2011).

Research conducted in different regions of Portugal suggested that the main users of *Magalhães* were children. Contrary to what was expected, the use of the computer at home was significantly superior to its use in school. Either alone or with peers, children explored *Magalhães* far beyond its educational content and on their own initiative (Viana, Silva, Coelho & Fernandes, 2012).

The programme *e-Escolinhas* was discontinued in 2011-2012, as a consequence of a policy change in education. Data on children's activities drawn during the two academic years the programme was in place (2009-2010 and 2010-2011) showed that by the end of the second year, the use of educational games and the number of Google searches had dropped drastically. By contrast, the number of visits to You Tube, commercial game websites, Facebook and other synchronous communication media (e.g. MSN, Skype) as well as the use of email accounts had increased. The activities Portuguese children tended to take up online were therefore consistent with patterns observed internationally: despite the wealth of possibilities available on the Internet, children tend to invest their energies in a handful of websites developed by adults and owned by large corporations (ChildWise, 2011).

Moving between portable computers and mobile phones

As noted by Dafna Lemish (2013), in the current multifunctional convergent media ecology, formerly presumed categories – information, entertainment and advertising; formal and informal learning; studying and playing – are becoming increasingly blurred. By the same token, the ways in which the Internet is accessed have also become more flexible, personalized and mobile.

In Europe, the first comparative results concerning children's access to and use of mobile media are emerging. The *Net Children Go Mobile*[3] project highlights that the privatization of Internet access and use has been accompanied by an increasingly pervasive presence of the Internet in everyday life, and implies the creation of different social conventions of freedom, privacy, sociability and supervision by parents and adults (Mascheroni & Ólafsson, 2014). In this context, school education is a central arena.

While the results from the Portuguese participation in the above-mentioned project are not yet available at the date of this writing, this text can already voice the experiences of nearly 80 children aged 8-12 who own a personal mobile phone with Internet access. Interviews were conducted with children of various social backgrounds, living in the metropolitan area of Lisbon[4]. Although most children continue to refer to *Magalhães* as something belonging to them ("my Magalhães"), the laptop has been put aside. They say the computer is "broken", or that it has been replaced by other laptops or tablets shared with family members. They claim to have stopped using *Magalhães* because it is "too slow" or "no longer fun". A laptop designed for children thus appears to have rapidly become obsolete in their eyes, or worse, to constitute an identity constraint ("the kid's computer") from which they desire to free themselves.

The interviews about mobile use (either devices bought first-hand or obtained from family members), confirmed that the social functions mobiles play for teenagers are already relevant at these ages. As Ling and Bertel (2013) identified, these functions are: the security link in case of danger, the means to coordinate in space and time; the generator of written messages (texting); expressive communication; Internet and multimedia. While the younger children limit themselves to games and family contacts, by the time they reach 10-11 years, the change in school cycle is often associated with the acquisition of a new mobile device, chosen by the child, sometimes as a learning experience about the management of limited resources:

> – When I started to have some money, I started to look around to see what I could do with it. The possibility of a tablet came up. It was a recent thing. Some were affordable, so... (Pedro, 12 years)

Despite having mobile devices with Internet access, the costs involved in using the Internet outside the house restrict its use. For this reason, these devices continue to be used essentially in the domestic setting. Another frequent trait emerging from the interviews is that of the children's role as the technological leader in their families:

> – I have mostly taught my family how to use Bluetooth. As we have a baby in the family, everyone wants to take photos of him... My mother wanted to send a contact to a friend, for instance. Therefore she sends a business card. You insert it in the text and send it. (Maria, 11 years)

> –My father is going to have Facebook and I am going to create his profile. (Nuno, 11 years)

For children, the predominant online activities are the exchange of text messages and games, a great deal of which are played on Facebook. Children whose parents have higher levels of education tend to experience greater restrictions in the access to this social network. The non-use of Facebook may be presented by the child as a result of parental restriction, or can arise from the child's personal decision:

– Some of my classmates have it [Facebook] because their parents allow them. At my age, my parents do not allow me to have it yet. (Carlos, 8 years)

– I have already been asked many times whether I want it or not... but it is not something that appeals to me. (Maria, 11 years)

The multimedia potentialities linked to image and music are mostly highlighted by children who set up their own playlists, download, reshuffle and sometimes share content. Contrary to the image of passivity usually associated with children's relationship with screens, in a culture of convergence it is possible to choose to be passive or active on various levels with each screen, depending on interest, context, personality and circumstances (Lemish, 2013):

– Sometimes, when I am making a Power Point, I go on You Tube and add music. (Patricia, 11 years)

– I do translations on Google; Sometimes I put the tunes on and go on Google to translate so that I know what all of that means. (Madelena, 10 years)

– Sometimes, I'm on You Tube and I'm on Facebook at the same time... for instance, I like Tim Burton very much, so I am usually on the website and share pictures and things related to his movies. (Violeta, 12 years)

Apart from searching for songs, pages with drawings, or information about cars, recipes, movies, TV shows or the weather, there are also children who search for something to surprise them, like the opening Google page illustrations:

– Sometimes, when those strange drawings pop up on the Google front page, I click on them to see what it is... (Daniel, 10 years)

Some children view with care and preoccupation issues of privacy concerning the images they capture with their mobiles, one of the most appreciated functionalities of these devices:

– I have already recorded my mother walking up the street and me playing with my cousin. I have also recorded my mother in the garden with me and my cousin.

Interviewer: And have you posted it on the Internet or not?

– No, and I would not like someone else doing it to me. (Lara, 10 years)

– I am going to make a video on my computer but I will not post it on Facebook because I don't want to identify anyone. It's like a video album. I have photos, I transfer them to my computer, join them together and make a movie with the ones I want, the ones I select. (Leonor, 10 years)

The digital culture of these children is marked by their pleasure in playing, experimenting, communicating and being with others. They want to use "real", powerful and fast equipment, even if this means sharing it with other members of the family. Their responses confirm that, more than mere technologies, media represent new cultural forms that transport images and fantasies and offer ample opportunities for self-expression and games (Buckingam, 2007). At these ages, children identify the relevance of humour for successful communication with peers:

– This is a special tool for people to be able to communicate well... for when something funny is needed because we can send some funny messages to make people laugh... (Daniel, 12 years).

Two years after the end of the *e-Escolinhas* programme, we found among the *Magalhães* generation only a few references to Internet access in the school context[5]. Mobile phones, the digital technology they usually carry with them and that offers multiple functionalities, are formally banned from the classroom. References to its use in the school context are residual. João (10) says that one day he took a picture of the summary written on the board in the classroom as he did not have enough time to write it down. André (11) once filmed a lab experiment in biology class and gave it to the teacher for her to have a look at. Daniel does not understand why this resource cannot be used in class:

– At the moment in our Maths class we are always using our calculator. The teacher asked us to use the calculator... I could use this [mobile phone] if the teacher allowed it... (Daniel, 10 years).

The use of mobile phones to capture images is most cited in the context of field trips, where it can originate elaborated records. Along with technical ability and revealing the pleasure of the production and remix, this practice may draw attention to the important discussion on copyright issues:

– When I went on that fieldtrip for the herbar project, I took maybe 20, 30 photos. Now my teacher is saying that we could make an album with the photos we took. I am saving my photos to a memory stick and will give it to her, for her to create an album. I am even recording data on a USB card. My grandfather has a device to listen to music in the car and I am recording songs onto that card. As my printer is HP and reads memory cards, I stick the memory card in there and check it out... I will get the songs. (Ruben, 10 years)

Final comments

In 2010, most Portuguese children entering the school system had contact with digital technology, even if under different access and parental or teacher mediations. The *e-Escolinhas* programme led to a democratization in Internet access. It was received with enthusiasm, but also resistance, from schools due to a lack of training and of favourable organizational conditions. It is also important to take heed of the reservations or indifference expressed by families from less privileged economic backgrounds or digitally excluded families, mainly in rural settings. The highest levels of endorsement of the project were registered among families seeking to provide their children with opportunities they themselves had lacked during their childhood. The findings from the *EU Kids Online* survey offered evidence that the programme had an impact on the pedagogical relationship, also showing that teachers were an important source of mediation for children and teenagers.

Assessments of the use of *Magalhães* in the classroom indicate that facilitating the means and infrastructures is by itself insufficient to guarantee that schools incorporate technological resources in their educational practices or take into account children's cultures and interest, making them constitutive parts of the learning process. Schools have the potential to become reflective environments that may promote the critical use of technology and the full exercise of digital citizenship rights and duties. Not every child is able to enjoy such an environment at home, even though households are increasingly well-equipped with technology. For this reason, it is essential to keep up with the changes in schools and households as concerns the use of digital means and in regard to teacher and parental mediation.

The Portuguese data from the *Net Children Go Mobile* survey will improve our understanding of the present context, while simultaneously advancing the discussion of what needs to be done in order to let children exercise their right to better communication and digital citizenship.

Notes

1. http://www.pte.gov.pt/pte/PT/index.htm
2. For more information on the history of this programme, please read about the project *Navegando com o Magalhães*, coordinated by Sara Pereira from the University of Minho, available at: http://www.lasics.uminho.pt/navmag/
3. Financed by the European Safer Internet Plus programme, it initially involved Denmark, Italy, Romania and the United Kingdom. Portugal, Ireland and Belgium joined the project later, supported by national funding. More information on http://www.netchildrengomobile.eu/
4. The interviews were conducted by Karita Gonçalves, in the context of her ongoing PhD dissertation on the access and use of mobile phones among children aged 8-12 in Portugal and Brazil. We also thank Juliana Doretto for the interviews conducted for the project *Net Children Go Mobile Portugal*.

5. This tendency towards low levels of Internet use in schools is consistent with the patterns observed in Italy and Romania. which in turn contrast with the patterns observed in Denmark and the UK, as shown in the first national results of the project *Net Children Go Mobile* (Macheroni & Ólafsson, 2013).

References

Buckingham, D. (2007). *Beyond Technology. Children's learning in the age of digital culture.* London: Polity Press.

ChildWise (2011). *ChildWise Monitor. The Trends Report* 2011: Childwise 2011 http://www.childwise.co.uk

Eiras, M. O., & Meirinhos, M. (2012). *O computador Magalhães no distrito de Bragança: factores restritivos à utilização em contexto de aprendizagem.* Dissertação de mestrado em TIC na Educação e Formação. Escola Superior de Educação: Bragança.

Esteves, B. (2012). *O computador Magalhães na transformação das práticas educativas: projecto desenvolvido no agrupamento de escolas de Miranda do Douro.* Dissertação de mestrado em TIC na Educação e Formação. Escola Superior de Educação: Bragança.

Lemish, D. (2013). Introduction. Children, adolescents and media: creating a shared scholary arena. In D. Lemish (Ed.), *The Routledge International Handbook of Children, Adolescents and Media* (pp.1-10). London: Routledge.

Ling, R., & Bertel, T. (2013). Mobile communication culture among children and adolescents. In D. Lemish (Ed.), *The Routledge International Handbook of Children, Adolescents and Media* (pp.127-133). London, Routledge.

Mascheroni, G., & Ólafsson, K. (2013). *Mobile internet access and use among European children. Initial findings of the Net Children Go Mobile project.* Milano, Educatt.

Pereira, S. (2013). More technology, better childhoods? The case of the Portuguese 'one laptop per child' programme. *CM– asopis za upravljanje komuniciraniem 8(29)* 171-197

Ponte, C. (2011). A rede de Espaços Internet entre paradoxos e desafios da paisagem digital. *Media & Jornalismo, 19,* 39-58.

Ponte, C., Jorge, A., Simões, J., & Cardoso, D. (2012). *Crianças e internet em Portugal.* Coimbra, MinervaCoimbra.

Silva, P. & Diogo, A. (2011). Usos do computador Magalhães entre a escola e a família: sobre a apropriação de uma política educativa em duas comunidades escolares. *Arquipélago, 12,* 9-48.

Viana, J., Silva, P., Coelho, C., & Fernandes, C. (2012). Sobre os usos do computador Magalhães pelos alunos. *II Congresso Internacional TIC e Educação.* Lisboa: Universidade de Lisboa. http://ticeduca.ie.ul.pt/atas/pdf/364.pdf

Brands, Media Literacy and Pre-teenagers

Conceição Costa

The commercial world offers children important opportunities in terms of entertainment, learning, creativity and cultural experience; but, on the other hand, there are significant and growing concerns over the negative impacts of commercialism on children's welfare (U.K Department of Children, Schools and Families [DCFS], 2008, p. 3).

One of the most recent tactics in children's marketing entails recruiting children as brand ambassadors to their peers, at the playground, at home and on social networks. GIA (Girls Intelligence Agency) is a company that presents itself as owning forty thousand "agents" that provide very important data on the juvenile girls' market. One of their services – "Pyjama Party in a Box" – consists of one child inviting ten to twelve best friends for a sleepover. Having received a "secret box" with cool products, the child (agent) invites his/her friends to try them and give their opinion. GIA has an impressive customer list in the food, toy and entertainment industry (Nairn, 2010, p. 110).

Another novelty in children's marketing is the development of "celebrity brands". An example of this is the recent product lines from Disney meant for pre-teenagers: Hannah Montana, Selena Gomez and the Jonas Brothers. The narrative of the movies and TV series revolves around teenagers' common situations (the close cliques in school and their rivalries), but uses show-business success characters that easily create the *fandom* phenomenon (Jenkins, 2006).

Children being regarded as consumers is considered by some authors to be a recent phenomenon, a result of the confluence of two trends that started at the end of the twentieth century: on the one hand, the expansion of sales through children; and on the other, a view of family and society influenced by the discussion of children's rights and infant sociology (Marshall, 2010). For Daniel Cook, this view of childhood – a child different from adults and closer to nature – has its origin in the middle class of the nineteenth century and created favourable conditions for the development of children's commercial culture through their parents' investment (Cook, 2004, p. 13).

The discovery of children as a market segment is thus not new. However, it is only in the last two decades of the twentieth century that we see the unprecedented growth of commercial branding strategies aimed at very small children (Buckingham, 2009; Wasco, 2008). On the economy side, what seems to be new is the extension of the relationship the brands seek to establish with the youngest children.

On the one hand there has been an institutionalization of children's marketing, and on the other, there an increasingly commercial approach is being aimed at younger children. Not long ago, branding strategies were aimed at teenagers, but currently it is the *tweens*[1] segment that has acquired the status of a powerful market.

The hybridization of marketing and entertainment in online and offline media gave origin to truly "commercial" spaces blended into children's everyday life, and these constitute an identity experience of meanings in the peer group: a place of entertainment, communication, development and inclusion in/exclusion from society (Tufte & Ekstrom, 2007, p. 12).

In the case of pre-teenagers, what role do the brands play in these negotiations? Do pre-teenagers with different social conditions have the necessary media literacy to analyse media environments in a critical way?

Regulation and media literacy

More and more educators have begun to recognize that, despite their students' familiarity with the Internet and other technologies, young people may or may not have the necessary skills to access, analyse and evaluate the information or entertainment available online (Hobbs, 2008, p. 431).

The European Commission's current policy regarding media is limited to recommending self-regulation between industry and the markets, and a higher accountability of parents in regulating children. It is in the context of self-regulation that the issue of media literacy is questioned, which, despite its multiple definitions, seeks to be a way to empower citizens through media.

The particularly fast growth of the Internet created a need to redefine the concept of literacy to incorporate technology, media and pop culture. Besides this, the increasing influence of brands in pop culture brings to the discussion the need to incorporate into the concept of literacy the critical analysis of the messages conveyed through brands (Bengtsson & Firat, 2006).

Research on media literacy has always been divided into two perspectives, depending on its goal: to provide the audience with the skills needed to be protected from the harmful effects of media, and to empower the audience (e.g. Drotner, 2008); that is, the acquisition of the skills needed to efficiently use the creative and analytic resources available in media (Livingstone, Wijnen, Papaio-annou, Costa, & Grandio, 2013, p. 2).

Media literacy cannot be amputated of its context, opening up a social and cultural discussion that emphasizes its plurality, beyond its analysis as an individual skill. People do not create meanings individually, but through their participation in "interpretive communities" (Buckingham, 2007, p. 38) that stimulate and value particular ways of literacy. This is the preferred model in northern Europe, where media education programmes for young people involve collaborative projects and take place in formal and informal learning environments. The school's role is mostly empowering, creating conditions for participants to learn and apply this knowledge in diverse situations. Media literacy projects in Iceland, Norway, Denmark, Sweden and Spain encourage students to use digital media while expressing their artistic and civic interests (Livingstone et al., 2013, pp. 5-7).

According to the results of the European study EU Kids Online II (2009-2011), there are not many differences in social-economic status in the use of Internet at school in Portugal (Ponte, 2012, p. 30). But besides access, are Portuguese children and young people ready to deal with the online risks and opportunities?

Still according to EU Kids Online II, only a minority of young European Internet users are involved in creating content, so media education should focus more on the active participation of children in online environments (Livingstone, Haddon, Görzig, & Ólafsson, 2011, p. 25). The research also shows that children do not all have the same ability to access, navigate and evaluate media content and services (*idem*).

In Portugal, despite the considerable advances in Internet access at school in the past decade, it was only at the beginning of 2014 that the General Board for Education provided for public consultation a Referential Media Training proposal, in the context of the Educational Guidelines for Citizenship.

In the following section, we will look at an empirical study of media education in the school context (2009-2012) in which the philosophy was to use media as a means of empowerment.

A media education experience: methodology orientations

The current study took place under the scope of the working field of the author's PhD thesis, entitled "Brands, Media Literacy and Pre-Teenagers' Identity Expressions", seeking to respond to the research goals presented in Table 1.

The theoretical models that serve as a starting point for this research work are the Activity Theory and the interactional perspective on identities, according to which the development of children is not just an individual act but rather results from their progressive involvement in social activities in their cultural environment. Consequently, the relevant analysis unit is not the individual child but the joint activity that occurs within an interaction: between a child and an adult, between a child and another more experienced child, between a child and his/her communities (de la Ville & Tartas, 2010, p. 32), and between a child and media objects (Van den Berg, 2008).

In this study, children are recognized as competent social actors who participate in social transformation and, in this process, also transform themselves. Children have their own culture different from the adult one, and the ethnographic perspective is particularly suited for channelling their voice.

Table 1.   Research goals, activities and tools

Research Goals	Research Activities	Tools	School 1	School 2	School 3
Understanding in which way teens establish a difference between commercial (and persuasive) communication and news, entertainment and educational content;	Diagnostic evaluation of brands and advertisement	Script with images and closed and open questions	x	x	x
	Advertising commercials analysis	Speech analysis	x	x	x
	Favourite celebrities	Speech analysis		x	
	Focus Group: Celebrities	Focus group		x	
	Focus Group: Hannah Montana	Focus group	x		
Knowing the activities related to consumption;	About Christmas gifts	Individual interview	x		
	Forum theme: "Do you enjoy going to stores?"	Speech analysis	x		
Understanding how pre-teenagers see each other (and themselves) through brands;	Design "Gift for my best friend"	Image analysis	x	x	x
	Interview about "Gift for my best friend"	Individual interview conducted by a team of children	x	x	x
	Brand party	Content analysis	x		
Understanding the role of digital media, particularly the Web, in building cultural identity;	Observation of online navigation	Field diary	x	x	x
	Analysis of the interaction between children through email and in the forum	Social network analysis tool	x	x	x

The research design is presented in Figure 1. The first study case took place from October 2009 to June 2010, and the remaining from January to March 2012.

The Social Education for Media Workshop was proposed by the researcher to schools in the context of the subject "Civic Education", presenting its philosophy, skills to acquire (Table 2) and resources to use. Its duration was one weekly hour per class.

It was sought as a contribution to increasing media literacy in children, through learning activities that at the same time allow the researcher to participate openly

Figure 1. Research Design

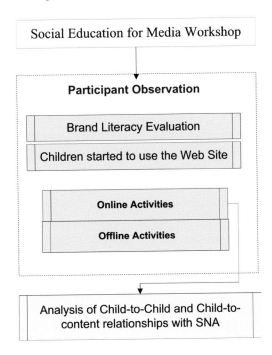

or covered up (observing) in children's lives, for a wide period of time: listening to what is said, watching their activities and asking questions – in order to answer the research questions (Hammersley & Atkinson, 1995, p. 1). The workshop was supported by a website designed with the participation of children (Costa & Damásio, 2010, pp. 103-104). The sample was selected based on a convenience criterion, and the social economic condition was obtained from an interview with those in charge at each school. The children from School 1 belong to families

Table 2. Skills and activities

Skills	Learning-Teaching Activities
Informative and persuasive communication in media	News, brands and advertisement; Watching and analysing advertising commercials
Writing in multimedia environments	Using the "myStoryMaker" app to build stories in animation; writing small news on the Amigos website
Creating audiovisual and web content	Video-recording an interview with a colleague on the drawing "Gift for my best friend"; creating an avatar for the profile on the Amigos website
Interpersonal communication and participation	Group activities; using email and the forum; electing the moderators and editors of the forum; games
Online safety	Using the "SeguraNet" app; forum discussion

in which the parents have mainly medium-and high-class status; at School 2 the parents have mostly medium-class status; and at School 3 the parents have mainly low-class status, and the majority of them are unemployed. A total of 59 children participated in this study.

Diagnostic and summative evaluation of brands and advertisements

As expected in ethnography, several additional instruments were used. The diagnostic evaluation around brands and advertisement was made at the beginning of the workshop at all three schools. The tool used was a script (Figure 2) with product images, brands and media drawn from websites aimed at pre-teenagers. In the script's construction, (global and local) media and entertainment product brands aimed at children aged nine to ten years were selected, also including other images like the Ministry for Education logo or misleading advertisement pop-ups on websites.

The script was filled in by each child individually. At the first stage, the children were invited to point out the images they recognized. At the second stage they were asked to indicate all images that, in their opinion, were brands, and lastly, those that were advertisements. The script also included a question about their favourite brand of clothing and another, multiple-choice question about what advertisement is. Since the studies at Schools 2 and 3 were conducted two years later, some additional images were included in the script to reflect changes in media "celebrity brands". At all three schools, the least recognized image was the Ministry for Education logo and the most recognized is the package of CHOCAPIC. This is certainly related to the levels of mass communication aimed at children and families, which is very high in the latter case and almost non-existent in the former.

As concerns the categorization of images as brands, the top choice of children from all schools was CHOCAPIC. As for the least rated images as brands, the Jonas Brothers, Hannah Montana and Shake it Up! were understood by a great number of children as stars and celebrities.

The commercial "Win an Apple iPhone" was categorized by the majority (even those who did not recognize the image) as an advertisement. This can be explained by the visual structure of the commercial, which is identical to that of traditional printed advertisements.

Three months after the beginning of the workshop and after all the brand and advertising spot analysis sessions, a summative evaluation was made. For this, the same script was used and the children were asked in individual interviews if they wanted to change it, and why.

The results were compared with those of the diagnostic evaluation, using only the images that were recognized by all the children: SAPOKids, Hannah Mon-

Figure 2. Script for Diagnostic Evaluation

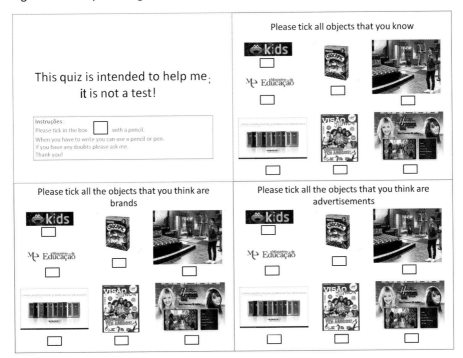

tana and CHOCAPIC. In the case of Hannah Montana's picture, it is notable that the number of children who considered it a brand increased from 11% to 30%, and those who considered it an advertisement increased from 54% to 70%. This means that concepts were learned, but it is through other activities (interviews, focus groups, messages in the website's forum) that the appropriation of brands in the context of peer groups is better understood.

From the interviews, we conclude that most children understand the function of brands and advertisements in the context of commercial activities. Brands are understood as the representation of products and commercial activities, and advertisements as an incentive to purchase products.

The relationship between "selling a product" and a brand is established by a child, referring to the images of Hannah Montana and the Jonas Brothers: "*I think they're brands because there's stuff to sell on the website, like clothing…*". However, this only occurred when the child was invited to reflect on this subject. From the age of around eight years, children have the ability to attach symbolic meaning to brands, but it is not until around 12 years of age that they incorporate this dimension into their judgment of brands and their corresponding consumers (Achenreiner & John, 2003, p. 216).

Figure 3.   Images Considered to be Brands and Advertisements

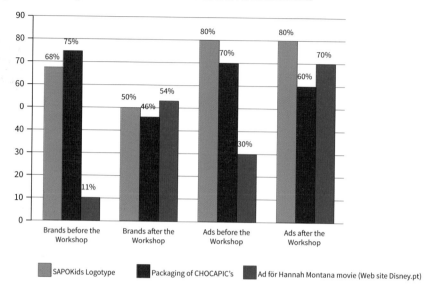

Branded gifts, no brand, and celebrities

Brands appear in the best friend's gift design, evidencing differences associated with gender and the wider cultural environment in which the children live. It is at School 1 that most of the toy brands and other entertainment products appear (Figure 4 for boys; Figure 5 for girls). At School 2, consisting mainly of girls, fashion accessories dominate the drawings (Figure 6); and at School 3 the children's drawings portray "playing in the street in green spaces", typical of the practices in the neighbourhood where the children live.

It is important to mention that in a forum debate about favourite celebrities in which the children from Schools 2 and 3 participated, pop musicians and TV series actors who are massively promoted through TV and the Internet were mentioned by both groups of children: Justin Bieber and Hannah Montana. There were also differences in taste, which seem to be markers of the wider cultural environment in which the two groups of children operate. Therefore, the favourite celebrities of one of the boys at School 2, who takes music lessons in the conservatory, are the Feist brothers, Nuno and Henrique (composer and actor, respectively). Names like Mickael Carreira, David Carreira and Michael Teló are only mentioned by children at School 3. (Mickael and David Carreira are brothers and the sons of pop singer Toni Carreira. David is known through the soap opera "Morangos com Açúcar", and Mickael is a Latin pop singer.)

Figure 4.   Lego and Playstation

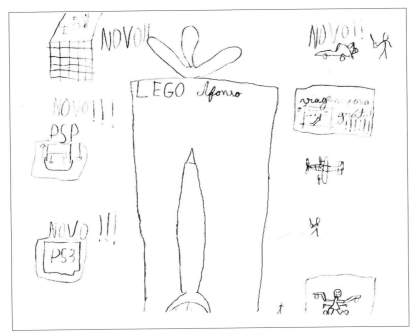

Figure 5.   Hannah Montana's wig

Figure 6. Perfume and accessories

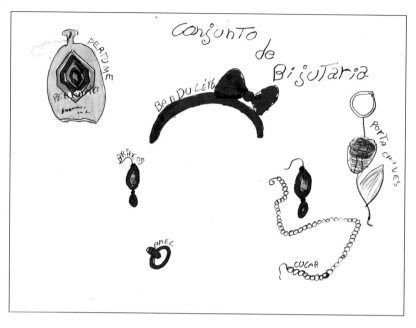

Figure 7 A "friend's forever heart"

Figure 8.   Playing soccer with my buddy

Conclusion

The knowledge demonstrated by children at all three schools about brands is a result of their daily contact with peer groups, TV, Internet and proximity communities such as the family.

For most children, advertisements and brands are evidence of commercial activities. Children recognize advertisements by their structure, even when they do not know the product being advertised.

The persuasive intentions of reference groups, which are simultaneously brands and "celebrity brands", are rarely identified by children. Brands are better understood at a perceptual rather than conceptual level; hence, the brands are more identified by their product category than their lifestyle. This does not mean that children in these ages do not have the ability to abstract or any knowledge about lifestyles associated with brands, but this is only manifested when reflection is explicitly requested of them (Livingstone & Helsper, 2006; Brucks, Armstrong, & Goldberg, 1988).

It was observed that while children were online, they closed pop-up windows and tried to ignore advertisements. From the interviews, it was concluded that the majority of children understand the function of brands and advertisement in the context of commercial activities. A small group manifested a negative attitude towards advertisements: *"They mislead; they lie; they say the products are better than what they actually are"*.

The analysis of the theme "Do you enjoy going to stores?", proposed at the initiative of a young boy in the forum, revealed that most children enjoy shopping and that the type of store differs according to gender. Most girls enjoy going to clothing stores, while the boys prefer sport, computer and video-game stores.

In the activity "Gift for my best friend", brands were more present at Schools 1 and 2, which are matched with a higher social class status.

The summative evaluation of brands and advertisement literacy revealed some learning about brands, but this does not mean the children became more immune to the effects of commercial messages.

What the study seems to make clear is that children do not possess a critical literacy that allows them to understand that their idols in show business are brands operating in their culture.

The ubiquitous corporate communications directed at children and the increased bargaining power of children in the family and at school, in line with a policy of self-regulation, could be seen as enablers of "the sponsorization" of childhood in contemporaneity. This does not mean that the majority of children are materialistic or consuming. However, for these pre-teenagers of different social backgrounds, their favourite celebrities, the TV or music characters, serve as role models in tastes and behaviours, as female and male symbols, as beauty and success ideals.

Lastly, the implementation of media literacy in school demands not only teacher training, but also a new perspective on the role of school in society, and its limits.

Note

1. There is a generalized agreement among researchers that the *tween* concept associates pre-teens (8-12 years old) with consumption. The word "tween" was first used in 1987, in an article by Carol Hall: 'Tween PowerZ: Youth's Middle Tier Comes of Age', Marketing and Media Decisions (Oct.): 56-62.

References

Achenreiner, B. G., & John, R. D. (2003). The Meaning of Brand Names to Children: A Developmental Investigation. *Journal of Consumer Psychology, 13*(3), 205-219.

Bengtsson, A., & Firat, A. F. (2006). Brand Literacy: Consumers' Sense-Making of Brand Management. *Advances in Consumer Research, 33*(1), 375-380.

Buckingham, D. (2007). *Beyond technology – children's learning in the age of digital culture.* Polity Press, Cambridge.

Brucks, M., Armstrong, M. G., & Goldberg, E. M. (1988). Children's use of cognitive defenses against television advertising: A cognitive response approach. *Journal of Consumer Research, 14*, 471-482.

Costa, C., & Damásio, J. M. (2010). How media literate are we? The voices of 9 years old children about brands, ads and their online community practices. *Obercom Journal, 4*(4), Lisboa.

Cook, D. T. (2004). Daniel Thomas Cook. *The Commodification of Childhood: The Children's Clothing Industry and the Rise of the Child Consumer.* (Kindle Locations 389-392). Kindle Edition.

de la Ville, V. I., & Tartas, V. (2010). Developing as Consumers. In D. Marshall, *Understanding Children as Consumers* (pp. 23-40). London: SAGE Publications Ltd.

Drotner, K. (2008). Leisure Is Hard Work: Digital Practices and Future Competencies. Youth, Identity, and Digital Media. In D. Buckingham (Ed.), *The John D. and Catherine T. MacArthur Foundation Series on Digital Media and Learning*. Cambridge, MA: The MIT Press. doi: 10.1162/ dmal.9780262524834.167

Jenkins, H. (2006). *Fans, Bloggers, and Gamers*. NYU Press academic.

Hammersley, M., & Atkinson, P. (1995). Ethics. In M. Hammersley & P. Atkinson (Eds.), *Ethnography: Principles in Practice* (pp. 263-287). London: Routledge.

Hobbs, R. (2008). Debates and Challenges Facing New Literacies in the 21st Century. In K. Drotner & S. Livingstone (Eds.), *The International Handbook of Children, Media and Culture* (pp. 431-437). London: SAGE.

Livingstone, S., & Helsper, E. J. (2006). Does Advertising Literacy Mediate the Effects of Advertising on Children? A Critical Examination of Two Linked Research Literatures in Relation to Obesity and Food Choice. *Journal of Communication, 56*, 560-584.

Livingstone, S., Haddon, L., Görzig, A., & Ólafsson, K. (2011). *EU kids online final report*. http:// www.lse.ac.uk/media%40lse/research/EUKidsOnline/EU%20Kids%20II%20%282009-11%29/ EUKidsOnlineIIReports/Final%20report.pdf

Livingstone, S., Wijnen, W. C., Papaioannou, T., Costa, C., & Grandio, M. d. (2013). Situating media literacy in the changing media ecology: critical insights from European research on audiences. In N. Carpentier, K. Schroeder & H. Hallet (Eds.), *Audience Transformations: Shifting Audience Positions in Late Modernity* (pp. 210-227). Routledge.

Marshall, D. (2011). *Understanding Children as Consumers*. London: SAGE Publications Ltd.

Nairn, A. (2010). Children and Brands. In D. Marshall (Ed.), *Understanding Children as Consumers* (pp. 96-115). London: SAGE Publications Ltd.

Ponte, C. (2012). Acesso, Usos e Competências. Resultados Nacionais do Inquérito EU KIDS ONLINE. In C. Ponte, A. Jorge, J. A. Simões & D. S. Cardoso. *Crianças e Internet em Portugal* (pp. 21-40). Coimbra: Edições Minerva Coimbra.

Ekström, K. M., & Tufte, B. (2007). Introduction. In K. M. Ekström & B. Tufte (Eds.), *Children, media and consumption* (pp. 11-30) (Yearbook 2007). Göteborg: Nordicom.

Van den Berg, B. (2008). *I – Object – Intimate technologies as 'reference groups' in the construction of identities*. The Media@LSE Fifth Anniversary Conference: Media, Communication and the humanity 2008. London: LSE.

UK Department for Children, Schools and Familes (2009). *The Impact of the Commercial World on Children's Wellbeing*.(Report number DCSF-00669-2009). UK: Crown. https://www.education. gov.uk/publications/standard/publicationDetail/Page1/DCSF-00669-2009

Wasco, J. (2008). The Commodification of Youth Culture. In K. Drotner & S. Livingstone, *The International Handbook of Children, Media and Culture* (pp. 460-474). London: SAGE.

The Internet in Young People's Everyday Life

Listening to Portuguese Teens' Voices

Sara Pereira

Children and young people today go about their lives in an increasingly media-tized fashion. Their daily lives are inhabited by a variety of media, ranging from the so-called new media to the more traditional ones, which have an impact on how they perceive, get to know and represent the world, how they interact with others, how they build their identity, and how they study, have fun and organize their daily lives. The media ecosystem, namely the digital environments, opened up opportunities to communicate, participate, create and produce information. Apparently, children and young people now have more means and opportunities at their disposal to express and share their ideas, interests and opinions, but are they actually taking advantage of such potential? What uses are they making of these means? Does the Internet, in fact, enable the younger generations to create a new communication culture of expression and participation?

This study set out to ascertain the relationship teenagers have with digital media, particularly the Internet and social networks. Furthermore, it sought to determine the types of access and uses teenagers aged 12 to 15 make of those media, as well as the digital literacy skills they claim to have. This led to a further goal of the study, which was to understand the role of teenagers as consumers and producers and to identify which of these roles is more relevant in their experience with the abovementioned media. Lastly, revealing the students' perceptions of the importance of actions and contexts that promote their media literacy constituted another purpose of this research.

In order to meet these objectives, an online questionnaire was administered to students of the third cycle of basic education, aged 12 to 15, attending a public school and a private school in two municipalities in the north of Portugal. All the classes comprising this cycle of education at both schools took part, resulting in 513 completed and validated questionnaires. The schools had a partnership agreement with the research project, which was why they were selected to participate. Taking into account the representations of public schools and private schools in Portugal, the latter being connoted with high socioeconomic levels, it was our intention to ascertain whether there are in fact discrepancies between students of these types of schools as far as the object of study is concerned.

The questionnaire data were treated and analysed using the IBM SPSS Statistics programme. It should be mentioned that the present text does not cover all the objectives of the study, focusing only on access, uses, online activities, Internet usage in the school context and the students' perceptions of the need for actions and initiatives that will enable them to have a critical use of the digital media.

Characterization of the teenage group and media access

Some 60% of the 513 students attend the private school, while 40% go to the public school. In terms of age group, the vast majority (84%) is between 12 and 14; however, 3% are 11 years old and 13% are 15 or over. The numbers are roughly balanced with regard to gender: 51.5% of the students are female and 48.5% are male.

And what preferences do these young people have in their daily lives; what do they do in their free time? The activity they rank, clearly, in first place is sports, with only 6% of the sample stating that they do not spend time on sports activities. All the other preferred activities which obtain significant results are connected with using media and playing on the computer, watching television, playing on the game console and listening to music. These teenagers show that watching television is not an activity they have stopped doing; it is still very present in their daily lives, despite the fact that they spend a great deal of time online.

It was observed, however, that television plays a more prominent role for younger children, i.e. those aged 11-12, in addition to being preferred slightly more by females. Using the computer is mentioned more often than watching television and, in the boys' case, the computer is more often associated with games. In fact, playing games – on the computer or the console – is an activity preferred mainly by males and in the 13 to 15 age group, being mentioned more often by students of the private school. Listening to music is another activity which stands out, although it is more frequently mentioned by girls.

As far as access to different media and technologies is concerned, this group is definitely connected. Although there was a reasonable number of non-responses to this item and it is not possible to determine their exact meaning, the fact is all the respondents have a television, 84% state that they have a mobile phone, 81% a laptop, 59% a desktop computer and 78% a game console. Only one student mentioned not having Internet access. Some 92% stated that they used social networks, with Facebook being their network of choice.

Uses and online activities

Having become acquainted with the type of access the participants have, a further step is to determine the uses they make of the Internet and social networks in an attempt to learn what motivates their use and to ascertain whether the Internet boosts communication and expression among young people. While it may be true that the Internet offers and facilitates new forms of communication and participation, the issue may be whether young people are taking advantage of these opportunities. It has been established that this group of participants has easy access to this medium; however, and moving away from the technological determinism perspective, it is my understanding that neither technology nor access to it ensures or promotes, in itself, expression and communication skills. It is vital to understand and analyse the manner in which children and young people use media while taking into account their cultural and family environments, and ascertain the extent to which they draw on the potential these media can offer them.

To this effect, the study sought to identify the activities teenagers carry out regularly, and those they never do, on the Internet. Table 1 shows the five activities most often mentioned by the participants, i.e., the five they state they do most frequently and the five they report never doing.

Figure 1.   The five activities the participants do every day and the five they never do on the Internet

Activities on the Internet

Every day	Never
Listen to music/watch video clips (67%)	Write on my blog/site (59%)
Use social networks (59%)	Participate in discussion groups (50%)
Communicate with my friends/family (55%)	Read online newspapers (47%)
Study and do homework (44%)	Write/comment on blogs and sites (41%)
Play games (37%)	Listen to the radio (25%)

These activities occupy the first five positions in both the responses given by the public and private school students, albeit with differences in terms of percentages for each activity. The most significant differences regarding the activities carried out daily pertain to 'study and do homework' and 'use social networks', with the result in these two cases being statistically significant ($p < 0.05$); i.e., there is a dependency relationship between the type of school and the regularity of the activities. The percentage of students from the public school who report using the Internet every day to study and do homework is higher (60% of the public school students compared to 40% of those at the private school), with a similar situation regarding the use of social networks (mentioned by 69% of the public school students in comparison with 64% of those at the private school). As far as the activities that are never carried out, the differences that stand out the most in terms of percentages are 'write on my blog/site' and 'participate in discussion groups'. Interestingly, the percentage of students who never write on their own blogs or sites is higher among those who attend the private school (61% as opposed to 55% at the public school). Likewise, 52% of the private school students state that they never participate in discussion groups, while this number drops to 45% for the public school students.

As far as gender is concerned, the most significant differences in the daily activities pertain to the use of social networks and game playing. Social networks are used more by girls (65%) than boys (52%), in contrast to games, which are played daily by 53% of the boys compared to only 23% of the girls. It should be said that in the girls' case, the activity 'look for information for school tasks' is actually ranked fifth on the list of the most frequent daily activities, whereas in the boys' case this position is held by 'play games'. There was also a ten percentage-point difference in the activity 'listen to music/watch video clips', favourable to the girls. In terms of the activities which are never carried out, the percentage of boys who never write on blogs/sites, either their own or others', is higher. Conversely, when it comes to participating in discussion groups, the percentage of girls who report never participating is higher (53% of the girls as opposed to 46% of the boys), although the difference is not significant. A larger difference is noticeable in the reading of online newspapers, as the percentage of girls who report never doing this activity is clearly higher (56%) than that of the boys (38%). Therefore, with regard to gender it was observed that there is a dependency relationship between this variable and the regularity of the following activities ($p < 0.05$): 'write on my blog/site', 'look up things of personal interest', 'play games', 'listen to music/watch video clips' and 'participate in discussion groups'.

When examining the age groups it can be observed that, in terms of the daily activities, using social networks and listening to music/watching video clips are two activities that increase with age. For instance, the latter is reported by 55% of students aged 11 and 12 while it is reported by 80% of those aged 15 and over. Conversely, using the Internet to 'study and do homework' is mentioned by 55% of students aged 11 and 12, dropping to 23% when the respondents are 15 and over.

Regarding the activities which are never carried out, it is interesting to observe that, although activities such as listening to the radio, reading online newspapers, and writing/commenting on blogs and sites obtain high percentages of 'I never do it' responses across all the age groups, they do decrease with age, which may suggest that these activities become more interesting to teenagers as they grow up. Similarly, the activity 'keep up with what is happening in the world' is mentioned by 23% of 11- and 12-year-olds, and then jumps to 40% for those 15 and over.

For the activities 'keep up with what is happening in the world', 'download videos, films and music', 'study and do homework', 'read online newspapers' and 'listen to music/watch video clips', the result is statistically significant ($p < 0.05$); i.e., there is a dependency relationship between the age group and the regularity of these activities.

These data, as well as other data collected from the questionnaire, suggest that the Internet is integrated into the daily life of this group of students, being used primarily as a means of entertainment and of communication with friends (and family). In fact, the Internet is a tool that can be resorted to daily for both amusement and communicative purposes, and as such is an excellent means for keeping in touch with and talking to peers. The use of social networks to talk to friends is mentioned by both boys and girls, with a significant difference noted in terms of game playing, as boys are more likely than girls to use social networks for online games.

Based on what these data reveal, i.e., that teenagers use the Internet as a means of communication *par excellence*, the issue that arises is to determine whether it brings something new to this process or is instead a conversation mediating tool. The participants agree that the Internet facilitates communication with others (84%), and also consider that it has enabled them to make new friends (86%). Social networks are above all a means of establishing a connection with peers, making it possible for students to continue their school interactions at home, and it is this extension of conversation that appears to cement friendships. This seems to be confirmed by the fact that approximately half of the respondents state that with the use of the Internet they go out less often to meet their friends. Indeed, today meetings with friends are mediated by computer or mobile phone screens, through social networks, in an almost permanent connection with the other. In these meetings, as well as in more extended networks, boys and girls share essentially music, photos and videos, regardless of their age group. They report not discussing many issues, for instance, current events or school affairs, opting rather for short comments, very often resorting to symbols (emoticons, punctuation marks, acronyms, etc.). In other words, these students seem to be highly agile when it comes to maintaining social networks and managing their contacts, but make little use of online media to comment or express an opinion in a more substantiated manner. Activities connected with the expression of ideas and opinions in addition to those related to editing and reading information are those which get the least attention from the teenagers. As can also be observed in their responses, the Internet is used by less than half of the respondents as a source of information about news and current events; even though, as mentioned before, interest in these issues increases with age.

Generally speaking, it can be said that although these teenagers are frequent users of the Internet and spend a substantial amount of their time on social networks, they do little to explore the potential and opportunities these media may offer, thereby demonstrating a high level of access and use but with a limited variety of activities which are only lightly developed; even though age, as stated before, is a significant variable regarding the type of activities carried out.

The question that is raised following these data is whether students have the opportunity to discuss and reflect on the Internet while at school. The vast majority of the respondents (96%) state that the Internet is an issue that has already been discussed at both schools. Based on the answers obtained, it can be inferred that this discussion focussed mainly on safety issues, with the purpose of warning students about the risks of the medium so that they could learn to protect themselves. Less common is the critical approach, with the aim of preparing students for a critical use, reading and production of information and thereby providing them with the tools for safe Web surfing. It thus becomes clearer why activities such as learning to search for information and creating a site or blog have relatively low percentages: 37% and 22%, respectively.

Regardless of the different approaches to the discussions on the media at school, this study sought to determine whether teenagers would value actions and initiatives that would enable them to have a critical and safe use of the Internet. Surprisingly, although it was observed that the participants take little advantage of the potential digital media have to offer, they do not appear to have a need for initiatives to assist them in further developing a critical and creative approach in their use of the information and media ecosystem. For instance, 89% state that they do not require parental regulation; 77% say they do not need support at school; and 85% consider that no laws would be required to regulate online services in order to help them use the Internet safely.

Final remarks: towards media literacy

The findings of this study, partially reported in this chapter, cannot be extrapolated to all Portuguese teenagers since they pertain only to the group of participants; nevertheless, they do support some of the conclusions reached in other national and international studies (for example, Steeves, 2014). Without purporting to be representative, this study highlights the importance of learning about, through teenagers themselves, the relationship they have with this tool of daily communication, learning and entertainment (Albero Andrés, 2010) that is the Internet.

One of the conclusions that stands out the most is the limited variety of activities these young people carry out on the Internet. These teenagers go online for entertainment, to pass time and to keep in touch with peers, and much less for issues related to civic participation or even to study or to search for information. Considering the classification of the project EU Kids Online regarding the positioning of children on the Internet (Ponte, 2012), these teenagers are undoubtedly enthusiastic users of digital technologies, essentially taking on the role of content recipients and of participants in messages, contacts and conversations initiated by others or themselves. In fact, as other studies have shown (cf., for example, Holloway & Valentine, 2003; Livingstone & Bober, 2005), Internet usage is very much based on spontaneous, intuitive uses, often guided by banal objectives and mundane forms of searching for information.

Thus, despite the significant amount of time dedicated to digital media and the central role they assume in these teenagers' lives, an analysis of their practices shows that access in itself is insufficient to ensure the development of digital skills. The analysis of the results raises the question, in the words of Albero Andrés (2010, p. 22), of 'whether the Internet promotes a new form of creating a civic culture or whether we are dealing with just the application of a new technology to do things the way they have always been done'.

Up to this point, the expression 'teenage group' has been used; however, the children and young people surveyed do not form a homogeneous social group. Their families have different social and cultural standings, which means the participants have distinct social capital. The nature of their practices and motivations as far as the use of the Internet is concerned are also distinct; therefore, it is important to take into account that the ability to critically use, read and analyse the media, as well as the ability to creatively produce content, are not exhibited by everyone in the same manner, and nor is the possibility to develop these abilities made available to everyone in the same manner. Similarly, these abilities do not develop automatically from the mere fact of having access to and using digital media. This study, thus, moves away from technological determinism perspectives that place the driving force on technology itself, instead embracing a perspective that considers that the uses and practices, in addition to the access, are associated with the social and cultural environments of the subjects as well as with their needs, interests and motivations in using the means at their disposal. It was observed that gender and age are variables that differentiate the types of uses, activities, interests and motivations. It is thus not a question of fixed practices but rather of volatile ones, which either intensify or diminish as the teenagers grow older. In terms of gender differences, girls appear to have a preference for listening to music whereas boys tend to prefer playing online games. Both value the Internet as a means of communication with friends, although girls do so slightly more than boys. While issues connected with news and current events always register low percentages, boys are more likely to be interested in the news than girls. This was observed in the interest shown by boys in reading online newspapers as well as in reading and commenting on blogs. Nevertheless, it should be noted that the figures are low.

When it comes to the type of school, there are some differences in terms of the types of uses and the kinds of approaches to discussions on the Internet.

At both the public and the private school the protection approach prevails, but it is at the public school that the critical approach obtains higher percentages. This may help explain why activities such as the creation of blogs are more common at the public school. The more controlled nature of private education in terms of the staff's teaching activities and pedagogical projects, as well as of the educational guidelines in general, could help explain this difference. On the other hand, the greater social heterogeneity of the public school students and the higher relative autonomy of teachers at this level of education, in accordance with Ministry of Education guidelines, may facilitate and open up for further possibilities for critical and empowering guidance work to be carried out.

In an age of powerful technological advancements, it is essential that children and young people develop new skills that not only enable them to access and handle technology (functional literacy), but that also prepare them to use, understand, analyse, critically evaluate and produce content (critical literacy).

References

Albero Andrés, M. (2010). *Internet, Jóvenes y Participación Civicopolítica. Límites e Oportunidades.* Barcelona: Ediciones Octaedro.

Holloway, S., & Valentine, G. (2003). *Cyberkids: Children in the Information Age* London: Routledge Falmer.

Livingstone, S., & Bober, M. (2005). *UK Children Go Online: Listening to Young People's Experiences* London: London School of Economics and Political Science

Ponte, C., Jorge, A., Simões, J. A., & Cardoso, D. (Eds.) (2012). *Crianças e Internet em Portugal.* Coimbra: Minerva Coimbra.

Steeves, V. (2014). *Young Canadians in a Wired World, Phase III: Life Online.* Ottawa: Media Smarts. http://mediasmarts.ca/sites/default/files/pdfs/publicationreport/full/YCWWIII_Life_Online_Full-Report.pdf

Media Education: Public Policies, Curricular Proposals and Teacher Training

"Easy Pieces" of Film Literacy

Some European Cases*

Vítor Reia-Baptista

The increasing development of multimedia materials as supporting vehicles of filmic languages has raised some new questions and problems within media and cultural studies, demanding different pedagogical approaches. One of the most important problems enunciated in these contexts questions the extent of the media limits and implications of the different vehicles supporting the original works. That is, until what point are we still in the presence of a given film work when it is shown, no longer on a big screen projected from a celluloid reel (the presentation form for which it was usually conceived) but on a small television, computer or phone screen beamed from a site, a file, a DVD or laser disc, and controlled through sequences of computer commands, each implying different pedagogical appropriations. This problem is not completely new, and we can recognize some parts of it from earlier discussions about the differences between cinema and television, or cinema and video for educational purposes. Nevertheless, there are new aspects that confer a more multidimensional character on the problem within a multimedia network context. Approaching some of these aspects, as an effort to contribute to the global reflection on the increasing development of multimedia information and communication technologies and processes, must be seen as a major contribution to better understanding their real nature and pedagogical value for a higher degree of media and film literacy.

From the moving image to the moving mind

Since the very beginning of film history film enthusiasts of all kinds, but especially industrialists and other film entrepreneurs, have been rather optimistic about the great possibilities of using film in educational environments. According to Larry Cuban, in the early 1920s Thomas Edison said:

> I believe that the motion picture is destined to revolutionize our educational system and that in a few years it will supplant largely, if not entirely, the use of textbooks. (Cuban, 1986, p.9).

As we know today, it did not happen exactly that way. But, despite the failure of this prophecy, many other links and connections have been established between motion pictures and education to our day, and I believe this process is far from complete. These connections are not always clear or well known in the media and educational fields, the agents of which are, generally and intuitively, aware of the existence of some dimensions of mutual influence but do not often act, at least consciously, in consequence of their implications.

Some of these dimensions present quite a number of specific characteristics that have great importance for the global communication processes, and therefore also educational ones, occurring in modern societies, of which cinema, television, video, books, pictures, texts, sounds, computers, records and other media devices are integrated parts.

In fact, Edison was not the only one with optimistic visions for the integration between the fields of media and education. There were, indeed, many other links between the two fields, but we cannot say generally that today there are many stable institutional links between different nations' communication industries and their educational systems, although some exceptions can be noted.

Travelling in time and technology from Edison's time to our own, we could turn our attention to other industrialists or technology traders and note their beliefs, not only concerning film as a powerful pedagogical medium, but regarding multimedia as global phenomena, in which cinema and films are continuously playing a growing part. John Sculley, former CEO of Apple Inc., wrote in his foreword to *Learning with Interactive Multimedia*:

> Imagine a classroom with a window on all the world's knowledge. Imagine a teacher with the capability to bring to life any image, any sound, any event. Imagine a student with the power to visit any place on earth at any time in history. Imagine a screen that can display in vivid color the inner workings of a cell, the births and deaths of stars, the clashes of armies and the triumphs of art ... I believe that all this will happen not simply because people have the capability to make it happen, but also because people have a compelling need to make it happen. (Ambron & Hooper, 1990, p. vii).

It is very interesting to note that the differences between the two beliefs in the pedagogical power of the media are almost non-existent. However, this reveals more about how intensive and constant the industry's expectations to penetrate the educational markets have been over the years, than it shows truly tested perspectives for the different media within different pedagogical contexts. Nevertheless, we have to admit that these perspectives are much more ubiquitous now than ever before, thanks to the new technological multimedia network contexts. This means that we can no longer dismiss them as a bunch of new/ old prophecies based on the industry's best wishes. In fact, some of them are already happening – *YouTube* being a good example – as texts (words, images and sounds), contexts and pretexts of a constantly renewed film literacy.

Films as texts

One of the most important roles is that of the receiver, decoding the filmic message through the specific devices of the multimedia platforms. He is generally no longer the abstract spectator taken from the collective darkness of the movie theatre, nor is he, anymore, the single manipulator of a non-intelligent video cassette recorder with rather limited possibilities of intervention with the original work. The user/receiver of the filmic multimedia material is, indeed, a reader of multiple texts, and his role will not only be that of a reader, creating meaning through his mental capacity of recognition, interpretation and association, as Umberto Eco has presented him to us before.

He will also be a much more active reader, and especially a much more powerful one. So powerful that, probably, he will not confine himself to the *role of the reader* and will become, in fact, a new creator with almost unlimited possibilities to manipulate the original work and even preserve his manipulation as a new work to be watched and studied.

Do we need media education to achieve media literacy?

In fact, most of the time, we can become media literate just by being exposed to the media, without any formal media educational process, since all processes of media exposure contain some kind of media pedagogy that forms and conforms media users (senders and receivers) in many ways, developing production, reading, interpretation and reproduction mechanisms, of which the very same senders and receivers are often simply not aware. When this happens (and it happens quite often) the media users are perhaps functionally media literate to some degree, but they are nevertheless alienated in several ways concerning the pedagogical processes that take place within their public and private media spheres. Then, some more specific media education processes may become important in order to achieve better media literacy results, for both media readers and media makers.

It was with this in mind that a group of independent scholars and experts from different countries and institutions gathered to join their efforts in the attempt to produce some kind of common approach to media literacy, which came to be known as "The European Charter for Media Literacy", a public declaration of commitment to certain essential factors of media literacy, such as:

Raise public understanding and awareness of Media Literacy, in relation to the media of communication, information and expression; Advocate the importance of Media Literacy in the development of educational, cultural, political, social and economic policy; Support the principle that every citizen of any age should have opportunities, in both formal and informal education, to develop the skills and knowledge necessary to increase their enjoyment, understanding and exploration of the media[1].

This means that we will have to develop formal and non-formal media education strategies for school environments, parental environments and, necessarily, professional media environments. Since we know that the media industries are usually almost completely closed to such pedagogical approaches, this means that we will have to concentrate our efforts on the environments of academic media training, that is, universities and other media training centers. Within this perspective, besides journalism, the other fields of major importance for media education and media literacy are film, video games, music, advertising and, because all the media tend to converge toward it, the Internet.

Some of these aspects have already been raised in earlier contexts, in an attempt to encourage reflection and discussion on their nature:

The Internet is actually the largest database for information support in the daily life of individuals but even institutions and services. Among those we can count students and teachers, but also media and opinion makers, as well as information providers including journalists. When it is essentially used as a path for communication channels for electronic messages, the web contains a series of useful information, presented by individuals, institutions, governments, associations and all types of commercial and noncommercial organizations. But who are the gate-keepers of that electronic flow? Who makes up the major streamlines of the global agenda? How and where are the most powerful editorial lines shaped? Beyond the boundless and instantaneous allocation of data, the Internet developed new ways for cultural, economic and social life. This development is related to communication instruments and access to the communication and information industries. It is apparent in politics, education, commerce, and in many other fields of public and private character. All these areas contribute to the rapid change of our traditional paradigms of public sphere and space and we don't know yet if our position as individual and social actors in the above is changing as quickly and maybe we are not yet completely aware of the implications of such changes. The potential threat of widespread alienation in such new environments of media exposure should not be dismissed lightly. (Reia-Baptista, 2006, p. 123).

Do we need film literacy?

Film, probably the most eclectic and syncretic of all media, has an incredible power of attraction which is replicated in all other media through the use of film languages in any kind of media context: music videos to promote music; real footage to enhance video games; film genres and film stars to reach publicity targets; film inserts and excerpts of all kinds on *YouTube, Facebook, Myspace* and millions of other websites. Film, in its many different forms, became the most common vehicle for these new environments of media exposure, thus also becoming one of the most important instruments for a multidimensional and multicultural media literacy among the many different media users, consumers, producers and "prosumers" of all ages as well as social and cultural levels; although different levels of media literacy, their nature or even what they lack can show differences or similarities, according to the local and global contexts where they are developed and practiced:

> Appropriations and usage patterns of these media technologies are in many ways rather specific, so one of the main risks, in a media literacy context, is the danger of generalization about common patterns of appropriation. However, one general feature in our attitudes toward these media cultural effects has been taking them as they were often ambivalent: television is still seen both as educational and as a drug; mobile phones are perceived both as a nuisance and as a life-saver; computer games are viewed both as learning tools and as addictive timewasters and film has been looked at since the very beginnings of the 7th art as a medium of great educational power as well as a medium with an enormous range of escapism dimensions. (Reia-Baptista, 2008, p.155).

The urgency to approach film, its languages and appropriations as a main vehicle of media literacy also concerns the enormous importance of this medium in the construction of our collective memories. The richness and diversity of the film languages, techniques and technologies are seen as instruments of great importance, from the primitive films of Lumière and Méliès to the most sophisticated virtual contributions on *YouTube*. Their role as vehicles of artistic and documentary narratology and as factors of authentic film literacy acquires an absolutely unquestionable importance in any society that calls itself a knowledge and information society, as constructive contributions to our collective and cultural memories.

Having this in mind, especially within the new context of media policies that are expected to be developed all around the world, and consequently some possible new media and film literacy approaches, it was a task of major importance to produce a thematic dossier concerning the role of *Film Languages in the European Collective Memory*. (Reia-Baptista, 2010)

Let us examine, then, how such a contribution can help us establish some links to the global media literacy strategies that need to be drawn all over the world, especially concerning the training of teachers in order to be able to deal with multiple film and audiovisual literacy challenges.

Four *easy pieces* of literacy

Paraphrasing the film by Bob Rafelson (1970), one should always find some "easy pieces" to put together our capacities, cultural stories and memories. This was the challenge involved in gathering different film literacy approaches in an attempt to build cultural bridges among different generations, movements and appropriations concerning the European collective film memory, presented here as a case study and an example of many other possible film literacy approaches.

The conservation of the collective memory of sounds and images as a European cultural heritage means acknowledging the various evolutionary contexts of audiovisual communication in Europe, as well as their relations to the cultures of the world at large, as these processes never occur in geographical or cultural isolation. The language of film takes on a vital role in these processes of communicative and educational evolution, as a vehicle of collective communication and education; that is, as a factor for an in-depth learning of the most varied domains of human knowledge – i.e., multiple literacies, including media and film literacy.

It is also important to examine the evolution of the pedagogical dimensions of audiovisual communication in general, and cinematographic education in particular, as the true starting point for an entire cultural repository that we cannot neglect or ignore; otherwise, we risk casting into oblivion some of the most important traces of our European cultural identity which, by their nature, are often so fragile. We are therefore obliged to delve into the media, channels, technologies and language we have developed for over a century to add clarity to the collective creativity and necessities of the artistic and documentary narration that represents us and enables us to reflect on our own human condition. But, strange though it may seem, the societies, sciences and technologies within which these narratives develop can also suffer from memory loss, just as we as individuals are forgetful or get old and are unable to regenerate the hetero-recognition mechanisms, and sometimes not even self-recognition, or because we cannot distance ourselves sufficiently from our prevailing knowledge and narratives in order to gain a more holistic, universal and reflective perspective. It is not because artists, scientists or pedagogues, like other human beings, have a "short memory", but because the arts, sciences and technologies and their languages are closed off and isolated within their own particular spaces and sometimes separated from knowledge, application and even dissemination.

This can happen in any branch of the arts or sciences, even when the fundamental principles of their languages belong to education or communication, which in itself is an enormous contradiction. Thus, the technological and communicative supports for the records of the individual and collective production of knowledge turn inward in their apparent self-sufficiency from the standpoint of the evolution of communication, taking into account the technological and linguistic development of the past century, which has shown itself to be fairly redundant as well as being a reducing agent that has erroneously and inefficiently preserved the procedural knowledge of construction and communication of scientific or cultural learning. Consequently, we are now obliged to analyze the possible risks of the loss of this collective property, which is often incredibly insubstantial and thus all the more valuable. To do this, we must also preserve, articulate and systematize some of the main features of the processes of cultural communication as phenomena of collective memorization and learning. As so many scientists and researchers have stated over the years in the exercise of their scientific irreverence and theoretical restlessness, the scientist is hardly ever able to take a step back and view science, in space and time, in such a way that he can see it move, and yet, it moves. And, as mentioned, the role of cinema and film languages as vehicles of artistic and documentary narratives, in a comprehensive and holistic perspective, acquires an absolutely unquestionable importance as a factor of authentic media and film literacy, as can be seen in the different approaches gathered in the thematic dossier of *Comunicar* 35 (Reia-Baptista, 2010):

1. The BFI Department of Film Education, recognized by many authors for playing a vital, leading role in this field, develops some main pedagogical approaches, especially in what we call film pedagogy, clearly demonstrating that the study of cinema and films is absolutely essential for understanding the world and times we live in.

2. The Audiovisual Centre (CAV) in Liège, Belgium, develops a reflection on the theme *Film Education: memory and heritage*, within which film education is identified, especially in these times of transition and migration into digital environments, as an urgent need to construct a profound film literacy as the supreme art form of memory, be it individual or collective.

3. The Media Lab at London University's Institute of Education discusses the role of film language in this era of transition among media, channels and cultural environments, taking horror movies and video games as an example of the hybridization of genres and the transmutation of forms of interaction among youngsters.

4. The CIAC, Research Centre for the Arts and Communication at the University of the Algarve, emphasizes the huge importance of the historic avant-gardes in the construction of film discourse and how they were essential in gaining recognition for cinema as an art form, offering their perspectives within the crossroads of these key concepts toward a possible renewed film literacy.

Conclusions

Although these case studies are benchmarked by the cultural context of European cinema and European film literacy appropriations, it seems quite adequate to conclude that these reflections may well be considered for other similar literacy approaches in other places and within other cultural contexts, such as those that may be developed within the different Portuguese-speaking contexts.

Note

1. http://www.euromedialiteracy.eu/about.php

References

Ambron, S., & Hooper, K. (1990). *Learning with Interactive Multimedia.* Washington: Microsoft Press/Apple Computer.

Cuban, L. (1986). *Teachers and Machines.* New York: Teachers College Press.

Eco, U. (1979). *The Role of the Reader.* London: Hutchinson & Co.

Reia-Baptista, V. (2006). *New Environments of Media Exposure – Internet and narrative structures: from Media Education to Media Pedagogy and Media Literacy.* In U. Carlsson (Ed.), *Regulation, Awareness, Empowerment* (pp. 123-134). Gothenburg University: Nordicom.

Reia-Baptista, V. (2008). *Multidimensional and Multicultural Media Literacy – social challenges and communicational risks on the edge between cultural heritage and technological development.* In U. Carlsson, S., Taye, Jaquinot-Delaunay, G., & J. M. Pérez-Tornero (Eds.), *Empowerment through Media Education* (pp. 155-165). Gothenburg University: Nordicom.

Reia-Baptista, V. (2010). Film Languages in the European Collective Memory. *Comunicar, 35,* XVIII, 10-13.

* This text is a summary of the article "Film Literacy: Media Appropriations with Examples from the European Film Context" originally published in the Journal Report (2012). doi: 10.3916/c39-2012-02-0.8.

Defining a Media Literacy Policy through Networking

Manuel Pinto

Paraphrasing what Ortega y Gasset said a hundred years ago, we are what we are plus our circumstances[1]. We make the circumstances, and we are made by them. Therefore, this text's approach to media literacy policies begs a careful analysis of the socio-cultural and political context of their development. Specifically considered are public policies, with the Portuguese case as the object of analysis.

It is the author's view that a given policy, besides belonging in a specific social-historic context, is always guided by certain values and beliefs, and conditioned by the more or less shared and widespread degree of awareness of its relevance and need. It is also an outcome of the symbolic and economic resources, of the processes and methodologies of its formulation and implementation, as well as the degree of participation and involvement of the social actors.

There are public policies characterized mostly by a top-down logic, and others that are encouraged or even created by civil society opinion movements. Naturally, between these two poles there is a range of possibilities.

It should be stated that the author stands for an open and multidimensional literacy concept regarding the media (Peréz-Tornero & Varis, 2012): as a skill gained throughout life, especially in school, that is characterized by the acquisition and operationalization of resources oriented to a critical attitude and thought towards the media and towards communication activities and participation in the media environment which take advantage of the plurality of technologies and languages. Since no person lives isolated, but rather in interaction with fellow human beings, training is based on the social relationship that is the mainstay of communication proper. In this line of thought, and following the guidelines of pioneers in this field (Halloran & Jones, 1985; Kaplún, 1998), we can understand education for a careful and competent use of the media as an education for communication.

The purpose of this article is to reflect on the definition of a media education policy through networking involving several public institutions. To achieve this the article will start by contextualizing the status of media education in Portugal, with an emphasis on the post-25th April 1974 Revolution period, but without neglecting the previous political framework of the Salazar dictatorship. Subsequently, it will describe the experience of the so-called Media Literacy Informal Group (GILM), in the field since 2009, and will conclude with some reflections on the results, the potential and the weaknesses of the research, as well as the relevance of this assessment in the European and international spheres.

A context of citizenship discovery and learning

Twentieth-century Portuguese history is marked by almost a half-century of political tyranny, of surveillance and censorship of difference and diversity, by the imposition of a monolithic ideology and worldview, and by the repression of those who dared to challenge the status quo of Oliveira Salazar's dictatorship. The exhaustion and revolt caused by the Colonial War in Africa, the chronic backwardness in fundamental areas of social life like schooling, health, employment and social security, together with the longing for freedom in some segments of society, were the factors that fuelled the rise in contradictions that led to the 25th April 1974 military coup supported by a movement whose programme can be synthesized in the three Ds: Democracy, Decolonisation and Development.

It is in this framework that some relevant dynamics that can be traced back to what would later be designated as media education should be understood; these were mainly linked to school journalism and to the introduction to cinema language. In the former, the pioneering role fell to pedagogic innovation movements, mostly inspired by Célestin Freinet (Freinet, 1993). In the latter, the film-society movement and other school-focused initiatives[2] played a key role and, within their framework, new space was opened to cinematographies characterized by aesthetics clearly different from (and opposed to) the authoritarian and paternalistic culture of the Salazar regime.

In the post-25th April period, in an environment of freedom of movement and creation, initiatives and proposals proliferated. Some continued former experiences, but now with a new horizon. Others engaged in bringing journalistic activity into the classroom, aiming at helping the young understand the world so that they could intervene in it. Others yet relied on the new technologies that were gradually being created, to conceive of new paths for education. The media and journalism themselves became subjects of study in formal education, commanding remarkable interest and curiosity. Years ago, from this range of options, the author attempted to elaborate a critical review, which now needs to be updated due to the emergence of the Internet (Pinto, 2003). However, in many cases the reflective, critical and intervention assumptions that came to characterize the idea of media literacy were not present yet. The isolation from other countries that endured at least until the 1980s, due to the inertia of decades of ostentatious isolationism, has only recently started to fade.

In the democratic period, several attempts were made to include media education in formal education. The first comprised the recommendations formulated in 1988 in the final document by the Commission for the Educational System Reform (CRSE), reached after hearings and debate with the educational agents that had taken place since 1986[3]. The second occurred in 1994, when then Secretary of State for Primary and Secondary Education asked a team from the University of Minho for a document on the curricular options for the school levels under his supervision[4]. In both cases, the political tribulations arising from government changes impaired the implementation of the proposals.

In a post-25th April media education analysis, it was concluded that there were "fragmented and inconsequential experiences, incapable of articulating themselves in a political and educational platform. Nevertheless, they are important for those that were or still are directly involved" (Pinto, 2003, p. 121).

Put into perspective and at a distance, this reading could be considered hasty. It is true that remarkable work, developed in the later 90s within the framework of the Educational Innovation Institute (IIE) of the Ministry of Education, was discontinued due to a change of government in 2002, thus terminating studies, resources and a book collection on media education. It is also true that this Institute launched and supported dynamics at many schools. On the other hand, since the 1980s, higher education institutions linked to teacher training and to scientific research have emerged that have invested in media education, such as the Universities of Minho and the Algarve, and the Polytechnic Institute of Setúbal. It was also in this period that the "Público", a quality newspaper launched in the early 90s, appeared in the media sector with the declared purpose of including in its editorial project the media education dimension, with a programme that has seen better days but is still functioning.

This notwithstanding, by the end of the first decade of the 21st Century, there was a dossier in the Noesis magazine dedicated to the theme "Media Education: from the Analogic to the Digital". Maria Emília Brederode Santos and Teresa Fonseca, who had belonged to the IIE, coordinated this dossier and placed an emphasis on "the successive breakthroughs and setbacks" which media education has had "twenty-five years after the "Grünwald Declaration (Brederode-Santos & Fonseca, 2009). Surely "breakthroughs and setbacks", but more than that: although media education was a relevant dimension of citizenship, it was still absent from the public agenda and distant from political concerns and programmes.

Actually, major changes had been registered in the meantime, deriving mostly from the expansion of the Internet, Web 2.0 and the social networks, the exponential growth of contacts and the dissemination of experiences and information, the multiplication of content production and broadcasting initiatives by actors in the field and no longer exclusively by 'renowned' institutions. Simultaneously, especially since the late 90s and in the framework of Portugal's full integration into the European Union, contacts with academics and decision-makers as well as with initiatives and institutions in the field of media and media literacy multiplied, allowing for the emergence of international partnerships and the establishment of networks in the fields of research and post-graduate teaching as well as the publication of studies.

GILM: looking for ways to place media literacy on the public agenda

The framework presented above allows for the understanding of the internal circumstances which, articulated with the evolution of European policies, will be at the outset of a 2009 initiative aimed at changing this situation. During this period a letter, dated 4th June 2009, was written by the Communication and Society Research Centre (CECS) of the University of Minho to the Media Office (GMCS) and the Media Regulatory Authority (ERC). This letter referenced the civic and cultural relevance of media and digital literacy, the responsibilities taken on in this area by the European Union Member-States, and the range of entities in Portugal with an interest in the subject. Consequently, a meeting including other institutions was suggested in order to take stock of the situation and "conceive an action plan that, whilst safeguarding each partner's specificities, will enable a greater inter-knowledge, creation of synergies, information production and exchange and better working conditions for everybody".

The letter recipients welcomed the suggestion, and the GMCS organized the first meeting at Palácio Foz, in Lisbon, on 30th July 2009. Besides the three afore-mentioned schools, participants were the National Education Council and the UNESCO National Commission, represented by its top cadres. It was decided to hold a follow-up of the meeting and ensure that the group had a more informal nature, as this was judged to be the most adequate approach for pursuing the intended goals. As time went by, the acronym GILM, standing for Media Literacy Informal Group, came to be used internally. Also from the outset, the idea of a congress that would serve as a meeting point and a space of inter-knowledge for all actors involved in media education in Portugal started to take shape. The features of the congress would be defined at the beginning of 2010, with a methodology that provided for these actors to be consulted in the preparatory stage.

One aspect that can be associated with the emergence of GILM is Directive 2007/65/CE, 11th December 2007, from the Council and the European Parliament, concerning television broadcasting and other legislation from the EU and other international organizations[5]. Therein it is established that, from December 2011 on, every three years the Commission should present to the European Parliament, the Council and the European Socio-Economic Committee a report on the implementation of the directive in every Member-State, namely on the "levels of media education" (Article 26). The initiative to congregate institutions involved in media education, especially those that would be tasked with monitoring the directive's implementation and the preparation of the report it provided for, would be a way (and an opportunity) to take a step forward concerning what was already being done in Portugal.

The GILM's dynamic, in the meantime extended to new institutions[6], has contained two strands from the beginning: the initiatives of each partner-institution within the realm of their specific mission, and the initiatives of the GILM proper. Of the activities promoted by the Informal Group, the following stand out:

GILM	PARTNERS
1st "Literacy , Media and Citizenship" Congress (Braga, 2011) Braga	Study "Media Education in Portugal – Experiences, Actors and Contexts" (ERC/CECS, 2011)
Declaration-Manifesto on Media Education	Media Literacy Site (GMCS) www.literaciamediatica.pt
National Event "Seven Days with the Media" (annual, open to all; started in 2012 as "One Day" event)	Recommendation by the National Council for Media Literacy Education (no. 6, 2011) addressed to the Government and to Parliament
2nd "Literacy , Media and Citizenship" Congress (Lisbon, 2013)	MIL*obs –Media, Information and Literacy Observatory (GMCS/CECS)
Minutes of the 1st and 2nd "Literacy , Media and Citizenship" congresses	Each partner's own programme in the scope of the event "Seven Days with the Media"
	Study on the evaluation of the media literacy levels of 12th grade students (GMCS/RBE/CECS) (ongoing)
	Elaboration, with public consultation, of the Reference of the Media Education Curriculum for Preschool
	Education and Primary and Secondary Education (DGE-MEC/CECS) (currently in its final phase) Site "Ensina" (audiovisual resources for schools and family support, made available by RTP since January 2014)
	25+ONE. Agenda of Media Education Activities", (CECS/GMCS, 2011)

Especially since the congresses and the annual open initiative "Seven Days with the Media" (www.literaciamediatica.pt/7diascomosmedia/), the GILM has been realizing one of its goals: linking people, institutions and projects and, finally, establishing networks and partnerships that do not overshadow but rather enhance the actions of each entity.

There is no political directive that defines general targets, general or common methods or rhythms beyond what the GILM itself decides by consensus. The Group is autonomous, and so is each partner. This notwithstanding, the entities that play some direct or indirect role in policy-making are GILM partners. This is the case for: GMCS, a governmental department linked to the media; the Ministry of Education and Science; the National Education Council (an organism that derives from Parliament); and the ERC, the media regulatory authority.

In this framework, beyond its own actions, the Informal Group works as a space of information and debate, inter-knowledge and reciprocal learning and creation of synergies. In the informal events of the journey, one gradually defines what seems to be fundamental in a policy: being in sync in terms of the main goals, having a memory of a route, recognizing the diversity of paths, maintaining inter-institutional cooperation, and providing a public service.

An impact evaluation study of this Group is still lacking, and is not the objective of this text. In any case, alongside the different partners' satisfaction with the work achieved, there is an awareness that there is still much to be done to make media literacy a shared concern. Perhaps it will be possible, in the future, to involve more social actors (linked to media outlets, health, seniors, families, the arts…). The investment in the training of trainers, extending it to increasingly larger circles, and the creation and availability of resources to support the initiatives, programmes and self-training, constitute crucial factors to promote. Finally, the Group may have to reflect upon the role it will take concerning the creation of a permanent network of the societal institutions with which it has been interacting. From such a network, association or council could stem common needs and concerns, intervention priorities and new forms of cooperation, as long as it possessed a lean and independent structure.

Concluding remarks

Portugal has developed media education initiatives of great diversity and wealth, albeit with limited reach and impact (Pinto, Pereira, Pereira & Ferreira, 2011) and in a framework of a historically recent process of democratic learning. This paper has shown how, despite some ad hoc attempts, training citizenry in communication and media has never become a target or goal of public policies. Equally, there has never been a socio-cultural 'movement' capable of developing into a pressure group or lobby, despite the attempt by the Education and Media

Association, which existed during the second half of the 1990s. The awareness that it was necessary to take a step in the direction of opposing the atomization of experiences and the "breakthroughs and setbacks" of the very idea of media education led to the decision to create a common meeting space for public entities, which would become the Media Literacy Informal Group.

Lacking an official mandate, the Group consolidated itself through the activities that each partner developed and through what all partners achieved together, despite the incidences of political change, or the rotation of the top officials within the participating institutions. In itself this certainly does not constitute a policy. But it is a meeting, cooperation, initiative and mobilization platform, dimensions without which policies do not survive. Informality may be seen as a weakness, but at the same time it confers versatility and efficiency on GILM. The case shows that, despite the diverse scope of action of each institution involved, it is possible to make a common journey, guided by service to the community. In this sense the way it has been working is, in itself, an enriching experience.

Notes

1. "Yo soy yo y mi circunstancia" – Ortega y Gasset (1914).
2. One example: José Vieira Marques, the key figure at the Figueira da Foz Cinema Festival, who for years held wide-ranging free courses on the introduction to cinematographic language at different schools across the country (Pinto, 2003, p. 123).
3. Cf. CRSE (1988). *Global Reform Proposal*. Lisbon: Office of Studies and Planning.
4. The report, produced by a group coordinated by the author of this text, was titled "*School and social communication: challenges and proposals for action*".
5. For a presentation of this legislation, see Lopes (2011) and Pereira (2013).
6. At the beginning of 2014, the following institutions integrated the GILM: National Education Council (CNE); UNESCO National Commission (CNU); Communication and Society Research Centre of the University of Minho (CECS); Directorate-General of Education of the Ministry of Education and Science (DGE); Media Regulatory Authority (ERC); Foundation for Science and Technology – Dep. of Information Society (FCT); the Media Office (GMCS); Network of School Libraries (RBE); Portuguese Radio and Television (RTP). There are two individual, non-institutional, members: Maria Emília Brederode Santos and Teresa Calçada, two personalities who in diverse ways have a trajectory linked to literacy and media education.

References

Brederode-Santos, M.E., & Fonseca, T. (2009). O regresso da educação mediática. *Noesis*, 79, 30-35.

Freinet, C. (1993). *O jornal escolar*. Lisboa: Estampa.

Halloran, J., & Jones M. (1985). *Mass media education: education for communication and mass communication research*. Paris: UNESCO.

Kaplún, M. (1998). *Una pedagogía de la comunicación*. Madrid: Ediciones de la Torre.

Lopes, P. C. (2011). *Educação para os media nas sociedades multimediáticas*. Lisboa: CIES e-Working Paper, nº 108.

Ortega y Gasset, J. (1914). *Meditaciones del Quijote*. Madrid: Publicaciones de la Residencia de Estudiantes.

Pereira, L. (2013). *Literacia digital e políticas tecnológicas para a educação*. Santo Tirso: De Facto Editores.

Peréz-Tornero, J.M., & Varis, T. (2012). *Alfabetización mediática y nuevo humanismo*. Barcelona: Ed. UOC/UNESCO-IITE.

Pinto, M. (2003). Correntes da educação para os media em Portugal: retrospectiva e horizontes em tempos de mudança. *Revista Iberoamericana de Educación, 32*, 119-142.

Pinto, M., Pereira, S., Pereira, L., & Ferreira, T. (2011). *Educação para os media em Portugal: experiências, actores e contextos*. Lisboa: ERC.

An Overview of Practices in Portugal

Media Education Practices in Portugal

A Panoramic View

Ana Jorge, Luís Pereira & Conceição Costa

Portugal has witnessed an increased dynamism in the field of media education in recent years, as a result of incentives from international bodies such as UNESCO, and more especially European ones, not only through the Recommendation of the European Council in 2009 and the European Parliament, but also as a result of a strong impetus from both civil society and academia[1].

Several relevant initiatives, launched by public, private and civil bodies including the academic world (Pinto, Pereira, Pereira & Ferreira, 2011; Ponte & Jorge, 2010), have contributed to remarkable progress, especially if we bear in mind the historic delay caused by the dictatorship that lasted until 1974, which was characterized by media censorship as well as low levels of schooling.

In this chapter, we offer a general panoramic view of the field of media education projects in the past two decades, targeted mostly at children and young people. We present some of the projects that have been regarded as good examples, considering the parameters that were defined, namely their longevity and impact, or their innovation in encouraging youth participation, for instance. In this overview, we will report on the different social agents involved in the field of media education, making projects for different audiences and with different philosophies and methodologies, in the context of both formal and informal education; but we will also document the main deficiencies in this field. More than a picture of the Portuguese reality, we present some of the best frames of a movie whose plot has been enriched in recent years, but which is still far from over.

From school newspapers to digital media

Media companies themselves have been among the pioneers in the field of media education, encouraging the school community to become involved in the production of school newspapers. At a time of growth in the media sector, after decades of dictatorship and in the first years of democracy, in the early 1990s the private daily newspaper *Público* launched Público na Escola [Público at School], which included a competition for school newspapers and the creation of resources, such as themed pieces, to support media education in schools. However, the project's funding was gradually cut in the late 2000s. After this, the competing daily newspaper *Diário de Notícias* launched the MediaLab project in 2010, with the support of bodies such as UNESCO. This project involves the newspaper inviting schools and youth communities into the newspaper's offices to attend workshops on producing a newspaper front page. An important dimension of MediaLab is the inter-generational connection, which becomes relevant in a society where different generations have had differing access to education: groups of elderly people visit the project and sometimes interact with the youngsters.

The production of school newspapers was also prompted by the academic world and, additionally, was the topic of the research project Media Education in the Castelo Branco Region, which explored the connections between the new technological media and the traditional newspaper, as reported in another chapter of this book. The development of a tool in connection with this field is of particular importance. In fact, in schools, both in classrooms and outside, the Education and Science Ministry (MEC) also supports other initiatives such as "School Newspapers and Broadcasts", devoted to the creative work of young people in the different media. These opportunities were greatly supported by the technological facilitation of the past decade, with both the introduction of computers in schools and the delivery of laptops to students, through the Magal-hães and e-escolas programmes.

Also noteworthy is the work at the level of literacies of the Network of School Libraries (Rede de Bibliotecas Escolares – RBE), under MEC, providing support to and underpinning the whole learning project. Created in 1995, today the RBE covers almost the entire state school network, empowering students and teachers to develop reading, information and media literacies.

Acknowledging the importance of digital media in the lives of youngsters, MEC, with other governmental and civil society partners, also promotes SeguraNet, a project focused on educating for the safer use of the Internet. SeguraNet is also notable for its feature of having a youth panel, a dimension that is relevant for the true participation of the targeted audiences in media education programmes.

Media education does not exist in Portugal as a separate subject in the curriculum; it figures only in the field of 'Education for Citizenship', within which are also included financial, road safety and health education, among others, and which takes place in non-curricular spaces such as Accompanied Study or Project Area, which have been losing space in the present curriculum. MEC has scarce resources to develop this educational role, but has associated itself with some projects that make resources available for this purpose. One such project is Me-diaSmart, an advertising literacy programme for children aged 6 to 11, imported from Canada and the United Kingdom and launched nationally in 2008 by the Portuguese Advertisers Association (APAN), with support from MEC since 2012. The project distributes materials to primary and secondary schools that request them and promotes competitions in advertising production, as a way to increase literacy among children, particularly regarding commercial communication and marketing through the different media. However, this initiative can be used as an argument against the stricter legislative regulation of advertising for children[2].

Cinema constitutes a further area for attention within the field of media edu-cation in Portugal. After several regional projects promoted by cinema clubs at the end of the 1990s (Viseu, Faro), in 2012 the National Plan for Cinema was launched by academics as a pilot with the intention of integrating this plan into the curriculum of MEC. However, it has faced problems in implementation re-garding screening royalties.

In early 2014, several initiatives were created. On the one hand, *RTP*, the public service broadcast operator, launched the Ensina portal[3], with material and resources: 800 pedagogical videos at the time of launching. In Ensina, media education is one of the content categories, and several videos related to this theme can be found, for instance excerpts from the "Digital Natives" programme aired on *RTP2* from 2010 to 2012.

At the same time, the Referential for Media Education, targeted at Pre-School and Primary and Secondary Schooling, is also under public discussion. The Refer-ential was produced by Manuel Pinto, Sara Pereira and Eduardo Jorge Madureira, and was commissioned by the General Directorate in Education (under MEC). This document states the Guidelines for Media Education and the competences to be acquired by students in the different stages of compulsory education. The Referential and the process of its validation also represent progress of media education and its official inclusion in the Portuguese schooling system.

Agents and voices

Associations play an important complementary role in the energetic drive for media education in the country. Besides APAN, since 2009 MEC has been asso-ciated with a copyright awareness-raising project for children and young people, promoted by the Association for Private Copy Management (Associação para a Gestão de Cópia Privada – AGECOP). The competitions Pequeno© and Grande© invite children and young people from several school levels to produce lyrics, photography, videos, poetry and prose, for instance, to awaken them to notions of copyright in accordance with the present law, and to work on concepts of media discourses, media and audiences, empowered by support materials.

In fact, motivation through competition has proven to be a popular and flexible way to introduce projects by associations or companies to schools. Besides the school newspaper competition, promoted yearly by *Público na Escola*, the Consumer Defence Association (Associação Portuguesa para a Defesa do Consumidor – DECO) promotes SITESTAR, supported by the body in charge of the technology infra-structures, DNS.pt. Among this competition's goals, we can highlight "promoting digital media literacy among young people of school age"[4]. The challenge "Learn how to navigate before they catch you" ("Aprende a navegar antes que te apanhem"), also active in early 2014, is part of the project "Communicate Safely" ("Comunicar em Segurança"), by the telecommunication company Portugal Telecom. This initiative is intended to prompt the educative community to use the Internet and communication technologies safely, in line with the approach Portugal Telecom has taken since 2005.

If the agenda of these projects is targeted mostly at content creation and media production awareness, but in a sporadic way through the format of competitions, work around media envisaging inclusion and participation has been seen in community associations' projects, with governmental support, for children and young people at risk of exclusion, as in the case of the Escolhas [Choices] Programme. Some of the projects that can be highlighted by their longevity and the quality they have attained are *Claquete* e *Rádio XL*, television and radio projects, respectively, from the area of Greater Lisbon. *Olhares* and *RadioActive*, with an academic origin (which are also focused on in other chapters of this book), were mostly conducted in partnership with community centres supported by Escolhas, which reflects how ideas from the academic world and civil society can be articulated with support from the State.

In fact, even without a formal connection between research and intervention, the academic world has played a very relevant role in putting the topic of media education on the educational and political agenda. Examples of this at the international level are Mediappro (2005-06, Universidade do Algarve[5]), *Study on the current trends and approaches to media literacy in Europe* (2006-07, Universidade do Minho[6]) and EU Kids Online (2006-14, Universidade Nova de Lisboa[7]); and at the national level Media Education in the Castelo Branco Region (2007-10, Universidade de Lisboa), which we have mentioned, Escolinhas Criativas (2010, Universidade do Porto and Universidade do Minho[8]) and Navegando com o *Magalhães* (2010-12, Universidade do Minho[9]).

However, training in media education is still lacking. It is at post-graduate level (Masters and PhD) that we can find some teaching offered in the new literacies, in seminars such as "Media Education", "Media Pedagogy and Literacy", "Education and Media" or "Digital Transliteracy". The universities and polytechnic institutes in the areas of Education Sciences and Communication Sciences are those that offer the most courses (Costa, Jorge & Pereira, 2014).

After the establishment in 2009 of the Informal Group of Media Literacy (Grupo Informal de Literacia Mediática – GILM)[10], which brings together stakeholders from several sectors associated with the topic (Ponte & Jorge, 2010), such as governmental bodies in education and communication, academia and the media, two national conferences were organized. At the two events, in Braga (2011) and Lisbon (2013), there was broad participation by researchers, teachers, media professionals and librarians, as well as media education project managers and political agents. Besides this, academia is also involved in conducting initiatives in the field. In 2012 GILM promoted 'One Day with the Media' and, in 2013, 'Seven Days with the Media', during the week when UNESCO celebrates Press Freedom Day. This event intends to reflect and encourage diversity and cooperation on the ground, and celebrate the efforts of the social agents, including academia, involved in media education.

Final remarks

The range of activities in media education in Portugal has, thus, been growing and becoming more diverse, thanks to the efforts of several agents, demonstrating the freedom and creativity to design and implement projects with different methodologies and targets. These projects contain dimensions of analysis and empowerment for the use of media, media production and participation – for several media, although the digital media have prevailed in recent years – and several media discourses are looked at. This diversity is celebrated during 'Seven Days with the Media' in May each year.

However, the multiplication of projects in the country in the past two decades is the result of a certain lack of coordination, in the face of a non-existent clear public policy on the topic. The civil and private initiatives concealed this absence, but did not ensure sustainable projects and did not guarantee evaluation, accountability or the sharing of methodologies and results. The Media Education Observatory, created after the 1st Congress of Literacy, Media and Citizenship, is also falling short of its promise to document the initiative on the ground.

Notes

1. This chapter is based on research conducted for the project Media and Information Education Policies in Europe, ANR-Translit/COST, coordinated by the Sorbonne Nouvelle University, Paris, in which Portugal takes part together with 27 other European countries (*vide* Costa, Jorge & Pereira, forthcoming).
2. "Publicidade dirigida a crianças atinge taxa de cumprimento de quase 100%", http://www.briefing.pt/publicidade/21167-publicidade-dirigida-a-criancas-atinge-taxa-de-cumprimento-de-quase-100.html
3. http://ensina.rtp.pt
4. At www.sitestar.pt

5. Mediappro, 2006.
6. Pérez Tornero, 2007.
7. Livingstone, Haddon, Görzig & Ólafsson, 2011.
8. Cf. http://info.escolinhas.pt/escolinhas-criativas
9. Cf. http://www.lasics.uminho.pt/navmag
10. Cf. http://www.literaciamediatica.pt

References

Costa, C., Jorge, A., & Pereira, L. (2014). *Media and Information Literacy Policies in Portugal (2013)*. Paris: ANR-Translit/COST. Retrieved June 12, 2014, from http://ppemi.ens-cachan.fr/data/media/colloque140528/rapports/PORTUGAL_2014.pdf

Livingstone, S. Haddon, L., Görzig, A., & Ólafsson, K. (2011). *Risks and safety on the internet: the perspective of European children: full findings and policy implications from the EU Kids Online survey of 9-16 year olds and their parents in 25 countries.* London: *EU Kids Online.* www.eukidsonline.net

Mediappro (2006). *A European Research Project: The Appropriation of New Media by Youth.* Bruxelas, Chaptal Communication with the Support of the European Commission/Safer Internet Action Plan.

Pinto, M., Pereira, S., Pereira, L., & Ferreira, T. D. (2011). *Educação para os Media em Portugal: experiências, actores e contextos.* Lisboa: Entidade Reguladora para a Comunicação Social.

Ponte, C., & Jorge, A. (2010). Media Education in Portugal: a building site, *Journal of Media Literacy*, *57*, 1 (2), 56-61.

Pérez Tornero, J. M. P. (Org.) (2007). *Study on the Current Trends and Approaches to Media Literacy in Europe*, European Commission. http://ec.europa.eu/culture/media/media-content/media-literacy/studies/study.pdf

Production of School Newspapers in Portuguese Schools

When the Printed Newspaper is More Desired than the Digital

Vitor Tomé

In the networked society it is crucial to recognize the power and importance of participating and exercising citizenship through the media (Jenkins, 2006). But, to exercise this power it requires active participation with the media (Potter, 2005) and empowerment that must begin in childhood (Gonnet, 1999) and continue throughout life (Rivoltella, 2007), through structured and effective preparation (European Commission, 2009; UNESCO, 2013, 2007).

In the absence of consensus regarding the instruction and preparation of media literacy education (Tomé, 2008), we follow the curriculum designed by UNESCO: Media and Information Literacy (MIL), defined as the ability to access the media, to understand, analyze and critically evaluate the information provided by them, producing information in a reflective and creative way, and disseminating it through the different media (traditional and digital).

A curriculum that prepares students to critically engage in media should take place both formally and informally in schools. However, thus far traditional schooling has been unsuccessful in this task in many countries throughout Europe, including Portugal (Pinto et al., 2011). The difficulties causing the sluggish development of MIL at school are as follows:

I. Lack of research in real schools, with collaboration among researchers, teachers, the media sector entities and policy-makers (Rivoltella, 2007, UNESCO, 2007);

II. Lack of educational resources relevant for each reality, validated by experts, teachers and students (Tomé, 2008);

III. Weak or nonexistent initial and further teacher education (Tyner, 2010);

IV. Curriculum development (Frau-Meigs & Torrent, 2009).

The project "Media Education in Castelo Branco Region – Portugal" (2007-2011), funded by the Foundation for Science and Technology (National Research Centre) and the newspaper *Reconquista*[1], sought to overcome these difficulties, contributing to the development of MIL in Portugal and possible replication in other countries. To answer each of these difficulties, we proceeded as follows:

I. We involved 24 groupings/public schools, about 100 teachers and almost 500 students (10-18 years). We gathered in the team of researchers from five institutions linked to Portuguese higher education and three foreigners, a newspaper company, a software company, the local government, a development association and a teachers' training institute[2];

II. We designed, produced and validated (along with experts, teachers and students) the DVD "Let's make school newspapers", which explains and illustrates all stages of production (team organization, journalistic genres, writing techniques, pagination...) of a school newspaper (in paper and online), with practical exercises and other resources (free download from www.literaciamedia.pt). We created a production platform for online school newspapers and a manual to support the project;

III. We organized, certified and administered (free of charge) an action of further training "Media Education and the School Newspaper to the Promotion of Reading and Writing", aimed at teachers of all levels of education;

IV. We defined as a goal the importance of integrating MIL into the various curriculum subjects, but with no need for teachers to change their prepared lesson plans. They were to achieve them by associating the development of skills of critical analysis and reflective production, through the use of media and its content.

Project: justification, aims and concretization

The school newspaper is one the most common collective media in the school environment (Barata, 2012; Público, 2005). Easy and inexpensive, it is "an important resource to develop critical thinking, styles and habits of thought and creativity, respect for diversity of opinion and interest in current issues" (Pinto, 1991, p.7). It can be used in the classroom as "a valuable pedagogical and didactic aid, to the various disciplinary areas" (Pinto, *idem*), and provides a bridge between school space and social space, which can otherwise form an obstacle to learning about citizenship (Remy, 2003). It can develop an interest in research and encourage the comparison of ideas. "Education for citizenship passes (passed) for press freedom. And passes (will pass) for connecting the school to the newspapers, and the newspapers to school" (Abrantes, 1992, p. 66).

The project had the following objectives: i) provide students and teachers with a better understanding of the different stages of the production of newspapers in print and online; ii) contribute to promoting the reading of newspapers; iii) help students gradually become critical decoders of, and reflexive producers of, media messages; iv) help increase students' motivation to use new media (CD-ROM, Internet); v) contribute to improving (graphics and content) existing school newspapers; and vi) connect schools and their community.

The implementation of this project involved the following stages:

I. Data collection at schools in the region (interview with the newspaper coordinators, library or school board) and an invitation to join the project;

II. Production and validation of the DVD: accomplished with five experts (media and journalism), four teachers and 104 students (Tomé, 2008);

III. Creation of the platform for newspaper production online and a manual to support the project;

IV. Application of a questionnaire on the relationship of young people with media/school newspapers (463 students at 24 schools);

V. Presentation of the DVD to teachers and students at each school;

VI. Work in schools (supported in loco by the research team), copies of the DVD provided to schools, accessible to teachers and students, used more by those working on the school newspaper, either in classes and/or in the journalism club, where the content of the school newspaper was produced by students and teachers;

VII. Intermediate evaluation: meeting of staff and 40 teachers of the network; presentation of results; defining future action. A discussion group (Google) was created and an internal competition launched for school newspapers, with the following criteria: number of newspaper articles signed by students; diversity of journalistic genders by edition; diversification of sources; diversity of topics;

VIII. Certified training for teachers: 192 teachers signed up, 150 started (maximum possible) and 128 completed;

IX. Data collection (questionnaire to students and interviews with teachers) and analysis of issues of newspapers published by schools;

X. Final evaluation (international conference).

Results

At the end of the project, all participating schools were regularly producing a printed school newspaper, but only five did so online, and sporadically.

Teams from schools produced 105 editions of newspapers, which we analyzed afterwards. The results show that students can gradually produce more articles for the school newspaper (from September 2009 to October 2010, the number of articles produced and signed by students increased by 74%, from 951 to 1,658). They use different journalistic genres (news dominated, followed by chronicle, opinion piece and only after the interview), a growing number of information sources (people first, followed by Internet, books and TV/movies) and a greater diversity of issues, especially when they had the opportunity to choose or negotiate the topics covered, instead of using those imposed by teachers (school themes dominated: study visits followed by Environment, Science/Technology/Health and Sports; Violence, Music or Medium).

The newspaper production teams were collecting staff and students, spending more time (weekly) on the endeavor, and using better spaces than at the beginning (e.g., moving from the common room to the ICT room).

According to the teachers, the DVD was important in the production of different journalistic genres, and contributed to increasing students' motivation and autonomy and to developing their ability to understand and produce media messages. It was also used to teach the unity of journalistic text (from the Portuguese curriculum). The platform and manual were used less, but were regarded as useful when used.

In terms of the project implementation, the difficulty most often mentioned by the teachers was lack of time. Therefore, teachers' selfless dedication, the free printing of school newspapers (which increased printings, improved frequency and contributed to the ability to offer them for free) and the continued support of the research team (offered and requested) were crucial.

Teachers stated that the project helped students develop a capacity for critical analysis and reflective production of media content, but also the ability to relate the content of the media to school subjects. The production process was organized, and the school newspaper as a product improved, contributing to a closer relationship between the school community and the educational community. Furthermore, the newspaper won second prize at a school newspaper contest held by *Público*, a Portuguese newspaper.

The teachers demonstrated how to integrate MIL into their lesson plans when they had in-service training. They worked in an interdisciplinary and practical way, which resulted in the production of media content by the students. However, it should be noted that training in ICT and digital literacy should be provided, because only 10% of the teachers proposed encouraging students to produce multimedia content and only 5% managed to do so (Tomé, 2011).

Teachers were eager to continue working in the area of media education, be it through the school newspaper or some other channel. They proposed extending the online newspaper project to all levels of education, integrating teachers of digital literacy into the team, creating a "space in schools, with proper equipment and enough time", and integrating media literacy into some curricula, with content that will engage teachers and students to collaborate with the school newspaper programs. The developers of the project (companies, schools and political stakeholders) reaffirmed their willingness to continue participating.

As for the students, their media habits changed. The 463 participants (234 girls and 229 boys) used the Internet, but preferred that the school newspaper be printed (85%, while only 15% preferred online publication), citing reasons of portability ("easier to read", "more serious and rigorous"), culture ("habit of reading on paper", "I'm the most proud to be published on paper"), ecology ("doesn't use energy", "it's recyclable") and physiology ("reading on-screen is more tiring"; "I like the smell of the newspaper"). And they produced media messages to be published. Today, on social media, young people are more reproducers than producers, as they prefer the share to the publication (Tomé, 2014). But not when it came to the printed school newspaper! What they publish allows them to show others and say, "Look, this is me."

Conclusion

The project objectives were fully achieved, as students and teachers participated more and improved the production of the school newspapers. Students improved their performance in terms of critical decoding and the reflective production of media messages, as they used the Internet more as a source of information as well as the DVD. The school newspapers improved in terms of graphics and content, while helping to bring the school and educational communities closer together. Finally, developing practical MIL activities, integrated into the curriculum, focusing on producing and analyzing media messages provided a growing level of media literacy for the citizens involved.

Notes

1. *Reconquista* took part in the project, offering: free printing of school newspapers during the period of the project (estimated commercial value 89,000 Euro); regular publication of news stories about the project before, during and after their term; and publication of two special supplements (16 pages each) with selected news stories written by the students. However, schools and students were free to use different newspapers and educational resources. The use of *Reconquista* in school activities was not compulsory.
2. The institutions involved were: University of Lisbon, New University of Lisbon, University of Algarve, University of Beira Interior, Polytechnic Institute of Castelo Branco (Portugal), CLEMI – Centre de Liason de l'Enseignement et des Médias d'Information (Paris, France), Catholic

University of Milan, University of Huelva (Spain). Other partners were: the newspaper *Reconquista*, the software company Netsigma, Governo Civil de Castelo Branco (regional government), Câmara Municipal de Castelo Branco (local government), Associação de Desenvolvimento da Raia Centro Sul (Adraces) and Centro de Formação Leonardo Coimbra (National Association of Teachers).

References

Abrantes, J. (1992). *Os Media e a Escola: da imprensa aos audiovisuais no ensino e na formação*. Lisboa: Texto Editora.

Barata, L. (2012). *Educação para os Media: As notícias das escolas do Ensino Básico na Imprensa Regional*. Tese de Mestrado. Faculdade de Artes e Letras da Universidade da Beira Interior, Portugal. http://www.bocc.ubi.pt/pag/m-jornalismo-2012-lidia-barata.pdf

Comissão das Comunidades Europeias (2009). *Commission Recommendation on media literacy in the digital environment for a more competitive audiovisual and content industry and an inclusive knowledge society*. http://eur-lex.europa.eu/LexUriServ/LexUriServ.do?uri=O-J:L:2009:227:0009:0012:EN:PDF

Frau-Meigs, D., & Torrent, J. (2009). Media Education Policy: Towards A Global Rationale. In D. Frau-Meigs & J. Torrent (Eds.), *Mapping Media Education Policies in the World – Visions, Programmes and Challenges* (pp. 15-25). New York: UN – Alliance of Civilizations.

Gonnet, J. (1999). *Éducation et médias*. Paris: PUF.

Jenkins, H. (2006). *Convergence Culture: where old and new media collide*. New York and London: New York University Press.

Pinto, M., Pereira, S., Pereira, L., & Ferreira, T. (2011). *Educação para os Média em Portugal: Experiências, actores e contextos*. Lisboa: Entidade Reguladora para a Comunicação Social.

Pinto, M. (1991). *A Imprensa na Escola: guia do professor*. Lisboa: Público, Comunicação Social SA.

Potter, J. (2005). *Media Literacy* (3rd edition). London: Sage Publications.

Público. (2005). *Livro de Estilo*. Lisboa: Público – Comunicação Social SA.

Remy, M. (2003). Le rôle des technologies de l´information et de la communication dans l´espace éducatif européen. Des médias-miracles? In J. M. Ferry & S. De Proost (Orgs.), *L´Ecole au défi de l´Europe – Médias, éducation et citoyenneté postnationale* (pp. 139-166). Bruxelles: Editions de l´Université de Bruxelles.

Rivoltella, P. (2007). Realidad y desafíos de la educación en medios en Italia. *Comunicar, 28*, 17-24.

Tomé, V. (2014). Usos e relações nas redes sociais: um estudo com jovens, seus pais e professores. Artigo aceite no II Congresso Mundial de Comunicação Ibero-Americana, 13 a 16 de Abril, Universidade do Minho, Portugal.

Tomé, V. (2011). Educação para os Média: é urgente formar professores. In S. Pereira (Org.), *Congresso Nacional "Literacia, Media e Cidadania"* (pp. 59-70). Braga, Universidade do Minho: Centro de Estudos de Comunicação e Sociedade
www.lasics.uminho.pt/ojs/index.php/lmc/article/download/527/496

Tomé, V. (2008). *CD-Rom "Vamos fazer jornais escolares": um contributo para o desenvolvimento da Educação para os Média em Portugal*. PhD Thesis not publiched, Faculdade de Psicologia e de Ciências da Educação da Universidade de Lisboa, Portugal.

Tyner, K. (2010). *Media Literacy: New Agendas in Communication*. New York: Routledge.

UNESCO (2013). Alfabetização midiática e informacional: currículo para formação de professores. Brasília: UNESCO, UFTM.

UNESCO (2007). Agenda de Paris ou 12 recommandations pour l'Éducation aux Médias. http://www.diplomatie.gouv.fr/fr/IMG/pdf/AgendaParisFinal_fr.pdf

RadioActive

A European Online Radio Project

Maria José Brites, Ana Jorge & Sílvio Correia Santos

Context: RadioActive Europe

The main aim of the RadioActive Europe[1] project is to use the production of on-line radio to empower young people and adults at risk of social exclusion, with regard to education and employment. Funded by the European Commission's Lifelong Learning Programme, RadioActive uses radio as an informal educational tool for groups of different ages, though mostly young people, through partners in the United Kingdom, Germany, Malta, Romania and Portugal. This chapter describes the Portuguese experience of this project, which has been running since March 2013 at three youth centres (two in Porto and one in Coimbra[2]) set up under the government project *Escolhas* ("Choices") to support youth communities throughout the country.

The project is organized in accordance with European guidelines on informal education, lifelong learning and action research with a social dimension[3]. However, it also has strong affinities with the development agenda in Latin America, where there is a long tradition of community intervention projects and where the history of radio is connected to that of education and the struggle for citizenship rights. The philosophy underpinning RadioActive is particularly inspired by the participative methods promoted in the 1960s and 70s by the Brazilian educator Paulo Freire. Following Freire (1977), this European project understands the need to consider the research reality from the inside out, respecting its idiosyncrasies. Consequently, the idea of active community participation underpinned the initial platform (Ravenscroft, Attwell, Stieglitz & Blagbrough, 2011) and the innovative research proposal: to promote and develop personal and social rapprochement to stimulate informal learning through online radio and the social media. One of the most important differences between formal and informal learning is precisely the increased opportunities that the latter offers for negotiation, which increases the chances of the task being appropriated by whoever carries it out (Underwood, Parker & Stone, 2013, p. 485).

Unlike many other radio projects that are designed to be close to citizens and that have emerged from their communities, RadioActive was developed in academia; though it too aims at being an idiosyncratic community process. This is one of the innovations of this research: it aims to empower the community by supplying tools, spaces and environments that enable these people to reflect upon and identify common problems and participate in their solutions, and also to develop a critical and artistic voice. The skills acquired are valuable when transposed to the various multidimensional needs of daily life; indeed, this empowerment aims to improve the community's quality of life (Perkins & Zimmerman, 1995, p. 571), with regard not only to problem-solving, but also to having the self-confidence to pursue dreams and desires. There is also an individual dimension to collective empowerment in that users, by manipulating digital tools, acquire skills and critical abilities that are useful for learning and development (Erstad, 2013, p. 79-80). In contemporary society, citizen empowerment is dependent upon media literacy (Jacquinot-Delaunay, Carlsson, Taye & Tornero, 2008, p. 28). Thus, RadioActive offers a means for informal, reflexive and creative communication.

This empowerment principle is aligned with the European Parliament and Council Recommendation (2006) concerning the eight essential skills for lifelong learning: communication in one's mother tongue; communication in foreign languages; digital skills; learning to learn; social and civic competences; sense of initiative and entrepreneurship; cultural awareness and expression, and mathematical competence and basic competences in science and technology.

Problematization: tools to act

Another of the main innovations of this project is problematization, along the lines stipulated by Paulo Freire. Practice is the starting point for an understanding of the reality in question, and is absolutely necessary; however, it is not enough in itself and therefore needs to be complemented by theoretical tools for interpretation (Freire, 1977, p. 26). The intervention strategy was defined collaboratively in the field (and not only through a literature review), taking into account the willingness, needs and characteristics of each community. Thus, it began with a systematization of the community's characteristics and profiles, in which the members themselves participated together with the researchers. The problematization phase, implemented in the first months of the project, involved direct participative observation of focus groups and informal conversations at different centres, as well as interaction during the technical and content workshops.

In one of the communities, we identified two levels of key participants/actors: a) coordinators in areas such as Information and Communication Technologies (ICT), or Education and Communication Sciences, who work directly with the communities; and b) children and young people at the centre, who have needs on the level of essential skills for lifelong learning. At the other two centres, there was also another intermediate group consisting of young adults who showed interest in being direct interlocutors, and indeed had the skills to do so, in some cases because they had prior experience of online radio at school. Unlike the previous group of children and young people, this group of young adults clearly had digital skills (which improved even more over the course of the project) and a spirit of initiative and entrepreneurship. Thus, they took over running the radio production, coordinating programmes, organizing formal and informal meetings with the children and young people in the community, and encouraging them to participate in the production.

Thus, this initial knowledge about the communities involved proved essential to RadioActive's success in the terrain. Its ability to adapt to differences, rather than imposing fixed models of intervention, allowed it to overcome unexpected problems more effectively. The two Porto centres illustrate the importance of problematization. At one of them, the group rapprochement is made through its young leaders and community facilitators with strong recourse to technology, as for them, the programme's technical quality is essential. At the other centre, the young people use conventional tools such as pen and paper, and distribute the radio tasks on posters stuck to walls: it is only after this that the possibility arises to use the computer, participating in the technical part and in making music, where the lyrics are paramount. One of the youngsters most committed to this task explains that the radio project got her interested in writing, as it led her to play with the Portuguese language in an attempt to write song lyrics – despite the fact that she did not appreciate Portuguese much as a subject at school.

> Now I try to do more [lyrics], this programme existed... before I didn't write anything at all. I didn't like it. But now this radio [project] exists and now that I know that I can do the music programme, I'm more inspired and I've begun to write more. (Inês, 15 years, interview, 2014)

Implementation: assessment and challenges

Given the levels of disaffection that some of these young people feel in relation to school and formal education, RadioActive operates mostly in an informal atmosphere. In these contexts, young people are commonly truant from school, are reluctant to explore digital tools and have little confidence in speaking in public. It is thus particularly important that they get the chance to use technology and online environments, do voice work, write texts, develop communication

179

skills and take responsibility for the execution of tasks. However, this does not preclude an important relationship between RadioActive and the school. All the groups participating in the project explore the possibility of using the online radio in the school. In Coimbra, one of the youngsters who had never produced radio before was invited to develop a radio project for children under 10. The second programme produced by *Metas*, in Porto, was broadcast, upon the suggestion of the young people involved, at the secondary school where they had previously had experience of online radio. For the third, the young people chose to debate the subject "Young people and education", focusing upon both formal and informal aspects. According to Jonas, community leader and one of the participants in the radio production, *"the value of informal education is that it gets them to experiment and do it themselves – they're not just listening but also trying it out"* (Jonas, 21 years, interview, 2014). Renato, 23 years, a monitor at the Digital Inclusion Centre (CID) and participant, also points out: *"They learn a lot with the radio* [project] *– how to do an interview, how to be objective. We learn that in school in the 7th grade in Portuguese in the part about communication."* With the radio project, they learn how to ask a question in a more objective way or to structure what they say: *"In the last programme, I asked a question and he didn't answer the way I wanted him to. Now I'm going to have to be more objective in my questions to get a better answer"* (Renato, 23 years, interview, 2014).

The school connection has also been activated by the technicians. For example, Joana, CID monitor at *Catapulta*, holds a series of workshops about RadioActive and the use of the audio recording and editing programme Audacity at a third-cycle school (7th to 9th grades) in the context of ICT lessons. She recognizes that learning takes place on a step-by-step basis: *"Even after I've explained* [that it is necessary to get copyright] *some of the children are still surprised, because they can't just go to YouTube and download music. I give them some alternatives, explain that they're free, the copyrights, then there are more technical aspects, such as how to download, how to record, how to organize my sound library"* (interview, 2014). This is also a way of ensuring the project's sustainability through learning by a cascade system.

Construction: promoting self-confidence and efficiency

Internet radio plays a very important role in helping these young people develop certain skills. The researchers on the ground have noted that levels of interest amongst the young participants tend to fluctuate due to lack of self-confidence; however, it returns when a particularly arduous or difficult task is accomplished and properly acknowledged. Thus, the lifelong learning skills prescribed by the European Parliament are shown to be profoundly related to self-confidence and self-efficacy, qualities that these young people acquire in the project. When Joana was questioned about the benefits that the radio project brought to *Catapulta*, she replied: *"For some, it functions very much on the level of self-esteem, the value they attribute to themselves and to their work. To realise that it might be appreciated, even if these are skills that aren't valued at school, like writing music, for example. Or singing. School doesn't usually give good grades for that, but here it's important, it's of value and it's good. They also commit themselves to a long-term project and for the question of writing that's very important indeed. It's not just about writing well, without mistakes, it's about expressing an idea"* (Joana, interview, 2014). Inês, who participated in *Catapulta*, claimed: *"I learned new things, I learned how to work with Audacity, I didn't know how. I learned many things that I didn't even know existed. Things that... well... I think working on the radio is something to be proud of* [smile]*!"* (Inês, 15 years, interview, 2014).

The connection between skills, efficacy and confidence is essential to encourage young people to participate and engage (Haste, 2004). An active model of education for citizenship presupposes agency, the search for knowledge, narrative and interpretation, and proactive engagement. This perspective on the role of efficacy in skills development is also decisive when we think of the way a project develops and the challenges that arise before it is concluded.

Sustainability: surviving to the end of the formal project

In many media education projects, there is a recurrent problem that affects the research and intervention on the ground: the fact that these projects only exist and yield results when there is funding. With this in mind, RadioActive has proposed the ambitious objective of creating structures in each of the participant countries that will enable the philosophy of the project to continue beyond its official end in December 2014. This continuity results from continued investment in a dialogic pedagogy which, from the outset, involves the participants in processes of reflection and analysis and in the conception and execution of activities. In Portugal, this is particularly important in the light of the economic situation, with rising unemployment and a general lack of investment, particularly when no financial returns are expected.

Notes
1. RadioActive Europe: promoting engagement, informal learning and employability of at-risk and excluded people across Europe through Internet radio and social media (531245-LLP-1-2012-1-UK-KA3-KA3MP).
2. *Metas* and *Catapulta* in Porto and *Trampolim* in Coimbra.
3. European Parliament and Council Recommendation of 18th December 2006.

References

Erstad, O. (2013). The Agency of Content Creators: Implications for Personal Engagement and Media Industries. *The Public, Javnost, 20*(2), 67-82.

Freire, P. (1977). *Educação e consciencialização política.* Lisbon: Livraria Sá da Costa.

Haste, H. (2004). "Constructing the citizen". *Political Psychology, 25*(3), 413-439.

Jacquinot-Delaunay, G., Carlsson, U. Tayie, S., & Tornero, J. M. (2008). Empowerment through Media Education: an intercultural approach. In U. Carlsson, S. Tayie, G. Jacquinot-Delaunay & J. M. Tornero (Eds.), *Empowerment through media education: An intercultural dialogue* (pp.19-33). Göteborg University: The International Clearinghouse on Children, Youth and Media/Nordicom.

Perkins, D. D., & Zimmerman, M. A. (1995). Empowerment theory, research, and application. *American Journal of Community Psychology, 23*(5), 569-579.

Ravenscroft, A., Attwell, G., Stieglitz, D., & Blagbrough, D. (2011). "'Jam Hot!' Personalised radio ciphers through augmented social media for the transformational learning of disadvantaged young people. *Proceedings of the Personal Learning Environments (PLE).* Conference 2011, Southampton, UK, 11-13 July 2011. http://journal.webscience.org/557/

Recommendation 2006/962/EC of the European Parliament and of the Council of 18 December 2006 on key competences for lifelong learning [Official Journal L 394 of 30 December 2006].

Underwood, C., Parker, L., & Stone, L. (2013). Getting it together: relational habitus in the emergence of digital literacies, *Learning, Media and Technology, 38* (4), 478-494.

Olhares em Foco (Glances in Focus)

A Participatory Photography Project to Promote Social Development Among Young People in Brazil and Portugal

Daniel Meirinho

This article uses the importance of visual culture in contemporary society to investigate how images can be used as a tool for reflection and empowerment for young people from social exclusion backgrounds. The participatory research-action project *Olhares em Foco (Glances in Focus)* reflects on how photography-based visuality can produce individual and collective change based on the personal perspectives and experiences of youth groups (Marshall & Shepard, 2006).

We draw extensively on the theories proposed by Paulo Freire (1970), which underlie the perception that each individual produces culture and critical thinking to reflect on his/her daily problems. In the *Olhares em Foco* project, participatory photography was explored as a major element of identity representation and reflection among three groups of young people from social exclusion backgrounds in both Brazil and Portugal.

Methodologically, the present work is based on the use of participatory photography (Clover, 2006; Prins, 2010; Singhal, Harter, Chitnis & Sharma, 2007), and on an approach inspired by some elements of the *Youth Participatory Action Research* (YPAR) methodology (Schensul, Berg, Schensul & Sydlo, 2004; Cammarota, 2007). However, the research was structured around the concepts of the *Photovoice* method (Wang, 2006). Created in the 1990s by researchers Caroline Wang and Mary Ann Burris (Wang & Burris, 1997), the "voice" in *Photovoice* stands for *Voicing Our Individual and Collective Experience*. The "voice" has been used during discussions, aiming to stimulate the participants "to reflect on their own living conditions, and also to share their own experiences" (Palibroda, Krieg, Murdock & Havelock, 2009, p.6).

The Olhares em Foco project

The fieldwork, performed between 2011 and 2013, involved 56 young people aged 12-20 years and living in three different social contexts. The project was planned as a series of social intervention workshops in which there was a relative age and gender equality among participants. Within each context there were 15 three-hour meetings for each group, and the learning experience was divided into three parts: the first contained recreational exercises, dialogues with the participants about the images to be produced and their experiences; the second focused on the production and discussion of the images taken by the participants; and in the third phase, there was a final exhibition of the photographs in all three social contexts – family, members of the community, youth groups, community leaders and political and social stakeholders were all invited.

The action-research project was implemented in three different locations, with the aim of widening the scope of the social analysis. In Brazil two social contexts were selected: in the state of Minas Gerais, the rural *quilombola* community known as *Pega* located at the Jequitinhonha Valley; and the urban environment of *Vila Santana do Cafezal*, with 65,000 inhabitants, located at the Algomerado da Serra in the city of Belo Horizonte. In Portugal, research was carried out in a social rehousing neighbourhood known as *Quinta do Mocho*, composed mainly of descendants of African immigrants, located on the outskirts of Lisbon. The participants produced a total of 5,499 photographs.

Photo 1.   Landscape view of Vila Santana do Cafezal. Camilo, 12 years (Vila Santana do Cafezal)

© Projeto Olhares em foco

Photo 2.   Landscape view of Pega community. Márcia, 18 years (Pega Community)

© Projeto Olhares em foco

Participatory photography as a tool for social intervention

The results of the *Olhares em Foco* project showed us that one of the major benefits of participatory photography was its ability to provide a clear and stimulating depiction of the participants as well as a wide range of possibilities for analysis regarding how they observe their own relationships, contexts and how they are visually depicted. This enabled participants to reveal their concerns, anxieties, and worries as seen through their own eyes. As the project advanced, the photographs revealed an increasingly general view of what was important to each participant in this particular phase of their life:

> *With the photography we can expose what's happening in the community and maybe by doing so we will engage the government and raise awareness among the people within the community to improve everybody's quality of life* (Keila, 16 years, Pega Community)

> *Through photography I can show my own reality and the things that need to be changed. I can see that my community has many good things, things I wasn't aware of in my daily life; it was through the photographic camera that I was able to discover them* (Tânia, 13 years,Vila Santana do Cafezal)

The images and dialogues from the meetings with the participants showed the importance that peer groups, family and social environment hold for them. This finding supports the ideas advanced more than 20 years ago by the *Center for Documentary Studies* at the University of Duke, North Carolina, regarding *Literacy Through Photography*, where since the 1990s researchers such as Wendy Ewald (2001) have been developing a sound learning and methodological philosophy that encourages children and young people to explore their own realities by photographing their own lives. Using the media-education approach, it was possible to develop a critical consciousness based on a changing learning process strengthened by the diversity and real experiences of each participant.

The photos create numerous dialogue possibilities as well as opportunities to question issues such as social representations of boys and girls, gender issues, and stereotypes – topics dear to the field of media education (Wilson, 2011). In the photos taken by the female participants, it was noticeable that they tended to focus on gestures and body poses they viewed as essential features of femininity – they posed with their hands on their hips, slightly leaning the body, with pouty lips, kissing or even stretching their tongues as a sign of debauch. Sometimes, more often in the groups of participants from Vila Santana do Cafezal and Quinta do Mocho, teenage girls took sexualized photos of themselves and their friends with their back to the camera, but looking directly at the lens with a finger on their mouth, their body leaning forward, and their other hand on their knee. As it was summer in Brazil, the young girls were wearing short and sexualized clothes. Therefore, we decided to hold a session on the issues associated with posting these types of sexualized full-body pictures on their social network profiles. Many of them did not recognize the risks associated with their sensual photographic poses; their intention was to come closer to the adult

Photo 3. Photos of gestures and poses, Quinta do Mocho. Gustavo, 12 years (Quinta do Mocho)

© Projeto Olhares em foco

Photo 4. Photos of gestures and poses.
Andrea, 14 years (Vila Santana do Cafezal)

© Projeto Olhares em foco

feminine world and the aestheticization of women in the media as a symbolic and iconic object of sexuality.

At the beginning, the boys showed no interest in the project. Their attitude was summed up by Jean, a 13-year-old young man: "Photography is a girly thing". Many did not even attend the first workshops, and when they did show up they would fall asleep while seated on the chair, thus showing their lack of interest in this activity. They are used to engaging in activities involving physical skills such as football, basketball, and capoeira, rather than dialogic or reflective skills, and stated that at their houses the responsibility for taking pictures on special occasions such as birthdays, Christmas, family meetings, etc., fell upon the women, their mothers and sisters. The women were also in charge of organizing and classifying family albums, assuming the role of "guardians" of family memories, as described by Leite (2000).

The photographs of affection displays and friendship relationships were another important variable in peer relationships featured in the visual representations of the participants. The participants from Quinta do Mocho and Vila Santana do Cafezal more often represented physical affection, such as hugs, kisses, and faces closely touching each other. In both urban communities, the girls took twice as many images as the boys, a result that reveals the extent to which physical affection is an important aspect of friendship bonds and a determining feature among girls. In the majority of pictures depicting affection boys were shown side by side, and in some cases displayed seemingly violent affection gestures such as strong hugs and neck locks, as ways of showing their male strength. Whereas

Photo 5. Photo of her friends. Ingrid, 12 years (Quinta do Mocho)

© Projeto Olhares em foco

Photo 6.   Photo of his friends from the neighbourhood. Dorival, 11 years (Vila Santana do Cafezal)

© Projeto Olhares em foco

the girls' photos of affection displays were mostly with their female peers, the boys took more pictures of mixed groups and with girls.

A specific aim of this research was to identify *which problems, needs, and resources in the community were visually captured, and which solutions were presented towards possible change.*

Issues such as racial and ethnic prejudice, the stigma of living in peripheral neighbourhoods and social integration were not clearly depicted in the images, and were only perceived in the collective debates with the groups.

To illustrate how we used the analytical composition tools based on visual narratives and interviews with images (photoelicitation), we present as an example a picture taken by a participant from the rural community. This participant photographed a member of the community standing next to a large amount of rubbish. Although the member of the community was meant to be the central focus of the image, the debate centred on what was surrounding him, namely the large quantity of rubbish. At this point it was discussed whether this problem stemmed from the fact that there was no regular rubbish collection by the city council, or whether it was due to poor environmental awareness by community members regarding where they should dispose of their household rubbish. The problem identified was the rubbish issue; the need was for regular rubbish collection and the creation of a schedule detailing the weekdays on which one could either put out his/her household rubbish or burn it. This was then presented to the hosting organization, which was involved in local development, so that it could be addressed in future, more long-term actions. This also represented an opportunity to engage young people in the process of change within the community. Table 1 summarizes the topics discussed at the workshop from the participants' perspective.

Table 1.   Resources and problems identified by the participants when talking about the images they have produced

Pega Community

Resources and strengths	Problems and needs
• The residents of the quilombola community; • Community vegetable garden; • Contact with nature; • The spirit of community and support from neighbouring communities; • Acknowledgement of a regional identity as residents of Jequitinhonha Valley; • The Araçuaí River is the water treatment plant; • Cultural traditions associated with the quilombola community, its roots, gastronomy, values and elders; • Social welfare assistance provided by the government; • Agricultural schools at which young people can learn how to grow crops resistant to the semiarid climate.	• Rubbish and the lack of regular rubbish collection by the public authorities; • Long dry season and the lack of agricultural assistance; • Child prostitution on the national roads and petrol stations close to the community; • Early alcohol consumption; • Unreliability of school transport; • The roads that serve the community are in very poor condition; • Lack of spaces and activities aimed at young people; • The schools have very low quality and standards, and are far from the community; • Lack of opportunities and social mobility; • Isolation and lack of communication; • An entrenched patriarchal and male chauvinist system.

Table 1. Cont.

Vila Santana do Cafezal

Resources and strengths	Problems and needs
• The residents of the community and of the other seven villages located in the Aglomerado da Serra region; • The dynamics of local and informal commerce; • Services offered by the community, such as school, health centre, and several social projects; • Geographic localization and the views of the city; • The Favela Radio station and local identity; • Community events and parties; • Several multisports facilities; • Several goods and services offered within the community; therefore residents don't need to leave the community; • Transport service between the villages of the Aglomerado da Serra region.	• Closed health units without GPs; • Lack of sanitation; • The number of organizations and associations targeted at young people; • Low level of young people's engagement in organized social movements; • Drug trafficking; • Public safety and violence; • Lack of opportunities and future prospects; • Prejudice and stigma of being "favelados"; • The power of police vigilance and the force used by the police; • Police corruption associated with drug trafficking; • Domestic and gender violence; • Single-parent and restructured families; • Child exploitation (parents place their children near traffic lights to beg for money); • The presence of the State is not felt.

Quinta do Mocho Neighbourhood

Resources and strengths	Problems and needs
• The neighbourhood residents; • Strong local identity and pride of belonging to the Quinta do Mocho neighbourhood; this can be seen in graffiti and tattoos displaying the neighbourhood name; • Community vegetable garden, • Services provided to the neighbourhood by the Loures City Council; • The supermarket; • The school is outside the neighbourhood; therefore young people have to socializze with people from outside Quinta do Mocho; • The Esperança (Hope) project and its activities; • Local shops, etc. • Peacefulness and street social life; • Friends and family live in the neighbourhood; • The parties promoted by the Esperança project; • The community nursery.	• People are pessimistic; • Safety and violence; • The power of police vigilance and the force used by the police; • Police violence against young people; • Violent settings created by some young groups; • The high rate of unemployed young people; • Drug trafficking; • Poor integration of young people from the neighbourhood in the school, and they are subject to prejudice for being residents of a social housing neighbourhood; • Lack of activities aimed at young people; • Mobility issues associated with lack of public transport; • Selective waste collection; • Isolation; • Few common spaces for parties and community meetings; • Poor integration and low social interaction with people outside the community.

We observed that their engagement in the process of critical consciousness, and the fact that there was someone willing to listen to their concerns, was regarded as valuable by the participants; furthermore, because they had produced their own photos they felt sufficiently acknowledged to discuss a wide range of issues that were troubling them (Pink, 2006). Based on their experience of reflecting on these issues, some young people stated that they were considering the possibility of paying more attention to the problems afflicting their own communities. As they became more aware of their own community problems and resources, their knowledge about their own community increased; they ceased to ignore local needs, and were willing to support future processes of local intervention promoting change (Prins, 2010).

Conclusion

The project *Olhares em Foco* illustrates how participatory photography (Wang & Burris, 1997) can be an essential tool in promoting recreational and dialogical activities developed within the media-education framework.

This is in agreement with Street (2001), who argues that when literacy is engaged together with the Photovoice visual method it provides social practices which enable children and young people to construct meanings out of media education and to interpret content associated with the repertoire and personal experiences of daily life. The use of photographic images within a participatory model raises questions which force the participants, regardless of their social background, to take a position regarding visual representations of socially intrinsic stereotypes which are reinforced in the media by both media and advertising companies.

References

Cammarota, J., & Fine, M. (Eds.) (2007). *Revolutionizing education: Youth participatory action research*. New York: Routledge.

Clover, D. E. (2006). Out of the Dark Room Participatory Photography as a Critical, Imaginative, and Public Aesthetic Practice of Transformative Education. *Journal of transformative education, 4*(3), 275-290.

Ewald, W. (2001). *I Wanna Take Me a Picture: Teaching Photography and Writing to Children*. Boston: Beacon Press.

Freire, P. (1970). *Pedagogia do oprimido*: Paz e Terra.

Leite, M. M (2000). *Retrato de Família* (2nd ed.). São Paulo: Editora da USP.

Marshall, A., & Shepard, B. (2006). Youth on the margins: Qualitative research with adolescent groups. In B. Leadbeater, E. B. B, C. Benoit, M. Jansson, A. Marshall & T. Riecken (Eds.), *Ethical issues in community-based research with children and youth*. Toronto: University of Toronto Press.

Palibroda, B., Krieg, B., Murdock, L., & Havelock, J. (2009). *A practical guide to photovoice: Sharing pictures, telling stories and changing communities*. Winnipeg: Prairie Women's Health Network.

Prins, E. (2010). Participatory photography: A tool for empowerment or surveillance? *Action Research, 8*(4), 426-443.

Pink, S. (2006). *The Future of Visual Anthropology: Engaging the Senses*. London and New York: Taylor & Francis

Schensul, J. J., Berg, M. J., Schensul, D,. & Sydlo, S. (2004). Core elements of participatory action research for educational empowerment and risk prevention with urban youth. *Practicing Anthropology, 26*(2), 5-9.

Singhal, A., Harter, L., Chitnis, K., & Sharma, D. (2007). Participatory photography as theory, method and praxis: analyzing an entertainment-education project in India. *Critical Arts: A South-North Journal of Cultural & Media Studies, 21*(1), 212-227.

Street, B. (2001). Contexts for literacy work: the 'new orders' and the 'new literacy studies. *Powerful literacies*, 13-22.

Wang, C. C. (2006). Youth Participation in Photovoice as a Strategy for Community Change. *Journal of Community Practice, 14*(1-2), 147-161.

Wang, C. C., & Burris, M. A. (1997). Photovoice: Concept, methodology, and use for participatory needs assessment. *Health Education and Behavior, 24,* 369-387.

Wilson, N., Dasho, S., Martin, A. C., Wallerstein, N., Wang, C. C., & Minkler, M. (2007). Engaging Young Adolescents in Social Action through Photovoice: The Youth Empowerment Strategies (YES!) Project. *Journal of Early Adolescence, 27*(2), 241-261.

Media Education and Intergenerational Communication

Inclusive Practice for Children and the Elderly[1]

Simone Petrella

New needs, new challenges, new responses

Within a context of economic crisis which reproduces new educational and relational needs, and in a society characterized by new technological innovations and communicative changes (Cardoso, 2009), media education faces unprecedented challenges and a need for new, more collaborative and inclusive practices.

The consequences of various phenomena affecting Portugal, such as the economic and financial crisis and the ageing of the population at an unprecedented speed (INE, 2011; EAPN, 2013), feed into 'the fourth world', characterized by the digital and social exclusion affecting mainly, and in various ways, the more vulnerable generations, children and the elderly (Castells, 2008; CE, 2011). All this in a society where new, not only technical but also cultural and social, competences are increasingly necessary for one to be 'included' (Castells, 2003), in order to be able to exert one's own citizenship in an autonomous and critical manner. In this scenario, media education based on critical, cultural and relational competences could and should represent an instrument and a way of including and empowering disadvantaged groups at risk of social exclusion (Gomes, 2003; Pérez Tornero, 2008). Building on these reflections, we have started an action research project, currently taking place in the city of Braga in northern Portugal, aimed at children and elderly people at the Cultural and Social Centre of Santo Adrião, whose objective is the promotion of communication between distant generations and mainly deprived communities, and the acquisition of media skills, at the same time analysing the exchange of knowledge arising from this meeting between generations and the direct influence on process of media literacy and social inclusion. Taking advantage of the flexibility and the amount of resources for media education, the project includes the creation and enlivening of informal spaces for playing and shar-ing[2], using the media as educational and relational resources (Rivoltella, 2003) and emphasizing the potentialities and the cultural and intellectual knowledge of all the participants.

Media education and intergenerationality: a precious alliance

The project, articulated with one of the nine workpackages composing the work plan of the European Media Literacy Education Study[3], the WP5: European Re-search on Inclusion of Disadvantaged Groups in Media Education, for which a team from the Communication and Society Research Centre of the Universidade do Minho (Minho University) is responsible, aims at responding to the lack of national programmes that join together media education, inclusion and intergen-erationality. Thus, our purpose is to promote the diffusion of good intergenera-tional practices potentially replicable in different contexts, mainly in contexts in which illiteracy, lack of motivation, illness or a risk of social exclusion apparently close people's door to the media and to intergenerational communication. This is the case at the Santo Adrião Cultural and Social Centre (CCSSA) which wel-comes our research, an institution of social solidarity that works with children at risk, youngsters and the elderly from various social economical contexts of the Braga district.

Jointly with the media education, a precious resource that supports our ac-tion is represented by the tradition of the Intergenerational Programmes, created in order to approach social problems related to economic, social and cultural needs and that develop social competences, problem-solving, critical thinking and an exchange of intergenerational knowledge (Newman & Sanchez, 2007), thus sharing some objectives and working tools with the media education. A more positive perception of elderly people's transmission of traditions and cul-ture, reduced isolation, the development of technical and social competences, increased self-esteem, and alternative activities for dealing with problems (drugs, violence and antisocial behaviour) are some of the benefits of the programmes based on intergenerational learning and communication, noted by researchers in this area (Kaplan & Pinazo, 2007). Our action research encompasses three groups of users of the CCSSA: two groups of youngsters and children (from the ATL and the CATL, the support organization for Children at Risk) and a group of elderly people (the retirement home day care centre). The assumptions that distinguish and support our work are the following:

- The reciprocity of the intergenerational exchanges in a collaborative and bidirectional learning process based on the blending of modern and tra-ditional knowledge (Dumazedier,1992);

194

- The conception of media literacy as a group of social and cultural competences stems from a training project of autonomous, critical and participative citizens.

InterGerAções Mediáticas (Media InterGenerAtions) into action

Considering the core of the project, we will briefly present some of the activities that have already taken place, highlighting the development and strengthening of the media skills, and the dimensions of critical analysis and of the responsible, autonomous and collaborative expression (Petrella, Pessôa, Silveira, Carvalho & Pinto, 2013).

• My grandmother is in the press[4]

For this activity, the young participants became journalists with the objective of interviewing a number of 'specialists', the elderly people, on issues such as, family, values and technological advances. The interviewees had the opportunity to share stories, the expertise and values they had consolidated throughout their life, with very interested journalists who were sometimes flabbergasted by the historical and cultural richness of the narrated facts. "Simone, the story of Dona Nair would make for a film!", was comment by one of the children. At the end of the interview, the young journalists had to write a brief journalistic text to summarize the enriching conversation, accompanied by a photo of the interviewer and interviewee. Our work aimed at bringing generations close together, stimulating curiosity and the capacity to listen and develop competences in journalistic writing amongst the young and promoting the sharing of stories and "forgotten" learning about the value of work and family as well as the media and its development in the lives of the elderly.

• Photo contest in Santo Adrião[5]

This activity consisted of organization of a photo contest in which participants were to portray in a photo "what the Centre represents for you". One contest was an exercise of reflection on the role of the CSSA in the life of its users, of their expression and verbalization through the photographic language and the power of the image.

After a brief *excursus* on the development of photographic devices and a brief talk about the use of such devices by the participants, various intergenerational pairs were formed. In order to stimulate reflection and the sharing of ideas in relation to the photos to be produced (subjects, framing, background, etc.), each pair was given a questionnaire about the Centre. Once this phase was finished, all pairs went out to take the chosen photos, using cameras and mobile phones. Once the photos were made the pairs answered a number of questions on the experience they had had together: "It was fun to teach the older people and to learn about their daily life at the Centre". This was one of the comments by the children involved in the project, while the most common comments among the elderly were: "I learned how to take photos with the mobile phone, something new indeed!", "I learned with the younger children – this reminds me of what happens when I'm with my grandchildren" and "I had a very good time!"

A vote was then taken for the best photo, and a public photographic exhibition was held at which the two generations presented their own productions, instantaneous moments of everyday life shared between the young and old friends.

• Storytelling… with advertising[6]

The main objective was to learn how advertising moulds stereotypes and social representations and through what language it communicates with us, stimulating creativity in an activity that led the two generations to co-operate in the creation of unique narratives. Small intergenerational groups were challenged to create a visual narration that would talk about everyday life within and outside the Centre, representing favourite activities (regarding the elderly) as well as activities they had done before they retired. The participants used newspapers and magazines to search for advertisements that could be part of the narration itself. The search was arduous, and the participants had the opportunity to reflect upon the ways advertising interprets and reproduces our needs and wishes, and how it represents social reality.

• Christmas at Santo Adrião

The last activity in 2013 consisted of making a Christmas film. The idea was to make a video to wish the users of and the workers at the Centre and their families a happy festive season, with the objective of reflecting upon the role of the CCSSA in the city of Braga and upon the specificity of the various activities involved in the action, to stimulate collaborative work between generations, and to develop competences in the creation of multimedia content.

After having formed small intergenerational work groups, we tried to give life to different film scenes in which each child and elderly person could wish everyone, in their own way, a happy Christmas. The way to do this was left to the creativity and criteria of the groups: the choice of wording, the kind of film, the setting, background music, etc. After a brief editing of the videos, we produced a trailer of a short movie[7] that was shown at Christmas time.

• Discovering the PC

For this activity, we invited four intergenerational pairs to share their personal likes and dislikes and their preferences regarding media consumption: radio, television, searching for information, reading, the computer, etc. This offered an opportunity to better get to know the participants, their consumption habits and the media skills they possessed. This was possible due to the second phase of the activity, in which the children played an important role in the process of digital inclusion of the elderly users, showing the potentialities of the computer (regarding the possibility to aggregate various types of media, enabling a convergent media consumption and the use of software for long-distance communication). Interested, and at the same time enjoying themselves, the elderly recognized the importance and value of the activity which represented the culmination of a gradual path that had begun in May 2013.

Conclusion

The freedom and informality we could perceive in the room during the activities, led to unpredictable results, such as the initiative of some children to stay beyond the established timetable to explain to the elderly the functioning and potentialities of platforms, such as *Facebook* and *Google Earth*, or merely to show school photos or photos of their favourite activities. The elderly responded to the different situations by overcoming their own limits, feeling completely "at ease", which would have been difficult to achieve without the intergenerational help. "This is funny, who would believe I would be sitting in front of this screen trying to understand how it works, I only completed primary school", said Dona Emilia in wonder enjoying herself due to the direct interaction (mediated by the children) with the computer while searching *Google* for the name of her nephew, a football player.

With the project we have just presented, we aim to stimulate symbolic and dynamic exchanges of collaborative learning, promoting the benefits of intergenerational communication and the acquisition and consolidation of media skills.

At the same time, we aim to develop educational and inclusive intergenerational practices centred in the media, not yet used in the national panorama. Due to its innovative nature and scope, this action research project, based on the participants' needs and potentialities, is not flawless. Difficulties and adjustments are constant, but the emphasis is continuously put on the benefits of the intergenerational relations and the use of the media as valuable educational and relational resources.

Notes

1. Project funded by the Foundation for Science and Technology (SFRH/BD/88503/2012)
2. One of the working tools is a blog, an open window to the activities undertaken: http://intergeracoesmediaticas.blogspot.pt/
3. http://www.emedus.org/
4. http://intergeracoesmediaticas.blogspot.pt/2013/11a-minha-avo-na-imprensa.html
5. http://intergeracoesmediaticas.blogspot.pt/2013/o8/concurso-fotográfico-intergeracional.html
6. http://intergeracoesmediaticas.blogspot.pt/2013/11/visual-storytellingcom-publicidade.html
7. The trailer: http://intergreacoesmediaticas. Blogspot.pt/2014/01/christmas-is-coming-movie.html; the film: http://www.youtube.com/watch?v=3wNAyO3bp_4

References

Cardoso, G. (2009). *Da comunicação de massa à comunicação em rede*. Porto: Porto Editora.

Castells, M. (2003). [1998]. *O fim do milénio*. Lisboa: FCK.

Castells, M. (2008). [1996]. *La nascita della società in rete*. Milano: UBE.

Comissão Europeia (2011). *Eurostat Education and Training Data*. http://epp.eurostat.ec.europa.eu/portal/page/portal/education/data/database

Dumazedier, J. (1992). Création et transmission des savoirs. *Gerontologie et société, 61*, 7-17.

EAPN (2013). Indicadores sobre a pobreza. Dados Europeus e Nacionais. http://www.eapn.pt/documentos_visualizar.php?ID=322

Gomes, M. C. (2003). Literexclusão na vida quotidiana. *Sociologia. Problemas e Práticas, 41*, 63-92.

INE (2012). *Censos 2011. Resultados provisórios*. http://censos.ine.pt/xportal/xmain?xpid=CENSOS&xpgid=censos2011_apresentacao

Jenkins, H., Purushotma, R., Weigel, M., Clinton, K., & Robinson, A. (2010). [2005]. *Culture Participative e Competenze Digitali*. Milano: Guerini.

Kaplan, M., & Pinazo, S. (2007). The benefits of intergenerational programmes. *Social studies collection, 23*, 64-91.

Newman, S., & Sanchez, M. (2007). Intergenerational programmes: concept, history and models. In M. Sanchez, D. Butts, A. Hatton-Yeo, N. A. Henkin, S. E. Jarrot ... A. P. C. Weintraub (Eds.), *Intergenerational programmes towards a society for all ages* (pp.34-63). http://www.intergenerational.clahs.vt.edu/papers/jarrott_weintraub_07_intergeneration_shared_sites.pdf

Pérez Tornero, J. M. (2008). Media Literacy. New Conceptualisation, New Approach. In U. Carlsson, G. Jauinot-Delaunay, & J. M. Pérez Tornero (Eds.), *Empowerment through media education: An intercultural dialogue* (pp. 103-116). Gothenburg University: International Clearinghouse on Children, Youth and Media/Nordicom.

Petrella, S. (2012). Repensar Competências e Habilidades para as Novas Gerações. Propostas para uma Nova Literacia Mediática. *Revista Comunicando, 1*(1), 205-222.

Petrella, S., Pessôa, C., Silveira, P., Carvalho, A., & Pinto, D. (2013). Entre a Escola e a Família: um Estudo em torno de Práticas de Educação para os Media em Portugal. *Revista Comunicando 2*, (2), 189-202.

SPAIN

Children, Youth and Media

You Have *New Connections*

Uses of Social Media among Children, Teenagers, and Young Adults in Spain

Ana I. Bernal Triviño & Josep Lobera Serrano

Youth and Technology

European societies tend to converge, so it is possible to observe a number of similar trends in them (Bendit, 2004). The characteristics of young European citizens also converge under more flexible labour trends, the erosion of social welfare systems and the rise of new technologies. However, some constraints remain among Spanish young adults, such as the highest rate of youth unemployment in Europe (57.7%) (Eurostat, 2014) and late emancipation. In recent years the economic crisis, which led to high unemployment rates and job insecurity, has affected young Spaniards significantly.

The impact of new information technologies on the habits of Spanish adults and teenagers has been remarkable in the last few years. Television and mobile phones have high penetration rates in Spanish homes. The preference for portable devices, such as mobile versus landline phones, or stationary computers versus laptops is also notable (Figure 1). The use of each device depends on age. The computer is the first technology to be used among children, followed by the Internet and mobile phones (Figure 2), which becomes one of the most valued devices. A survey shows that 53.7% of those aged 16 to 24 years considered mobile phones "very necessary" (Aranda, Sánchez-Navarro & Tabernero, 2009). In 2012, Internet access on mobile phones increased by 300% among youngsters. Other trends have also become established, such as the use of instant messaging services (56%) (Fundación Telefonica, 2013).

Home is the main point of access to the Internet, especially among children. For teenagers, the habit of going online from school is also increasing (Figure 3). The Internet represents a source of information and entertainment for young Spaniards: not only does it allow people to manage their contacts or send messages; they can also use social media to share content and interact with friends (Figure 4).

Despite the negative consequences reported on new technologies (social isolation, bedroom culture…), other investigations question these prejudices as they also promote personal autonomy, improve problem-solving skills, and strengthen social relationships with friends (Bringué & Sádaba, 2011). As an example that stereotypes are not always true, 92% of teenagers said they never met up with strangers contacted via the Internet (Sánchez Burón & Fernández Mártin, 2010). According to Del Rio, Sábada & Bringué (2010), attacks such as cyberbullying are minor phenomena. Both the digital world and social media can provide new opportunities for learning, participation, creativity, and communication (Livingstone & Haddon, 2009, p.15).

ICT and Spanish youth

Figure 1.   Household equipment regarding ICT products

Television	Mobil phone	Landline	Radio
99,4%	96,1%	78,0%	76,8%
Internet	**Laptop**	**Computer**	**Tablet**
69,8%	54,3%	45,1%	16,3%

Fuentes: INE, 2013.

Figure 2. Percentage of users by age and ICT   **Figure 3.** Internet and place of use

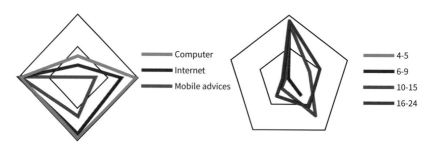

Source: 4-5 years (AIMC, 2009), 6-9 years (Bringué & Sádaba, 2009), 10-24 years (INE, 2013)

Figure 4. Main uses and Internet (by age)

	e-mail	Social network	Information access	Downloads
12-18	95,5 %	55,4 %	69,7 %	65,4 %
16-24	91,2 %	94,5 %	55,1 %	55,9 %
15-19	66,9 %	73,3 %	60,5 %	61,4 %

	Relate	Hang out	Share photos	Read news
12-18	50,8 %	75,7 %	35,7 %	
16-24	36,6 %			66,6 %
15-19	55,5 %	43,3 %	18,6 %	

Sources: 15-19 years (INJUVE, 2013), 12 -18 years (Aranda et al., 2009), 16-24 years (INE, 2013).

Impact of social media: practices and uses

Interacting through social media is one of the main activities teenagers and young adults use the Internet for (Figure 2). Some 57.9% of those aged 15 to 19 years visit one or more social media sites several times a day, spending an average of 1.28 hours a day on them (INJUVE, 2012). Tuenti, Facebook and Twitter are the most used social media in Spain (Figure 5), although their use varies by age. The Spanish social media Tuenti has the highest number of followers among adolescents. It also has a greater presence of commercial brands: 41% of users have had contact with companies tailored to their consumption profiles such as Coca-Cola, Nike, or McDonalds (The Cocktail Analysis, 2013). However, access to Tuenti has decreased in recent years (AIMC, 2013a). In the majority of social media, the presence of publicity grows on a par with that of news and entertainment (Lazo, Rodrigo & Martín, 2013). For this reason, the need for new media literacy is even more justified as it can help guarantee the respect of fundamental rights as well as develop critical awareness of the role of the media in society (UNESCO, 2013, p. 20).

Social media and youth

Young people mainly use social media to keep in touch with friends, share photos or videos and snoop around (Aranda et al., 2009) (Figure 6). Age and education are variables that make a difference in the quantitative use of social media (Espinar & González Río, 2009), although differences are also illustrated by gender:

205

Figure 5. Preferred social networks (by age)

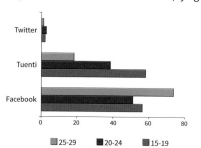

Figure 6. Main uses of social media (by age)

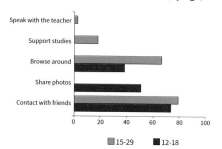

Fuentes: 15 a 29 años (INJUVE, 2013), 12 a 18 años (Aranda et al., 2009).

girls use them more to stay in touch with other people, whereas for boys the use is more individual (Colás Bravo, Ramírez & Pons, 2013). Social media have a private-public side: They allow users to share content with friends and, at the same time, establish new relationships (Frutos Torres & Vázquez Barrio, 2012).

Mass media, youth and politics

Both the Internet and the digitization of content favour a media convergence that has led to new behaviours in the use of mass media. Internet penetration has reached the heights of television among the youngest users (Figure 7). However, there is no exclusion but rather a merger through the promotion of social television. About four million Spaniards discuss television programmes in social media (Tuitele, 2013), especially series for teenagers (Deltell Escolar, Claes & López, 2013). Here, networks become an immediate tool for sharing reflections on programmes among friends and strangers. On the other hand, newspapers and radio stations have received a big push thanks to mobile phones and tablets (Figure 8) thanks to their ease of use, speed, and interactivity. Tablets are mostly used for entertainment applications, social media and information, whereas the use of social media and interpersonal communication is more predominant with mobile phones (Figure 9).

Since 2008, and with the onset of the economic crisis, there has been a decrease in the consumption of newspapers and magazines, whereas the consumption of online news and entertainment sites as well as radio stations has risen. As the crisis deepens, so does the attention of young people on politics (Figure 10). Television is the favourite medium for staying up to date, followed by the Internet, newspapers and radio stations (Figure 11). The Internet has become one "fundamental" source of political information for more than 80% of young adults (Figure 12). Although television is considered an "evasive" medium from which people casually hear the news, the Internet allows them to get more in-depth information on what they have already heard on TV (Bernal, 2009, p. 119).

Media, youth, and ICT

Figure 7. Media penetration, 16-24 years

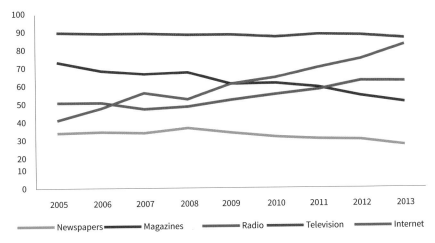

Source: AIMC (2013b).

Figure 8. Access by devices, 15-19 years

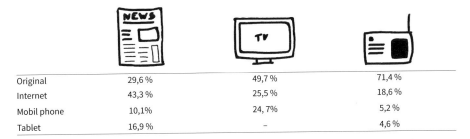

	NEWS	TV	Radio
Original	29,6 %	49,7 %	71,4 %
Internet	43,3 %	25,5 %	18,6 %
Mobil phone	10,1%	24, 7%	5,2 %
Tablet	16,9 %	–	4,6 %

Source: AIMC (2013c).

Figure 9. Mobile application download, 15-19 years

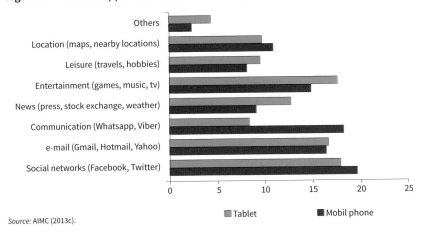

Source: AIMC (2013c).

Youth, politics and ICT

Figure 10. Evolution of interest in politics

	2004	2005	2010	2011	2012
Interest (15-29 years)	23,2 %	25,9 %	26,4 %	31,4 %	40,7 %

Source: AIMC (2013c).

Figure 11. Interest in political information (by age)

	15-19 years	20-24 years	25-29 years
Newspaper	12,2 %	16,1 %	18,5 %
Television	24,0 %	31,3 %	35,4 %
Radio	9,5 %	10,9 %	16,7 %
Internet	17,9 %	25,9 %	28,8 %

Figure 12. For staying on top of news, the Internet is...

	15-19 years	20-24 years	25-29 years
Fundamental source	39, 1%	42,4 %	38,9 %
Important source	43,3 %	42,2 %	45, 6 %
Total	82,9 %	84,6 %	84,5 %

Figure 13. Political and social networks

	15-19 years
Social networks make me interested in political affairs	37,8 %
The information/news gathered from social networking is unreliable	39,1 %
Social networking is a modern way to keep abreast of politics	46,3 %

Source: INJUVE (2013).

Therefore, social media are a common and close element in the life of teenagers and young adults (aged 15 to 29 years). They are considered as the right channel for staying up to date on political issues (Figure 10). Social media also contribute to a revitalization of informal political participation linked to a public display of discomfort, favouring the creation of a group identity (Rubio, 2012). The use of social media for political participation (formal or informal) has a dual nature: they are both inclusive and exclusive tools that allow an integration of the speech of young anonymous people. Still, technological and/or socioeconomic gaps limit the spread of an "e-democracy" (Hernández, Róbles & Martinéz, 2013).

The use of social media in education

Social media technologies are twofold: firstly, they facilitate communication and access to information; secondly, they have – as any other technology – specific risks that depend on their use, in this case related to privacy and harassment. This double dimension also arises in their educational use: we find activities aimed, on the one hand, at preventing social media risks and, on the other, at developing their techno-pedagogical potential. In Spain, both types of initiatives have been few and rarely interrelated. When developed, most of these initiatives have been geared toward preventing dysfunctional behaviour on the Internet, usually promoted from outside the academic sector[1].

Despite the limited effort promoted by educational authorities to boost the use of social media as an enabler of learning, each year more schools, colleges and universities introduce social media as an educational tool. Most of these experiences have been carried out through Ning networks (Infante Moro & Aguaded Gómez, 2012, p.171), while others have been gathered on *Red de Buenas PracTICas 2.0*, *Internet en el aula* and *Educ@conTic*. More recently, EduTwitter and EduFacebook joined this list; several schools are using these two social media sites for teaching and for promoting the educational possibilities of microblogging and social networking, among other functions. Furthermore, social media encourages the implementation and development of innovative teaching methods, such as the flipped classroom. On the other hand, some companies, in collaboration with a number of institutions, are providing free websites with interactive learning materials to the educational community, such as the website Escuela 2.0.

For the past two decades, technology investment in Spanish schools has been high. Several public programmes have been designed to provide technology infrastructure and connectivity to the centres – the latest, at the state level, is the "Programa Escuela 2.0". Today there is a computer for every 2.8 students in primary and secondary education, and 95% of schools have broadband Internet access. Each year new projects arise to strengthen and diversify the technological infrastructure in schools. Today, for example, the *mochila digital* ("digital backpack") is being piloted with 3,000 students at 45 schools in Castilla-La Mancha. This experience is expected to be extended to other regions this year (Fundación Telefonica, 2014).

However, efforts to acquire and improve technology in schools have not been accompanied in the same proportion by effective efforts in teacher training in the educational use of technology and social media. Two of three teachers do not feel trained in the use of ICT as educational tools, and to an even lesser extent in the use of social media. Area-Moreira's (2010, p. 95) reflection in the Canary Islands' case can be applied to all of Spain: "There is a strong presence of technology, but this by itself does not generate substantive processes of methodological change in the practices of teaching and learning". This lack of training can be found in the origin of why more than half of the teachers in primary and secondary education have not given way to incorporating ICT into their educational practice[2]. There is no coordinated effort from educational administrations in this direction yet. Some teachers turn to online resources of various kinds, some of them from abroad, in order to train themselves in technological and techno-pedagogical skills.

Although Spain has one of the highest prevalences of DIB (Dysfunctional Internet Behaviour) in Europe (Tsitsika, Tzavela & Mavromati, 2013), media literacy – especially digital media literacy – has never been a core element of the school curriculum. The LOGSE (*Act on the General Organisation of the Education System*) created two optional subjects, Process Communication and Communication Studies, which appeared and disappeared from the curriculum. It was not until 2006, when the LOE (*Act on Education*) was passed, that "Data processing and digital competence" became a core competency in the curriculum. "The initiation into the use of ICT, for learning, to develop a critical mind towards received and conveyed messages"[3] was regarded as an objective of primary education. The recently passed LOMCE Act will establish itineraries for teacher training in new technologies. The Ministry of Education, in consultation with the Autonomous Communities, is expected to develop a common frame for educational digital competence to guide teacher training and facilitate the development of a digital culture in the classroom

Currently, most teachers still do not dare use social media technologies in the classroom, or they do not see the techno-pedagogical potential in the content they teach. Thus, much of the potential of the technology infrastructure and connectivity already present at the centres is becoming diluted. Strategies should, therefore, incorporate the principles outlined by Jonassen, Howland, Moore & Marra (2003) to facilitate meaningful learning from the use of ICT. An adaptation of its principles to the use of social networking in educational strategies means that: 1) learning is intentional – students should know the goal of the use of social media and how it relates to what they are learning; 2) learning is constructive – students do not just use social media but the experiences derived from its use are linked to knowledge they already have; 3) tasks are authentic, close to the students' reality ; 4) we use the potential of social media to make learning collaborative; and 5) students are active subjects, involved in their own learning.

A reflection on the use of social media in the classroom is necessary from the perspective of the Pedagogical Content Knowledge (PCK), introduced by Shulman (1986), and its technological adaptation by Mishra and Koehler (2006, 2008)[4]. In this framework, any educational innovation based on the use of social media should dialogue with both the content and the pedagogical approach. Teachers need not only to know how social media works, but also how to apply it to favour a particular learning. Applying the principles of Mishra & Koehler (2008) to the educational use of social media, we identify that teachers need: 1) technological knowledge and skills in the use of social media; 2) technological content knowledge – the ability to apply social media to the content being taught; 3) techno-pedagogical knowledge – knowing how to use social media to facilitate student learning; and 4) techno-pedagogical content knowledge – involving the integration of the three preceding aspects, i.e. finding the proper use of social media to facilitate learning a particular subject or content. The debate on the right strategies to introduce social media to the classroom should be on a par with concrete efforts to promote techno-pedagogical teacher training in social media. This is perhaps the priority in order to teach students how to address the risks involved in the use of new forms of communication and exchange of information and, at the same time, take advantage of the numerous opportunities offered by social media to improve opportunities for learning.

Conclusions

Social media is being integrated, year after year, into the family, social and educational lives of the young. Young Spaniards do not see social media technologies as promoters of isolation, but as motivators of the relationship between peers and the exchange of information. The potential of social media have recently begun to be exploited by traditional media companies, advertising and education, and its development will be even greater in the future. Among the Spanish youth, interest in politics and political information has increased during this continued economic crisis. Internet and social media have facilitated the emergence of new spaces for political information and participation. In education the public initiatives to meet social media's new challenges and opportunities have been few and rarely interrelated, most of them focusing on the prevention of dysfunctional behaviour on the Internet. Although technology investment in Spanish schools has been high in the past two decades, there have not been effective efforts in techno-pedagogical teacher training: two of three teachers do not feel trained in the use of ICT in the classroom, and even less in the use of social media. This is the origin of the absence of a widespread change in methodology that leverages the potential of social media, and ICT in general, for meaningful, collaborative and connected learning. Despite the lack of momentum from the educational authorities, each year more schools, colleges and universities introduce social media as an educational tool.

Notes

1. Such as the Spanish Drug Enforcement Agency, Addictive Behaviors Prevention Units, Municipal Drug Prevention Plans, the Ombudsman, the Ombudsman for Children and NGOs.
2. Data on the use of ICT in educational practice come from the Fundación Telefonica report (2009).
3. On the other hand, it explains that "digital literacy involves making regular use of the technological resources available to solve real problems efficiently".
4. Shulman (1986) introduced the concept of Pedagogical Content Knowledge (PCK) as a specific category referring to the teacher's ability to transform knowledge into pedagogical knowledge adapted to the student diversity. Mishra & Koehler (2006) have added the category "technology" to this concept.

References

AIMC (2009). *Estudio General de Medios (EGM): Niños en Internet*. Madrid.

AIMC (2013a). *Audiencia Internet*. Madrid.

AIMC (2013b). *Estudio General de Medios* (EGM). Madrid.

AIMC (2013c). *Navegantes en la red*. EGM. Madrid.

Aranda, D., Sánchez-Navarro, J., & Tabernero, C. (2009). *Jóvenes y ocio digital. Informe sobre el uso de herramientas digitales por parte de adolescentes en España (UOC) 2009-2010*. Barcelona: UOC.

Area-Moreira, M. (2010). El proceso de integración y uso pedagógico de las TIC en los centros educativos. Un estudio de casos. *Revista de Educación, 252*, 77-97.

Bendit, R. (2004). La modernización de la juventud y modelos de políticas de juventud en Europa. In U. de Manizales, GTZ &UNICEF, *Construcción de Políticas de Juventud: análisis y perspectivas* (pp. 15-75). Programa Presidencial Colombia Joven, Centro de Estudios Avanzados en Niñez y Juventud CINDE.

Bernal, A. (2009). Los *nuevos medios de comunicación y los jóvenes. Aproximación a un modelo ideal de medio*. Madrid: Euroeditions.

Bringué, X., & Sádaba, C. (2011). *Menores y redes sociales*. Madrid: Generaciones interactivas.

Colás Bravo, P., Ramírez, T. G., & Pons, J. De P. (2013). Juventud y redes sociales: Motivaciones y usos preferentes. *Comunicar, 40*, 15-23.

Del Río, J., Sádaba, C., & Bringué, X. (2010). Menores y redes ¿sociales?: de la amistad al cyberbullying. Juventud y nuevos medios de comunicación, *Revista de Estudios de Juventud, 88*, 115-129.

Deltell Escolar, L., Claes, F., & López, J. M. O. (2013). Audiencias televisivas y líderes de opinión en Twitter. Caso de estudio El Barco. *Estudios sobre el Mensaje Periodístico, 19*, 347-364.

Espinar, E. E., & González Río, M. J. (2009). Jóvenes en las redes sociales virtuales: un análisis exploratorio de las diferencias de género. *Feminismo, 14*, 87-106.

Eurostat (2014). *Euro area unemployment rate at 12.1%*. http://epp.eurostat.ec.europa.eu/cache/ITY_PUBLIC/3-08012014-BP/EN/3-08012014-BP-EN.PDF

Frutos Torres, B. de, & Vázquez Barrio, T. (2012). Adolescentes y jóvenes en el entorno digital: análisis de su discurso sobre usos, percepción de riesgo y mecanismos de protección. *Doxa, 15*, 57-59.

Fundación Telefonica (2009). *La Sociedad de la Información en España, 2009*. Barcelona: Ariel.

Fundación Telefonica (2013). *La Sociedad de la Información en España 2012*. Barcelona: Ariel.

Fundación Telefonica (2014). *La Sociedad de la Información en España 2013*. Barcelona: Ariel.

Hernández, E., Róbles, M. C., & Martínez, J. B. (2013). Jóvenes interactivos y culturas cívicas. Sentido educativo, mediático y político del 15. *Comunicar, 40*, 57-67.

INE (2013). *Encuesta sobre equipamiento y uso de tecnologías de la información y comunicación en los hogares*. Madrid: INE.

Infante Moro, A., & Aguaded Gómez, J. I. (2013). Las redes sociales como herramientas educativas, nuevos escenarios de aprendizaje. In Y. S. Romero, A. H. A. Fernández, E. L. Meneses, J. Cabero-Almenara & J. I. Aguaded Gómez (Eds.), *Las tecnologías de la información en contextos educativos: nuevos escenarios de aprendizaje* (pp.163-176). Colombia: Universidad Santiago de Cali.

INJUVE (2013).*Informe de la Juventud 2012*. Madrid: Instituto de la Juventud.

INJUVE (2012). *Jóvenes y Nuevas Tecnologías*. Madrid: Instituto de la Juventud.

Jonassen, D. H.; Howland, J.; Moore, J., & Marra, R. M. (2003). *Learning to solve problems with technology: A constructivist perspective*. Ed.Columbus, OH: Merrill/Prentice-Hall.

Koehler, M., & Mishra, P. (Eds.) (2008). Introducing TPCK. En AACTE Commitee on Innovation and Technology. *Handbook of Technological Pedagogical Content Knowledge (TPCK) for Educators* (pp.3-29). New York, Routledge.

Lazo, C. M., Rodrigo, E. M., & Martín, L. S. (2013). La 'i-Generación' y su interacción en las redes sociales. Análisis de Coca-Cola en Tuenti. *Comunicar*, *40*, 41-48.

Livingstone, S., & Haddon, L. (Eds.) (2009). *Kids Online: Opportunities and Risks for Children*. Bristol: The Policy Press.

Mishra, P., & Koehler, M. J. (2006). Technological Pedagogical Content Knowledge: A framework for teacher knowledge. *Teachers College Record*, *108*(6), 1017-1054.

Rubio, M. (2012). Participación política de la juventud, redes sociales y democracia digital. *Telos*, *93*, 106-115.

Sánchez Burón, A. S., & Fernández Mártin, M. P. (2010). *Informe generación 2.0. Hábitos de los adolescentes en el uso de las redes sociales. Estudio comparativo entre Comunidades Autónomas*. Madrid: Universidad Camilo José Cela.

Shulman, L. (1986). Those who understand: Knowledge growth in teaching. *Educational Researcher*, *15*, 4-14.

Tsitsika, A., Tzavela, E., & Mavromati; F.I. (Eds.) (2013). *Research on Internet Addictive Behaviours among European Adolescents*. EU NET ADB Consortium.

The Cocktail Analysis (2013). *5ª Oleada Observatorio Redes Sociales*. Madrid.

Tuitele (2013). *Un año de televisión social en España*. Madrid: Tuitele.

UNESCO (2013). *Alfabetização midiática e informacional: currículo para formação de profesores*. Brasil: UNESCO, UFTM.

Digital Play and the Internet as ludic ecosystems

*The hierarchy of media for entertainment
and emergent literacies*

*Jordi Sánchez-Navarro, Daniel Aranda Juárez
& Silvia Martínez Martínez*

In the body of research and proposals for action in media education, young people's relationship with television has been the center of attention due to the ubiquity and influence of this medium in everyday life. We believe that such an approach should be reconsidered, as recent research (which has investigated not only the active media consumption by young citizens but also the hierarchy of media they establish in relation to their several interests) has revealed that, although the time they dedicate to watching television is greater than that dedicated to the Internet, the youth regard watching television as a habit "of the past," whereas the personal computer is the device that fits their leisure needs and audiovisual consumption. In this sense, the data show that young people perceive television consumption as an activity related to common spaces within the household, supplied in a way that does not match their interests. Moreover, they perceive the media and content consumption through the Internet as a "freer" activity; that is, an activity less regulated by parents and better adapted to their social, cultural, and psychological needs (Aranda, Roca & Sánchez-Navarro, 2013).

In these circumstances, the question "What do they use the Internet for?" becomes irrelevant: the youth use the Internet for everything, as reported by several authors in the case of Spain (Aranda, Sánchez-Navarro & Tabernero, 2009; Bernete, 2010; Rubio-Gil, 2009, 2010) and as we have again confirmed within the framework of an international research project, the World Internet Project (WIP)[1], from which some data and conclusions are shown and discussed on the following pages. The results of the WIP and other research projects give us clues toward an in-depth understanding of the Internet as a fundamental medium for the leisure of young people, who also establish a clear hierarchy of media for entertainment. In addition, we have observed that this form of entertainment is clearly related to the users' self-expression and that, at the same time, this self-expression is related to a ludic orientation of the use of the Internet. At this entertainment crossroads of self-expression and ludic orientation, a characteristic use of the media by the youth emerges. This use is the seed of a new model of media consumption that requires, therefore, a refocusing of certain aspects that are taken for granted in the field of media education.

Media for entertainment

The data collected in the WIP show that, among all the uses of the Internet, one seems to be especially relevant. Comparing the answers gathered in different waves, it can be observed that the percentage of youth who perceive the Internet as a suitable space for entertainment has increased slightly, to 86.8% in 2013 from 85.6% in 2011. This trend is confirmed when users between the ages of 16 and 24 are asked about their perception of the Internet as a medium for amusement and enjoyment.

The uses and activities of younger users are clearly coherent with this perception. Based on the data, 63.7% of the youth connect to the Internet on a daily

Figure 1. Perception on the Internet in terms of amusement and enjoyment among young users interviewed in 2013 (%)

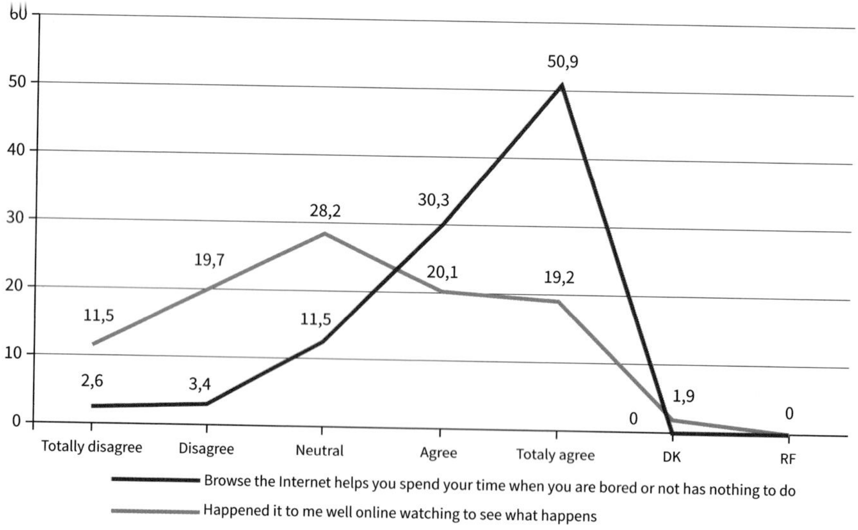

Source: WIP 2013, data from Spain (T= 234).

216

basis, and 48.7% do so to visit social networking sites or video websites; 24.8% look for jokes, cartoons, or other humorous content every day, whereas 36.3% do so every week. Other common activities among young people are downloading or listening to music (37.6% daily, 35% weekly) and watching videos (26.9% daily, 41% weekly). The results in 2013 show that, although 40% of the youth reported that they never connect to the Internet to play games, 60% of them play with variable frequency, which represents an increase from 2011.

Therefore, the Internet is clearly a basic tool for entertainment among the youth, as several previous studies have shown (Sánchez-Navarro & Aranda, 2011, 2013). In fact, this usage for entertainment is so integrated into daily life that one could say that Internet-based entertainment is no longer an area of interest for academic research because it belongs to the field of market studies. That is, because the Internet has become the basic infrastructure of entertainment for the youth, we have reached a point at which it no longer makes sense to continue studying something because it is simply there. However, from our point of view, whether we like it or not, the Internet is part of a complex ecosystem of media that is not getting easier but quite the opposite. Therefore, any project of media education must pay attention to the position the Internet holds in the landscape of contemporary media as far as the everyday life of young people is concerned. In this sense, it is interesting and necessary to compare the perceptions and uses of the Internet with those of other media.

This media hierarchy dominated by the Internet was confirmed in our research in 2012. Using a qualitative approach,[2] we gathered data through eight focus

Table 1. Assessment of media as sources of entertainment: a comparative study on the perceptions of users interviewed in 2011 and 2013 (%)

		2013							2011						
		Not important at all (1)	Not Important (2)	Neutral (3)	Important (4)	Very important (5)	DK	RF	Not important at all (1)	Not Important (2)	Neutral (3)	Important (4)	Very important (5)	NS	NC
Media for entertainment	Internet	1,3	1,3	10,7	31,2	55,6	0	0	2,3	2	10	33,1	52,5	0	0
	Television	6,4	15,7	23	28	26,8	0	0	6,4	13,4	17,4	38,5	24,4	0	0
	Newspaper	21,7	24,7	38,7	12,3	2,6	0	0	15,1	30,1	33,1	15,7	6	0	0
	Radio	19,1	20	33,6	17,4	9,4	0	0,4	16,7	23,7	21,1	24,7	13,4	0,3	0

Source: WIP, data from Spain in 2011 (T=299) and 2013 (T=234).

groups organized in at four centers of secondary education. The interviewees stated that, even in cases when the time they spent watching television was greater than the time they dedicated to the Internet, television was not perceived as the main source of entertainment. Regardless of the time spent, the Internet is the preferential medium. The data gathered in the focus group show that, as mentioned, television consumption is perceived, as previously mentioned, as a more restrictive activity, located in common areas of the household (such as the living room, dining room, and or kitchen), and offered in ways that do not fit the real interests of the young. On the contrary, going online for entertainment is a "freer" activity, that is to say, less regulated by adults (parents) and better fitted to their real needs. The fact that Internet consumption takes place in private spaces within the household (mainly in the bedroom) probably contributes to this perception by the youth.

Entertainment, self-expression, and playfulness

Entertainment, understood as a *set of contents*, is not the only factor that makes the Internet the preferred medium for young people. The InternetIt also offers the youththem a space for self-expression, which fits very well with their needs. There is already an abundant body of literature, derived mainly from the pioneering studies of Danah Boyd (2007) and Mizuko Ito (2009), on how the Internet and, especially, social networking sites offer young people a space to work productively toward managing their identity and status, and raising their awareness of social rules. As the work of a University of Amsterdam research group led by Patti Valkenburg pointed out very precisely pointed out, the correct psychosocial development of adolescents depends largely on the development of their identity, intimacy, and sexuality (Valkenburg & Peter, 2011). Teenagers have to develop a strong self-knowledge and must be sure about of who they are and what they want to become. It is also important that they develop a certain sense of intimacy, as well as achieve the skills necessary to form, maintain, and even conclude relationships with others that who are meaningful to them. To attain the correct development of these psychosocial aspects, teenagers need to develop two important skills: (1) how to presenting oneself to others (self-presentation) and (2) how to sharesharing intimate aspects with others (self-disclosure). The boys and girls with whom we have spoken in our research projects played down the potential risks associated with privacy management in social networks and other services of the Internet, because as their giving a bit of intimacy reverts to the achievement of greater knowledge and opportunities for sociability, as stated in Rheingold's studies about on social network capital. Users generate and manage a cultural capital that is based on and reverts to: 1) the flow of information, opportunities, and choices; 2) the ability to influence;

3) the certification of social credentials; and 4) the reinforcement of identity and the recognition of who we are and what we like.

As previously mentioned, entertainment, self-expression, sociability, and play appear to be clearly entwined in the cultural consumption and activities of young people on the Internet; this has also been confirmed in several researches research projects in which young people implicitly or explicitly mentioned implicitly or explicitly the ludic approach to the use of the Internet in everyday life (Aranda, Sánchez-Navarro, & Tabernero, 2009; Sánchez-Navaro & Aranda, 2010, 2012; Aranda, Roca & Sánchez-Navarro, 2013). Thus, as mentioned at the beginning of this chapter, we argue that the characteristic use of the Internet by the youth constitutes the origin of a new model of relationship with the media and requires an extension of the focus of media education. Hence, we think hold that *ludoliteracy* should be added unequivocally to the set of *media literacies.*

Emergent literacies: Ludoliteracy

It should be pointed out that the concept of ludoliteracy refers not only to video games, or to what is explicitly understood as a game, but also to that the current tendency of the digital society toward playfulness, in the form of either ubiquitous games on mobile devices or an the increasing gamification of art, marketing, or and social media. Ludoliteracy is a form of knowledge that implies understanding digital gaming as a semiotic system (Gee, 2004), as a different medium that generates its own meanings and pleasures, and requires its own analytic and creative skills. It has to do not only with functional abilities related to the act of playing, but also with analytic and reflexive capacities and skills, and with creative abilities oriented toward the production of meanings in playful contexts.

Insisting on the idea that ludoliteracy is related not only to video games, it must be pointed out that its origin can be found, precisely, in the confirmation that digital games are a characteristic medium of our contemporary culture. From the data obtained in the WIP 2013, we observed that 81% of the surveyed youth reported playing or having played video games on consoles, computers, mobile devices, or even social networking sites, and 41% admitted that they play often. These numbers are consistent with their perception of video games: 53% of the surveyed youth believed that playing video games was not a waste of time. Outside these data, the literature shows that, through the use of digital games, individuals improve their the abilities and skills they need needed in the digital society (Jenkins, 2008; Aranda & Sánchez-Navarro, 2009, 2010), obtain pleasure and fun (Huizinga, 1994; Sherry, 2004), participate in creative ways through fan communities (Wirman, 2009), socialize with peers while generating interchange networks (Jansz & Marten, 2005; Zagal, 2010), or learn both curricular and extracurricular contents and skills (Gee, 2004; Lacasa, 2011; Whitton, 2009).

Every ludoliteracy proposal must be fully framed within the principles of media literacy and media education in a global context. According to the UNESCO indications (2008), the objective of media literacy is to help filter the media and the messages they transmitted by them because these have an influence on the personal decisions of citizens. This point of view establishes that different processes and techniques (media education proposals) allow and help students, education professionals, and citizens in general to develop critical capacities and knowledge about the media.

Any definition of ludoliteracy needs to include the two dimensions of media education: education with the media and education in the media. Therefore, we need to pay attention to digital play as a didactic tool and as an object of study. Following classic authors (Masterman, 1993), we can distinguish between education with digital gaming and education in digital gaming. The first approach comprehends the use of digital play as an educative support, as a pedagogical help aid at the service of contents and educative programs (Jacquinot, 1996). Such a didactic use of digital games (Aguaded, 1999) would be aimed at enriching and diversifying contents, making them more attractive and closer to the reality of the students, by using a medium that motivates and fascinates them. Serious games or educative games have been and continue to be a very fruitful field, led by theoretical bodies and educative initiatives, such as the digital game-based learning (Prensky, 2007), edutainment (Egenfeldt, 2005), or the so-called *serious games*. The educative use of digital play would be related to contents competences, abilities, and skills present in actual educative curricula, such as problem-solving, teamwork, or values like effort and self-improvement (Lacasa, 2011; Aranda & Sánchez-Navarro, 2011; Wirman 2009). The use of commercial video games, casual games for tablets or smartphones, and, more recently, different dynamics of gamification have a prominent role in this kind these kinds of proposals. However, as previously mentioned, ludoliteracy is the understanding of digital play not only as a didactic tool but also as an object of study *per se*. According to Poulsen and Gatzidis (2010), understanding digital play is not only valuable *per se* as a pedagogical proposal but is also a prerequisite for those interested in its educative use. Thus, ludoliteracy would also be aimed at reflecting the technological, cultural, sociological, and economic context of digital games as well as media. From this point of view, one of the main goals of ludoliteracy would be to provide children, teenagers, and adults with knowledge toward obtaining a certain level of control over the media they use, in this case, digital games. In a nutshell, according to Roberto Aparici's arguments regarding media in general, if citizens are offered appropriate analysis guidelines and a reflexive, critical, and pedagogical (we would add creative) proposal, they will have the tools necessary to make autonomous decisions about the messages (products and discourses) they receive from media (Aparici, 1997).

Based on the work of James Gee (2004), José Zagal (2010, p. 24), defines ludoliteracy as (1) the ability to play, (2) the ability to understand meanings in relation to games, and (3) the ability to create games. These three aspects are common in most ludoliteracy proposals (Buckingham & Burn, 2007; Poulsen & Gatzidis, 2010; Caperton, 2010; Squire, 2005, 2008), all of them based on the following dimensions of skills: (1) functional skills (playing the game or reading); (2) analytic or reflexive skills; and (3) productive ability (writing). Zagal focused his proposal on the second dimension, arguing that the analytical and reflexive skills are aimed at improving the ability to explain, discuss, frame, and interpret games in the cultural context, as a cultural artefact, in relation to other games, by comparing games and genres, and within their technological contexts.

Beyond where the emphasis is putplaced, it seems clear that the academic community agrees that a good literacy plan must take into account reading competence, analysis, production, and pleasure. However, according to Squire (2005), a good literacy policy – media literacy in our case – is an attitude, not a destination. Thus, media literacy in digital gaming – ludoliteracy – must be a continuous process of inquiry, research, and self-reflection.

Notes

1. The World Internet Project (WIP), an international and collaborative project involving more than 30 research teams, analyzes the social, political, and economic impacts of the Internet and other new technologies. The data presented in this chapter were obtained from two fieldworks, conducted in June 2011 and December 2013. The universe of study in both fieldworks was formed by the general population aged 16 and above living in Spanish households with fixed telephone lines. The resulting samples in both fieldworks were proportional per autonomous community to the real distribution of the Spanish population, with margins of error of ±2.13% (2011) and ±2.45% (2013) for P=Q=50% and assuming maximum uncertainty.

2. Research conducted in the framework of the *Digital Convergence and Youth: The New Spaces of Audiovisual Consumption* project under a grant from the Catalan Audiovisual Council.

References

Aguaded, I. (1999). *Convivir con la televisión. Familia, educación y recepción televisiva*. Barcelona: Paidós.

Aparici, R. (1997). Educación para los medios. *Voces y Culturas, 11/12*, 89-99.

Aranda, D., Sánchez-Navarro, J., & Tabernero, C. (2009). *Jóvenes y ocio digital. Informe sobre el uso de herramientas digitales por parte de adolescentes en España*. Barcelona: Editorial UOC.

Aranda, D., Roca, M., & Sánchez-Navarro, J. (2013). Televisión e internet. El significado de uso de la red en el consumo audiovisual de los adolescentes. *Quaderns del CAC, 39*, XVI, 15-23.

Bernete, F. (2010). Usos de las TIC, relaciones sociales y cambios en la socialización de las y los jóvenes. *Revista de Estudios de Juventud, 88*, 97-114.

boyd, d. (2007). Why youth (heart) social network sites: the role of networked publics in teenage social life. In D. Buckingham (Ed.), *MacArthur Foundation Series on Digital Learning – Youth, Identity, and Digital Media Volume* (pp. 119-142). Cambridge, MA: MIT Press.

Buckingham, D., & Burn, A. (2007). Game Literacy in Theory and practice. *Journal of Educational Multimedia and Hypermedia, 16*(3), 323-349.

Caperton, H. (2010). Toward a theory of game-media literacy: Playing and bulding as reading and writing. *International Journal of Gaming and Computer-Mediated Simulations, 2*(1), 1-16.

Egenfeldt-Nielsen, S. (2005). *Beyond Edutainment: Exploring the educational potential of computer games*. Phd Dissertation. Copenhagen: IT- University of Copenhagen.

Gee, J. P. (2004). *Lo que nos enseñan los videojuegos sobre el aprendizaje y el alfabetismo*. Málaga: Aljibe.

Huizinga, J. (1994). *Homo Ludens*. Madrid: Alianza

Ito, M., Baumer, S., Bittanti, M., boyd, d., Cody, R., … Tripp, L. (2009). *Hanging Out, Messing Around, Geeking Out: Living and Learning with New Media*. Cambridge: MIT Press.

Jacquinot, G. (1996). *La escuela frente a las pantallas*. Buenos Aires: Aique.

Jansz, J. & Marten, L. (2005). Gaming at a LAN event: the social context of playing videogames. *New Media & Society, 7*(3), 333-355.

Jenkins, H., Purushotma, R., Weigel, M., Clinton, K., & Robison, A. (2008). *Confronting the Challenges of Participatory Culture: Media Education for the 21st Century*. Chicago: The MacArthur Foundation.

Lacasa, P. (2011). *Los videojuegos, aprender en mundos reales y virtuales*. Madrid: Morata.

Masterman, L. (1993). *La enseñanza de los medios audiovisuales*. Madrid: Ediciones de la Torre.

Poulsen, M., & Gatzidis, C. (2010). *Understanding the game: an examination of Ludoliteracy*. 4th European Conference on Games Based Learning, Copenhagen. http://mathiaspoulsen.com/Understanding%20the%20Game_An%20Examination%20of%20Ludoliteracy.pdf

Prensky, M. (2007). *Digital game-based learning*. St. Paul: Paragon House.

Rubio Gil, Á. (2010). Generación digital: patrones de consumo de Internet, cultura juvenil y cambio social. *Revista de Estudios de Juventud, 88*, 201-221.

Rubio Gil, Á. (2009). *Adolescentes y Jóvenes en Red*. Madrid: Instituto de la Juventud.

Sánchez-Navarro, J., & Aranda, D. (2010). Un enfoque emergente en la investigación sobre comunicación: Los videojuegos como espacios para lo social. *Anàlisi: Quaderns de comunicació i cultura, 40*, 129-141.

Sánchez-Navarro, J., & Aranda, D. (2011). Internet como fuente de información para la vida cotidiana de los jóvenes españoles. *El profesional de la información, 20*(1), 32-37.

Sánchez-Navarro, J., & Aranda, D. (2012). Desmontando tópicos: Jóvenes, redes sociales y videojuegos. In E. Martínez Rodrigo & C. Marta Lazo (Eds.), *Jóvenes interactivos: Nuevos modos de comunicarse* (pp. 119-135). A Coruña: Netbiblo.

Sánchez-Navarro, J., & Aranda, D. (2013). Messenger and social network sites as tools for sociability, leisure and informal learning for Spanish young people. *European Journal of Communication, 28*(1), 67-75.

Sherry, J. (2004). Flow and media enjoyment. *Communication Theory, 4*, 328-347.

Squire, K. (2005). Toward a Media Literacy for Games. *Telemedium 52*(1-2), 9-15.

Squire, K. (2008). Video-Game Literacy. A Literacy of Expertise. In J. Coiro, M. Knobel, C. Lankshear & D. J. Leu (Eds.), *Handbook of research on new Literacies* (pp 639-673). New York: Routledge.

UNESCO (2008). *Teacher Training Curricula for Media and Information Literacy. Report of the International Expert Group Meeting*. Paris: UNESCO.

Valkenburg, P. M., & Peter, J. (2011). Adolescents' online communication: An integrated model of its attraction, opportunities, and risks. *Journal of Adolescent Health, 48*, 121-127.

Whitton, N. (2009). *Learning with Digital Games: A Practical Guide to Engaging Students in Higher Education*. New York: Routledge.

Wirman, H. (2009). Sobre la productividad y los fans de los videojuegos. In D. Aranda & J. Sánchez-Navarro (Eds.), *Aprovecha el tiempo y juega* (pp. 145-184). Barcelona: Editorial UOC.

Zagal, J.P. (2010). *Ludoliteracy: Defining, Understanding, And Supporting Games Education*. ETC Press, paper 4. http://repository.cmu.edu/etcpress/4

Media Competence in Primary and Secondary School Education in Spain

M. Amor Pérez-Rodríguez & Paloma Contreras-Pulido

In the past few years several projects have been developed, with the backing of institutions such as the European Commission and UNESCO[1], that aim to define the dimensions, indicators and criteria to enable us to assess the levels and extent of media competence within various settings. In 2007, the *Study on the current trends and approaches on Media Literacy in Europe* (European Commission) highlighted the need to establish such criteria, and several authors (Celot & Pérez-Tornero, 2009; European Commission, 2011; Ferrés, 2007; Ferrés & Piscitelli, 2012; Pérez-Rodríguez & Delgado, 2012; Pérez-Tornero & Martínez-Cerdá, 2011) have followed a line of research that emphasizes the importance of achieving results that can provide the basis for promoting media literacy.

One result of this concern and the recognition of the importance of providing citizens with an authentic media education has been the development in Spain of a research project[2] of considerable scope over the past four years by more than 30 researchers at some 20 universities, to assess the level of media competence in various population settings. The study focuses on university teachers at education and communication faculties in Spain, media professionals, children and young people in all stages of state, state-funded and private education, families, senior citizens and a specific social exclusion setting, prisons. The results presented in this chapter are part of an analysis of *compulsory education and audiovisual communication competence in a digital setting*, in which researchers from 17 Spanish universities took part, the subjects being students in primary and secondary school education as defined in Spain.

ing images. The *Technology* dimension revealed higher levels of competence. In primary school students, almost 48% answered that they had a good level of technological competence, and 40% said they had some knowledge. Among secondary school students, 62.4% said they were aware of more than half the technologies named in the questionnaire while 62.4% said they could competently navigate the Internet; 54.3% classified themselves as fairly competent users. The data for *Production and programming* in primary schools showed that 45% had a thorough knowledge of this concept, while more than 25% were unaware of media dynamics and the technical development of an audiovisual production. In secondary school, 66% said they knew the jobs done by media production professionals, by identifying just under half the professions listed, while those careers linked to new forms of communication and the Internet were less well-known. In terms of data on production, 43% were able to successfully construct a visual sequence while only 33.7% could put the necessary phases in the correct order to make an audiovisual product. For *Ideology and values*, the study revealed that in primary school 53.6% could clearly identify aspects related to this dimension. When secondary school students were questioned on the critical reading and understanding of the audiovisual information presented to them, 22.3% stated that they planned their Internet searches taking into account objectives and the tools available, while 69% were unable to carry out an effective search because they lacked prior organization and planning skills, and even objectives, as well as the ability to assess the information found. However, 53.6% could identify aspects of advertising that most influenced them while 46.4% could not. For *Reception and audience,* 50.06% of the children surveyed in primary education were able to recognize what it meant to be a media recipient. In secondary education, data on the ability to recognize the influence of the media show that 25% acknowledged they could be affected by a particular advertisement, although 89.7% said that this influence might well affect others; 45.1% indicated that the influence of advertising was due to the use of emotions and catchy storylines. A total of 72.6% had never reported or complained about offensive images, videos, etc. in the media, and 27.5% declared that they actively participated in social and/or political activities either in forums (25.7%) or social networks (24%). The *Aesthetics* dimension registered low in primary school, with only 20% choosing the appropriate answer. In secondary school, 29.9% of those surveyed selected the pleasant visual effect and 25.9% opted to position the key element in the foreground, while a further 17.7% favoured the attractive design.

The future of media education

As can be seen, those dimensions most closely related to aspects linked in some way to schooling strategies are the most developed, as in the case of *Language* and *Technology*. Here the students show considerable competence in codes and genres, and in tools and resources when searching for information. In *Production and programming*, *Reception and audience*, and *Ideology and values* the level of competence is average, as demonstrated by the fact that half of those surveyed have some knowledge or recognize certain influences. To a certain extent, the data obtained coincide with studies by Mediappro (2006) and the European Commission (2011) in terms of critical skills; for example, young children considered advertising to be a form of entertainment and were unable to detect its hidden intentions. They had a rough idea that the content transmits certain ideologies and values, but could not always recognize this at the first viewing. The *Aesthetics* dimension scores lowest in both groups, perhaps because it entails the most complex indicators that require the use of skills for relating and recognizing aesthetic categories, as well as a certain sensibility among those surveyed.

The development of cognitive and instrumental skills related to media and technological languages is important but insufficient. Those that can implicitly promote media competence alongside the proper training of citizens are related to critical thought, responsibility, reflection, cooperation, tolerance, creativity, sensibility and innovation. If the level of student media competence is not very high with regard to those dimensions most closely linked to it – that is, *Production and programming*, *Reception and audience* and *Ideology and values*, and *Aesthetics* in particular – it is clear where our efforts need to be directed, and what the priorities are for all educational institutions.

Notes

1. European Commission (2007): "Un planteamiento europeo de la alfabetización mediática en el entorno digital", (http://ec.europa.eu/culture/media/literacy/docs/com/es.pdf); UNESCO: Grünwald Declaration (1982), Conference "Educating for the Media and the Digital Age" (1999), París Agenda or 12 Recommendations for Media Education (2007), and the Braga Declaration (2011), (www.unesco.org/new/en/communication-and-information/media-development/media-literacy/mil-as-composite-concept/).
2. R+D+I project developed and financed by the Ministry of Economy and Competition's Convocatoria de Proyectos I+D: EDU2010-21395-C03-03: "La competencia en comunicación audiovisual en un entorno digital. Diagnóstico de necesidades en tres ámbitos sociales", coordinated by Prof. Dr. Joan Ferrés of the Universitat Pompeu Fabra, Prof. Dr. Agustín García-Matilla of the University of Valladolid, and Prof. Dr. J. Ignacio Aguaded of the University of Huelva.
3. Celot & Pérez-Tornero, 2009; Ferrés, 2007; Ferrés & Piscitelli, 2012; Pérez-Rodríguez & Delgado, 2013; Pérez-Tornero & Martínez-Cerdá, 2011.

References

Aparici, R., Campuzano, A., Ferres, J., & García-Matilla, A. (2010). *La educación mediática en la Escuela 2.0*. www.airecomun.com/sites/all/files/materiales/educacion_mediatica_e20_julio20010.pdf
Celot, P., & Pérez-Tornero, J.M. (2009). *Study on Assessment Criteria for Media Literacy Levels. A comprehensive view of the concept of media literacy and an understanding of how media*

literacy level in Europe should be assessed. http://ec.europa.eu/culture/media/media-content/medialiteracy/studies/eavi_study_assess_crit_media_lit_levels_europe_finrep.pdf

European Commission (2007). *Study on the current trends and approaches on Media Literacy in Europe.* http://ec.europa.eu/culture/media/media-content/media-literacy/studies/study.pdf

European Commission (2011). *Testing and Refining Criteria to Assess Media Literacy Levels in Europe. Final Report.* http://ec.europa.eu/culture/media/media-content/media-literacy/studies/final-report-ml-study-2011.pdf

Ferrés, J. (2007). Competence in media studies: its dimensions and indicators. *Comunicar, 29,* 100-107.

Ferrés, J., & Piscitelli, A. (2012). Media Competence. Articulated Proposal of Dimensions and Indicators. *Comunicar, 38,* 75-82. doi: 10.3916/C38-2012-02-08

Masanet, M. J., Contreras-Pulido, P., & Ferrés, J. (2013). Highly qualified students? Research into the media competence level of Spanish youth. *Comunicación y sociedad, 26*(4), 217-234.

Mediappro (2006). *The Appropriation of New Media by Youth.* http://mediappro.eu

Pérez-Rodríguez, M. A., & Delgado, A. (2012). From Digital and Audiovisual Competence to Media Competence: Dimensions and indicators. *Comunicar, 39,* 25-34. doi: 10.3916/C39-2012-02-02

Pérez-Tornero, J. M., & Martínez-Cerdá, J. F. (2011). Hacia un sistema supranacional de indicadores mediáticos. *Infoamérica, 5,* 39-57.

UNESCO (2007). *Agenda de París o 12 Recomendaciones para la Educación en Medios.* http://www.diplomatie.gouv.fr/fr/IMG/pdf/Parisagendafin_en.pdf

Media Education: Public Policies, Curricular Proposals and Teacher Training

European Policies for Media Education and Competence

J. Ignacio Aguaded & Águeda Delgado

Various international institutions proclaim the urgent need to institute media education. In fact, the idea of a global development of media literacy has already taken root, as seen in measures and documents published by the European Commission, the Council of Europe and the UN (Alliance for Civilizations[1]).

One of the key measures within the European scenario is "Media Education" as a school subject. This European Parliament report emphasized the need to improve school infrastructure, and proposed that adults also be tutored in media literacy, which clearly demonstrates the importance of media education in today's information and communication society.

Many important steps have been taken in this direction, the most significant being the pioneering UNESCO Grünwald Declaration of 1982 "on media-related education", which stated that:

- Political and educational systems must assume their obligations to promote a critical understanding among citizens of the various communication phenomena;

- The school and family share responsibility for preparing young people to live in a world dominated by text, sound and images;

- A thorough integration of educational and communication systems is undoubtedly an important step towards ensuring that media education is more effective.

A series of conferences and seminars in various countries drove this idea forward by establishing the bases and framework for action on media education.

In 1990, the University of Toulouse in France held an International Conference, entitled "New Directions in Media Education", which aroused awareness in this new discipline of education in media, and highlighted the need for new methodological approaches.

Also in the 1990s, the European Commission launched measures as part of the "Learning in the Information Society (1996-1998)" action plan, whose general aims were to "boost school access to the information society by offering new openings to the world; to encourage the broad dissemination of multimedia pedagogical practices and the creation of a critical mass of users, products and multimedia educational services; and to reinforce the European dimension of education and training based on the instruments of the information society, with an appreciation of cultural and linguistic diversity" (European Commission, 1997).

This plan also included the Netd@ys Europe[2] initiative, whose aim was to "promote the use of new media in education and culture". Netd@ys Europe unified the various individual projects presented at the "Semana Netd@ys", which took place each November between 1997 and 2005; the tendency here was to prioritize pedagogical rather than technological content. The European Commission would define the thematic content each year to include topics such as citizenship, European diversity and cultural identity, equality of opportunities, education and training for enhanced usage of the media, and beyond Europe, with special emphasis on the nations of Central and Eastern Europe, and with the active participation of Australia, Brazil, Canada and Israel. This initiative was open to any organization willing to subscribe to its philosophy and objectives, and although the initiative was aimed at all citizens, it focused particularly on 15- to 25-year-olds.

In 1999, the Conference on *"Educating for the Media and the Digital Age"* (UNESCO, 1999) was held in Vienna, centring on the following three axes:

- *Media Education: Why?* The aim was to articulate the need to integrate media into formal education.

- *Media Education: How?* This showed the wide range of good practices at work among the nations represented at the conference.

- *Media Education: Strategies for the future?* A presentation of new perspectives for the 21st century.

The emergence of the Internet in the media scenario at that time led to a change in focus towards all things digital, not to mention the redirection of principles.

The European Union began to develop strategies, such as its *Safer Internet*[3] programme. These strategies were initiated among individual states and at the Europe-wide level, and their main aims were to make the use of the Internet and other communication technologies safe, especially for children and youngsters; other objectives included the education of users, particularly children, parents, carers, teachers and educators, and the struggle against illegal content and harmful behaviour online.

The development of infrastructure and media literacy also advanced with the Lisbon Council of 2000, which agreed to implement various short-term commitments to technology and the Internet. These included the pledge that, by the end of 2001, all schools would have access to the Internet and multimedia resources, and that within another 12 months all teachers would be trained to use the Internet and multimedia equipment. The installation of such technologies in the classroom required new actions, such as "the development of specific capacities for proper ICT use: the selection, analysis and later transformation of information into knowledge and skills" (European Commission, 2001).

In order to change the learning processes related to multimedia technologies and the Internet, the European Commission adopted the *"eLearning:* conceiving the future of education" initiative in May 2000. This initiative formed part of the *eEurope* action plan, whose "aim is to enable Europe to exploit its strong points and overcome obstacles to a greater integration and usage of digital technologies".

The *eLearning* 2001-04 plan centred on infrastructure, training, services, content and cooperation. In terms of competences, it emphasized the importance of possessing technical, intellectual and social competences beyond digital culture. It also integrated the critical and responsible use of the new technologies within the "new basic competences" for lifelong learning.

The *eLearning* programme for 2004-06 began to focus on digital literacy, particularly in terms of media literacy, which "constitutes one of the skills and competences that is essential for active participation in the knowledge society. Digital literacy is related to media literacy and social skills, and they have common objectives such as active citizenship and the responsible use of ICT". The development of digital literacy was to be one of this programme's main lines of action.

Meanwhile, at an event more closely related to the media, a call to action was sounded in the recommendations of the Seville Seminar on Media Education (UNESCO, 2002). This document reveals that media education was now deemed to be an issue that affected everyone, not just school children; and this included the regulatory authorities, state media, the media industry, and parents and citizens in general. It was not enough to worry about the negative effects of the media; it was important to tap into the enriching potential of such media – hence the need to instigate media education (Pérez-Tornero, 2007, pp. 131-132).

Another vital step undertaken by the European Commission and Parliament was the establishment in 2006 of a "group of experts in media education"[4] and the launch of a public survey that charted media literacy levels across Europe[5], which in turn led to the Audiovisual Media and Services Directive. This called for the promotion of media literacy in all sectors of society, given its importance in producing media-competent citizens "capable of selection with causal knowledge, understanding the nature of content and services, making the best use of a whole range of opportunities presented by the new communication technologies and protecting their families and themselves from harmful and offensive material". These actions are still in progress today, with an emphasis on Communication, "a European focus on media literacy in the digital environment" (European Commission, 2007), which added a new element to European audiovisual policy and complemented the new borderless audiovisual media services and the MEDIA 2007 programme for the development and distribution of European cinema.

In the same year, the Paris Agenda (UNESCO, 2007) announced recommendations for the development of media education programmes on all levels, teacher training, and research and international cooperation.

The launch of the Lifelong Learning programme gathered all previous initiatives on education and training, such as professional training and the *eLearning* programme that concluded in 2006. One of the four transversal lines of this programme consisted of Information and Communication Technologies (ICT) for education, which is also one of the priorities of its four vertical programmes (Erasmus, Comenius, Leonardo da Vinci and Grundtvig). The Lifelong Learning programme supports ICT for innovation based on pedagogy, technology and organization. In pedagogical terms, considerable importance was given to virtual learning as a way of improving learning strategies, especially those that promote creativity and innovation.

In this aspect, progress has been made over the years with the tackling of concerns about infrastructure and the handling of technologies to the use of ICT to create and innovate. This led to the designation of 2009 by that year's European Commission as the year of creation and innovation[6].

The same year also saw the Commission's presentation of its Recommendation on media literacy, in which it called on all EU member states and the media industry to commit to strengthening media literacy. It also launched a debate on the inclusion of media literacy in compulsory study plans and as a key competence in lifelong learning. To further promote this debate, the Commission established a group of experts to focus on media literacy in schools. All EU member states and those of the European Free Trade Association were represented, along with independent experts who presented a range of good practices, experiences and case studies. The aim of this gathering was to examine the current state of media literacy in the schools of all the nations represented, and to debate the possible inclusion of media skills in formal education programmes.

In March 2011, the Braga Declaration was signed at the National Congress on Literacy, Media and Citizenship, held at the University of Minho (Portugal); the resulting communique extended the notion of education to include an informed and critical use of the media as an important aspect of citizens' education.

Many of these initiatives are clearly still valid. Hence, the European Commission continues to encourage the exchange of good practices based on activities that are currently in action, such as MEDIA 2007, Media Mundus, the Directive on Audiovisual Media Services, and other initiatives. The institution also publishes reports on "media literacy levels" in each member state.

Instruments and studies on media literacy

Other instruments and studies related to media education have been undertaken and developed alongside these policies; these consist of tools, programmes and guides aiming to foment media literacy by clearly defining this phenomenon, proposals for new methodologies and teacher training as well as the necessary tools to assess and determine those media literacy aspects that need greater emphasis in order for citizens to acquire audiovisual communication competence.

One such instrument was UNESCO's "Media Education Kit" in 2006 for teachers, students, parents and professionals. It consisted of manuals that provided a perspective on the school curriculum that includes media education in all its dimensions: initiation in audiovisual language, content analysis, understanding the financial set-up of media groups, appropriation of citizens' rights and protection of young people from harmful material, and awareness of self-regulation and regulation in general (Frau-Meigs, 2006, p. 7), all of which could shape a unified, modular media education programme.

This programme was followed by an initiative that is still functioning today: *"Teacher Training Curricula for Media and Information Literacy"*. This aims to integrate media education and information literacy at the start of training for secondary school teachers, and is designed to be applied and adapted universally in accordance with the needs of each country[7]. This programme conceives of media education and information literacy as requiring five competences, the "5 Cs": understanding, critical thought, creativity, citizenship and intercultural communication.

This impulse led to the publication in 2011 of *Media and Information Literacy (MIL). A Curriculum for Teachers* (Wilson et al., 2011). This has become an important resource for EU member states as they continuously strive to achieve the objectives established in MIL-related declarations and at conferences. In the words of Jānis Kārkliņš (2011, p.11), this curriculum "is also pioneering for two reasons: first, it looks to the future, taking into account current trends that bring together radio, television, Internet, newspapers, books, digital archives and libraries in one single platform, and as such, it is the first time that the MIL has been presented in a holistic form; second, it is designed specifically with teachers in mind and aims to integrate a formal education system for teachers, so it initiates a catalysing process that should reach millions of young people and develop their capabilities".

This publication comes in two parts: the first contains the MIL Curriculum and Framework Competences, developing a general outlook around notions, fundamentals and main themes; the second part includes a more detailed explanation of basic and optional modules. It is mainly aimed at primary and secondary school teachers, and is thus a tool specifically designed for teaching institutions.

Of equal importance have been studies in Canada by the Media Awareness Network on how young people use the Internet[8], or the *Media Literacy Teacher Resource Guide* produced by the Canadian Broadcasting Corporation and the Ontario Institute, which aims to help students deconstruct the messages and images they receive from the media in order to be able to assess the huge quantity of data they are constantly subjected to in an appropriate way (Di Croce, 2009, p. 3).

The question of assessment is tackled in the "Study on Assessment Criteria for Media Literacy Levels" (2009), directed by Pérez-Tornero for the European Commission. It covers the 27 EU member states, and European Economic Area countries such as Norway, Iceland and Liechtenstein. Its aims are:

- To provide an analysis and most of the criteria necessary for assessing media literacy levels.

- To apply those criteria to EU member states.

- To provide an assessment of media literacy levels in EU member states.

- That the study should consider the possibility of consolidating common media literacy policies in practice in the EU.

This study emphasizes two dimensions within media literacy: one derived from the individual's capability to use the media, and another based on context and environmental factors, referred to in the study as Individual Competences and Environmental Factors.

Later, "Testing and Refining Criteria to Assess Media Literacy Levels in Europe" (2011) carried out a follow-up of this study, assessing and recommending methods for measuring national levels of media literacy. Among the aspects related to measuring media literacy was a strong recommendation to attend to critical understanding and the national context. In terms of promoting education in media, a series of recommendations covered three different areas: in terms of EU member states, the configuring of national panels of interest groups, the exchange of experiences, mutual cooperation among member states and with UNESCO and the OECD, scientific and educational research and collaboration with the media industry; with regard to educational policies, encouraging the integration of measures in media education, the promotion of creative and participative capabilities in educational systems and knowledge of media regulations; and in relation to citizens, the promotion of an active European citizenry and of media literacy in the context of an active citizenship and in initiatives promoting the inclusion of groups at risk.

Notes

1. www.aocmedialiteracy.org
2. http://europa.eu/legislation_summaries/education_training_youth/general_framework/c11045_es.htm
3. http://ec.europa.eu/information_society/activities/sip/index_en.htm
4. This group consisted of European media literacy experts, who met three times a year to analyse and define aims and trends in this field. They also aimed to promote good actions and practices in media literacy among fellow Europeans. See: http://ec.europa.eu/culture/media/literacy/act_prog/expert_group/index_en.htm [2011-10-13].
5. To improve media literacy in the digital age, the European Commission launched a public survey which ended on 15 December 2006. The aim was to identify media literacy foci and describe emerging trends across Europe. The questionnaire and survey results are available at: http://ec.europa.eu/culture/media/literacy/act_prog/consultation/index_en.htm
6. All information relating to *2009: The European Year of Creativity and Innovation*. www.create2009.europa.eu
7. http://portal.unesco.org/ci/en/ev.php-URL_ID=27057&URL_DO=DO_TOPIC&URL_SECTION=201.html.
8. Similar studies include: *Young Canadians in a Wired World* (http://mediasmarts.ca/research-policy); Taylor (2001), and Steeves & Webster (2008).

References

Celot, P., & Pérez-Tornero, J. M. (Eds.) (2009). Study on Assessment Criteria for Media Literacy Levels – *A comprehensive view of the concept of media literacy and an Understanding of how media literacy level in Europe Should Be Assessed*. Brussels: European Commission. http://ec.europa.eu/culture/media/literacy/docs/studies/eavi_study_assess_crit_media_lit_levels_europe_finrep.pdf.

Di Croce, D. (2009). *Media Literacy. Teacher Resource Guide*. Canadian Broadcasting Corporation.

European Commission (2011). *Testing and Refining Criteria to Assess Media Literacy Levels in Europe. Final Report*. http://ec.europa.eu/culture/media/media-content/media-literacy/studies/final-report-ml-study-2011.pdf

European Commission (2009). *Recomendación de la Comisión sobre la alfabetización mediática en el entorno digital para una industria audiovisual y de contenidos más competitiva y una sociedad del conocimiento incluyente*. Brussels. http://ec.europa.eu/culture/media/literacy/docs/recom/c_2009_6464_es.pdf

European Commission (2007). *Un planteamiento europeo de la alfabetización mediática en el entorno digital*. Brussels http://ec.europa.eu/culture/media/literacy/docs/com/es.pdf

European Commission (2001). Informe sobre los futuros objetivos precisos de los sistemas europeos. http://europa.eu/legislation_summaries/education_training_youth/general_framework/c11049_es.htm

European Commission (1997). Aprender en la sociedad de la información. Plan de acción para una iniciativa europea de educación (1996-1998).

Frau-Meigs, D. (Ed.) (2006) *Media Education. A kit for teachers, students, parents and professionals*. Paris: UNESCO.

Wilson, C., Grizzle, A., Tuazon, R., Akyempong, K., & Cheung, C.K. (Eds.) (2011). *Alfabetización mediática e informacional. Currículum para profesores*. Paris: UNESCO.

Kārkliņš, J. (2011). Introduction. In Wilson, C. et al. (Eds.), *Alfabetización mediática e informacional. Curriculum para profesores.* Paris: UNESCO.

Parlamento Europeo y Consejo (2007). Directiva «Servicios de medios audiovisuales sin fronteras». Unión Europea. http://europa.eu/legislation_summaries/audiovisual_and_media/l24101_es.htm

Pérez-Tornero, J. M. (2007). Educación en medios para Jóvenes, en Sevilla. *Comunicar, 28,* 125-132.

Steeves, V., & Webster, C. (2008). *Closing the Barn Door: The Effect of Parental Supervision on Canadian Children's Online Privacy.* Bulletin of Science Technology Society, 28 (1), 4-19.

Taylor, A. (2001). Young Canadians in a Wired World: How Canadian Kids Are Using the Internet. *Education Canada,* 41 (3). www.cea-ace.ca/sites/default/files/EdCan-2001-v41-n3-Taylor.pdf

UNESCO (2011). *Declaración de Braga.* Braga. www.cca.eca.usp.br/noticia/756

UNESCO (2007). *Agenda de París o 12 Recomendaciones para la Educación en Medios.* Paris. www.ifap.ru/pr/2007/070625ba.pdf

UNESCO (2002). *Seminario de Sevilla sobre Educación en Medios.* Sevilla.

UNESCO (1999). *Educating for the Media and the Digital Age.* (Conference). Viena. http://edu.of.ru/attach/17/3485.pdf

UNESCO (1990). *Declaración sobre educación para todos y marco de acción para satisfacer las necesidades básicas de aprendizaje.* Jomtien. www.oei.es/quipu/marco_jomtien.pdf

UNESCO (1982). *Declaración de Grünwald sobre la educación relativa a los medios de comunicación.* Grünwald. www.unesco.org/education/pdf/ MEDIA_S.pdf

Spain: 3 Key Aspects of Media Education in the Context of a Recession

José Manuel Pérez Tornero & Mireia Pi

A study by the Department of Communication and Education of the Universitat Autònoma de Barcelona (UAB) (Pérez Tornero & Martínez Cerdá, 2013) on the comparative development of media literacy in Europe place Spain, as a country, in an average position. In short, it is distant from the leading Northern European countries, close to the large central countries, and in line with the countries of Southern Europe.

The same study emphasized the fact that the evolution of media literacy in most European countries was equal between 2005 and 2010. All media literacy indices (Celot & Pérez Tornero, 2009; European Media Literacy Observatory, 2014) showed constant improvement, especially regarding access to, and availability of, technologies, and less so for factors related to critical understanding. In this context of general progress, Spain, in a phase of *moderate* progress, had moved up several positions and begun to assert its own strategy of media literacy policy (Martínez, 2010; Bernabéu Morón, 2011; Prats, Aguaded-Gómez & García-Matilla, 2012) linked to education, but also built on a much wider context (Pérez Tornero, 2009).

However, the Spanish economic recession – the severity of which has been felt since 2009 – has slowed this progress and has given rise to the appearance of serious problems that are threatening the levels of media literacy achieved. Some of the achievements reached in media literacy, which seemed to have become established in Spain, have since been diluted and the general media education system is currently in danger.

It is still early to statistically analyse the effects of the recession, and therefore to study its consequences. However, from a qualitative perspective, the most acute problems can be described.

An average development in media literacy

A study on media literacy indicators, carried out by an international consortium in which the UAB assumed scientific direction (Celot & Pérez Tornero, 2009), noted three main areas in media literacy: a) *environmental factors* – media availability, on the one hand, and the context of media literacy, on the other. The latter encompasses: media education policy, regulation of the subject by authorities, the role of civil society and that of the media industry. Next is the area related to b) *individual competences* – which is itself divided into use, on the one hand, and critical understanding, on the other. And, finally c) *social competences* – which is divided into three subgroups: participation, social relations and content creation.

Taking all these factors into consideration, the development of media literacy in Spain was considered to be moderate. In more specific terms, this meant that:

- The possibilities of accessing media, and especially the Internet, were improving and were available to nearly the whole population – yet not reaching the level of development of Northern European countries .

- An incipient strategy to promote media literacy existed: on the one hand, media literacy was part of the educational curriculum; on the other, teacher training in that discipline was being launched, and some resource centres were being developed.

- At the same time, certain regulation strategies were also being put into place to promote media literacy.

- Lastly, civic activity related to media literacy was growing: on the one hand in civic organisations (more companies with more activity; acceleration of all media-related communication activities), and on the other, more participation and more creation of content by citizens.

Moving from an average level of development to the next level and reaching the level of Northern European countries was just a question of maintaining current efforts and strengthening the system. However, the recession and its consequences seem to have curbed improvement of the system.

Characteristics and scope of the recession in Spain

Before delving into an analysis of the dimensions of the future of media literacy in Spain, it is important to get an overview of the recession. Although the origin of the recession in Spain is economic, the most striking aspect is the fact that it has spread to other areas: political, institutional and social, thus acquiring a more global nature. As regards the economy, the figures are conclusive.

Spain went into a recession in 2008 and was not able to begin to improve the situation until 2010. During that period, it lost some of the positions it had gained with regard to other European countries. As regards the country's Gross Domestic Product (GDP), it went from being 5% above the average to 5% below the average; thus losing 10 relative points[1].

During those same years, unemployment reached record highs, affecting 6,200,000 people, and in 2013, 27.16% of the population was unemployed – in 2007, a mere 7.95% of the population was unemployed. In this context, the most significant and worrying aspect is that the largest proportion of unemployment is amongst those under 25 years of age (57.2%), in a country with an already ageing population.

The social consequences were felt immediately. The at-risk-of-poverty rate surged dramatically in Spain, reaching 27% in 2012 (Eurostat, 2013), compared to more advanced European countries where the figures oscillated between 9% and 11%, positioning Spain amongst the worst in Europe.

At the same time, income inequality in Spain worsened and the *poverty gap* reached 30.6%, while the average amongst other European countries was 23.2%.

In addition, in line with all of this, state social spending and the funding allocated to education decreased radically: the investment in education in 2009 was 5.1% of the GDP, and this reduced to 4.7% in 2011. There were reductions in the number of teachers, in the number of grants and amount of funds granted and in aids for school supplies and canteens, whilst tuition fees increased.

The recession also struck the media and telecommunication industry, forcing the closure of or drastic reduction in several mass media[2], including printed, radio and audio-visual media, in both private and public sectors.

The consequences of the recession could also be felt in the civic sector. A growing indifference towards institutions, especially political ones, had emerged. Disclosure of numerous corruption cases generated a general feeling that a large proportion of the institutions had already lost the legitimacy and authority they had previously enjoyed. This climate of tension gave rise to movements of protest such as the 15 M, sporadic community movements and new political options, leading to a new wave of social and communicative activism.

How does all of this affect media literacy? To perform a comprehensive analysis, we will look at three extensive areas related to media education.

1. The development of the media education curricula

2. Teacher training

3. Infrastructures and digital services in educational centres

Curriculum development

In 2006, the educational curriculum in Spain introduced, although not explicitly, media education in teaching[3]. The EMEDUS[4] report about Spain completes this perspective: with regard to the curriculum in compulsory education, the report points out that the Organic Law on Education, adopted in 2006 and changed in 2013, stipulates that media literacy was within the sphere of "digital competence" and was one of the key competences (Tucho, 2008). However, the focus of this incorporation of media education was notably technological and was geared, almost exclusively, towards new media and ICTs. A more systematic and advanced approach was needed.

Subsequently, legal reforms were made, yet they did not lead to great progress in terms of media education. The Organic Law on Education was changed by the 2013 LOMCE (Organic Law for the Improvement of the Quality of Education). In this new law, the legislators suggested reinforcing perseverance in studies – what they referred to as the "culture of effort" – and bringing education closer to the requirements of the job market. As regards media education, although the critical training of students and the educational implementation of ICTs[5] were introduced as main objectives, the competence objectives set by the previous law, which were exclusively calculated in terms of digital competences, were neither systematized nor altered.

The most notable changes implemented by the LOMCE refer to the inclusion of certain subjects linked to ICTs and some optional subjects related to the audiovisual field in the curriculum. It is important to reiterate that, at this juncture, there is still no complete curricular systematization of media education, although recommendations and directives promoting media literacy have been passed at the European level. A purely instrumental and technological one-sided approach to media education still overwrites a more global, critical and semiotic approach.

The recession has therefore accentuated the Spanish legislating spirit – as regards media education – what could be called "technological and professional determination". As a result, the pragmatic and utilitarian nature of media literacy has been accentuated and consequently, its critical, cultural and civic dimensions remain marginalized.

Teacher training

At the start of the recession, in 2009, teacher training in Spain notoriously neglected media education.

As regards formal education, both primary and secondary school teachers barely received training in a subject called "educational technology" which, as its title indicates, adopts an instrumental approach to communicative tools and does not lead to the global approach introduced by media literacy. It is true that educational technology teachers, especially in faculties of education and teacher training, have gradually moved towards media literacy. This has been demonstrated in many international congresses on media education and digital competence[6]. Teachers of educational technology – as well as teachers and researchers in the communication field and other related fields – from throughout Spain played a significant role in the congresses. It is important to note that some Master's courses, focusing on educational technology, are beginning to open up the field for media education: Master's courses such as "Digital Technologies and the Knowledge Society" at the National Distance Education University[7].

The involvement of professors of didactics from the faculties of education regarding matters related to media literacy has also been significant. In fact, recently, the University Association of Professors of Didactics of Social Sciences (AUPCDS) dedicated considerable attention to mass media. The fruit of their collective work has recently been released: *Medios de comunicación y pensamiento crítico* (Mass media and critical thinking) (Díaz Matarranz, Santisteban Fernández & Cascarejo, 2013).

In this context and on a more positive note, it must be stated that the Master of Communication and Education at the UAB, created in 1994, has been promoting postgraduate training in media education for over twenty years[8]. Subsequently, other postgraduate studies have been created, namely the "Audio-visual and education communication"[9] course at the University of Huelva.

However, the translation of these initiatives into a firm curricular and systematic framework within media education, in initial training, is still a distant reality.

The authorities in charge of teacher training have been more concerned with the organization of courses focused on specific digital tools than on a global approach to the phenomenon of media literacy.

However, the recession has resulted in significant changes.

Firstly, the Ministry of Education launched a project aimed at creating a "Common digital competence framework for teachers" (Spain – Ministry of Education, Culture and Sport, 2013),[10] which seeks to establish standards of skills and knowledge for all teachers involved in education. It is the first time such an effort has been made in Spain, bringing together the various authorities with power in the area.

The common framework aims to serve as a reference for teacher training and promote the acquisition of knowledge in digital competence. It is true that it does not adopt a global approach similar to that of media literacy, nor does it entirely abandon the instrumental technological approach, but it does represent a step forward and an important coordination factor when establishing training policies related to media education.

Additionally, yet on a less positive note, the recession has affected the sustainability of postgraduate studies. University grants have been reduced, as have contributions to training from the authorities. University tuition fees have increased and the lifespan of courses and Master's programmes in media education training has suffered, as has occurred with other postgraduate studies.

Thus, we can state that, in the context of the recession, Spain has immersed itself in the theoretical definition of media education teacher training policies, but at the same time, in practical terms, resources and initiatives have begun to dwindle and are increasingly scarce. The question is whether, as the recession continues, all the theoretical achievements will come to nothing.

(3) Infrastructures and digital educational services

Around 2009, Spain had achieved a notable technological development in educational centres, as noted by some European studies (European Commission, 2013). However, the recession has meant an important reduction in the economic resources allocated to the technological and media transformation of education. This has slowed down some of the most important projects put in place.

The project Escuela 2.0[11] (2.0 School), which had promoted access to a laptop computer for all students, has been cut. Likewise, investment in technological resources in the centres has also suffered.

The project Escuela 2.0 has been replaced by another called Plan de Cultura Digital (Digital culture plan) (2012) [12] – which promotes the creation of actions such as: a) Connectivity of schools; b) Interoperability and standards; c) Common spaces with open contents: d) General catalogue of payable educational resources: Punto Neutro[13], and e) Digital teaching competence. However, during 2014, the dismissal or resignation of most of those in charge has led to the overall failure of the project.

The consequences of this situation are clear: there are not as many opportunities to move forward in the use of technological systems in education as there were a few years ago. All of this hinders the development of media education.

Paradoxically, in this critical context, some initiatives have emerged that – without the economic backing of previous plans – are gradually leading to and promoting the implementation of new digital services linked to new media competences.

We are referring to the implementation of digital textbooks within education. This phenomenon started in the Autonomous Community of Catalonia and soon reached other communities. It received the support of public authorities with technological improvement in educational centres, and led to an acceleration of media capacities within schools.

Along with this "institutional" launch some publishers have followed suit[14]. Traditional textbook publishers are finding themselves obliged to provide digital complements, and even digital service platforms, which are successively becoming more sophisticated. Gradually, new digital platforms of educational content and services are becoming established, and in many cases, are replacing the use of textbooks. This has immediate consequences for the media skills of students and teaching staff, who are forced to acquire informative and communicative skills and to introduce new cooperative and participation work practices. Therefore, unintentionally, a situation of economic hardship has accelerated the digitalization of education and the acquisition of communicative competences.

Paradoxically, the recession has served as a catalyst for change. In Spain, at present, subscribing to a platform of educational content and its subsequent updates is cheaper than purchasing textbooks, for both personal users and the administration. For this reason, many authorities and centres have started promoting what they call the "digital schoolbag", that is, the intensive use of digital resources in education with the aim of, partially or completely, replacing printed textbooks. Many centres have abandoned paper, and the authorities have created services to facilitate access to the digital world.

For example, the launch, by the Ministry of Education, of a platform called *Punto Neutro* to sell educational contents has helped to boost the digital immersion of the educational community. Other initiatives geared towards promoting open educational resources and teacher training in the subject should be understood in the same way.

Research reveals that teaching staff are open and willing to accept digital transformation, its new tools and particularly digital books (Pérez-Tornero & Pi, 2013).

The ambivalent effect of the recession is palpable. On the one hand, the cuts have become a barrier to access to ICTs and hinder progress in media education. Yet on the other hand, by encouraging the use of cheaper and more competitive services and technology, the cuts have catalysed progress in the form of adopting digital services – such as digital textbooks – thus encouraging the acquisition of new media skills. The empirical outcome of the situation will only be assessable in the next few years.

An undefined panorama

The media education curriculum, teacher training and access to digital technology and services are the three pillars of media education which have been significantly affected by the recession. On the one hand, economic shortages and cuts in investment have slowed down some of the most significant and promising lines of action in media education policy in Spain. More specifically, we are referring to the direct aids used to promote infrastructures in the educational centres and the direct or indirect aids aimed at didactic material. In the same regard, technological and utilitarian pressures have boosted the instrumental focus of media education and have ignored almost everything that was not linked to ITCs. All of this has occurred to the detriment of a more systemic and global construction of the paradigm that is media education and has represented a loss for the humanistic dimension of media literacy (Pérez Tornero & Varis, 2010).

However, the scarcity has boosted some processes which have been beneficial to media education. For example, digital textbooks and the resulting acquisition of new competences have found a catalyst for their expansion in the scarcity of assistance and the economic instability. The same has occurred with light technological equipment and the open resource platforms which competed in price with printed textbooks. All of this was driven by the growth of the cooperative economy, which emerged as an idea in the educational community.

Perhaps the recession has also reinforced the feeling of community among teachers, as well as their capacity to come together, take action and promote changes, thus bringing renewed energy to the sector.

The scarcity of economic resources is, most probably, what has driven the political sector to design action strategies aimed at helping to systematize efforts which until then had remained dispersed. This is how the new common framework of digital competence for teachers and the Plan de Cultura Digital (Project for Digital Culture) are perceived.

All of this has occurred in an atmosphere of communicative mobilization, especially in the educational community which, faced with the recession and job insecurity, has had to make its voice heard. In these sectors, there is increasing enthusiasm and optimism concerning technological change and the appeal to criticism currently represented by media education.

However, all of this is taking place in a panorama of doubts, uncertainties and scarce resources, which jeopardize a systematic policy of media literacy – a panorama which will only become clearer with the passage of time.

Notes

1. A good analysis of the recession in Spain (Juan, 2010) is accessible on Wikipedia http://es.wikipedia.org/wiki/Crisis_econ%C3%B3mica_espa%C3%B1ola_de_2008-2014
2. http://www.apmadrid.es/noticias/generales/informe-de-la-profesion-periodistica-2013-11151-empleos-perdidos-y-284-medios-cerrados-desde-2008; http://www.prnoticias.com/index.php/marketing/1103/20125006-2013-iel-ano-en-que-se-freno-la-caida-de-la-publicidad-prensa-ha-perdido-un-60-y-tv-un-48#Red1Y57IiEOy1QXs
3. Bernabéu Morón, N. (Coord.)(2011). To consult the law see, http://www.boe.es/buscar/pdf/2006/BOE-A-2006-7899-consolidado.pdf
4. http://eumedus.com/index.php/reports/reports-drafted-from-uab/178-report-formal-education-spain
5. http://www.boe.es/boe/dias/2013/12/10/pdfs/BOE-A-2013-12886.pdf
6. The first took place in Segovia (http://www.educacionmediatica.es/congreso2011), and the second in Barcelona (http://www.uoc.edu/portal/es/symposia/congreso_ludoliteracy2013).
7. http://www.uned.es/ntedu/master/index.htm
8. http://www.gabinetecomunicacionyeducacion.com/
9. http://www.master-educomunicacion.es/

10. http://educalab.es/documents/10180/12809/MarcoComunCompeDigiDoceV2.pdf/e8766a69-d9ba-43f2-afe9-f526f0b34859
11. http://www.ite.educacion.es/escuela-20
12. http://blog.educalab.es/intef/2013/04/16/plan-de-cultura-digital-en-la-escuela
13. http://educalab.es/recursos/punto-neutro
14. One of the most developed is that of the Planeta publishing group (aulaPlaneta), but there are others like Digitaltext or, simply, traditional publishers who are broadening their offers with digital resources and beginning to generate virtual educational services: *Aula Virtual* by Santillana, SM Conectados, Vicens Vives, *Espacio Digital GRETA* by Anaya, XTEND, etc.

References

Bernabéu Morón, N. (Coord.) (2011). *Alfabetización mediática y competencias básicas*. Secretaría de Estado de Educación y Formación Profesional. Ministerio de Educación. Publicaciones Mediascopio: Madrid. https://www.educacion.gob.es/documentos/mediascopio/archivos_secciones/156/ccbb.pdf

Celot, P., & Pérez Tornero, J.M. (2009). *Study on Assessment Criteria for Media Literacy Levels*. Bruselas: Comisión Europea. http://ec.europa.eu/culture/library/studies/literacy-criteria-report_en.pdf

Díaz Matarranz, J. J., Santisteban Fernández, A., & Cascarejo A. (Eds.) (2013). *Medios de comunicación y pensamiento crítico*. Alcalá de Henares: Servicio de Publicaciones de la Universidad de Alcalá.

España. Ministerio de Educación, Cultura y Deporte (2013). *Marco Común de Competencia digital docente, V 2.0. (Plan de cultura digital en la escuela)*. http://educalab.es/documents/10180/12809/MarcoComunCompeDigiDoceV2.pdf/e8766a69-d9ba-43f2-afe9-f526f0b34859

European Media Literacy Observatory (2014). http://eumedus.com/index.php/homepage/news/194-check-the-emedus-numbers.

European Commission (2013). *Survey on Schools: ICT in Education. Benchmarking Access, Attitudes on Technology in Europe's schools*. https://ec.europa.eu/digital-agenda/sites/digital-agenda/files/KK-31-13-401-EN-N.pdf

Eurostat, Estadísticas sobre la distribución de la renta (2013). http://epp.eurostat.ec.europa.eu/statistics_explained/index.php/Income_distribution_statistics/es#Tasa_y_umbral_de_riesgo_de_pobreza

Instituto Nacional de Tecnologías Educativas y de Formación del Profesorado (2013). *Plan de Cultura Digital en la Escuela*. http://blog.educalab.es/intef/2013/04/16/plan-de-cultura-digital-en-la-escuela/

Juan, J. (2010). *Nada es gratis: como evitar la década perdida tras la década prodigiosa*. Barcelona: Destino.

Martínez, J. M. M. (2010). *Retos y perspectivas de la educación mediática en España. Proyecto Mediascopio Prensa. La lectura de la prensa escrita en el aula*. Madrid: Ministerio de Educación.

Pérez Tornero, J. M. (2009). El nuevo horizonte europeo de la alfabetización mediática. *Telos*, 79, 6-7. http://ddd.uab.cat/pub/artpub/2009/106913/telos_a2009n79p6.pdf

Pérez Tornero, J. M., & Martínez Cerdá, J. F. (2013). *Midiendo la Alfabetización Mediática en Europa 2005-2010*. Barcelona: Observatorio Milion. http://www.gabinetecomunicacionyeducacion.com/files/adjuntos/Yearbook%202005-2010.pdf

Pérez Tornero, J. M. & Pi, M. (2013). *La integración de las TIC y los libros digitales en la educación*. Barcelona: aulaPlaneta.

Pérez Tornero, J. M. & Varis, T. (2010). *Media Literacy and New Humanism*. UNESCO Institute for Information Technologies in Education. http://iite.unesco.org/pics/publications/en/files/3214678.pdf

Pérez Tornero, J. M. (2010). *Promover la alfabetización mediática es ya una obligación legal en España para los poderes públicos y los medios audiovisuales*. http://jmtornero.wordpress.com/2010/04/03/promover-la-alfabetizacion-mediatica-es-ya-obligacion-legal-de-los-poderes-publicos-y-de-los-medios-audiovisuales-en-espana/

Martínez, J. M. M. (2010). *Retos y perspectivas de la educación mediática en España*. Ministerio de Educación: Madrid.

Prats, J. F., Aguaded-Gómez, I., & García-Matilla, A. (2012). La competencia mediática de la ciudadanía española: dificultades y retos. *ICONO* 14, 10(3), 23-42.

Tucho, F. (2008). La educación en comunicación en la LOE y sus decretos de Enseñanzas Mínimas. *Comunicar,* 31, 547-553. doi: 10.3916/c31-2008-03-049

An Overview of Practices in Spain

Media Literacy in Spain

A Brief Panorama and a Good Practices Proposal

Rosa García-Ruiz & Vicent Gozálvez Pérez

The growing interest in media education in Spain is bringing great advances in the comprehensive training of the citizenry, thanks to the involvement and commitment of many of the agents in the educational and communication spheres. To immerse ourselves in the origin, objectives and results of these shared interests, we present an overview of both the communication and education fields, beginning with the work published by the European Commission (2007), by addressing the initiatives and guidelines that will set the stage for the presentation of good practices in media education.

Media education in formal education

From the education system's General Organic Law of 1990 to the Organic Law of Education of 2006, many advances have been made in relation to media education. Media education becomes a fundamental and transversal element in the curriculum, complemented by digital and technological competency in response to the comprehensive training needed in the new information and communication society, so that citizens will be ethically responsible participants, critical and self-sufficient when facing new messages and the media.

The application of the proposed curricula in the classroom is backed by various initiatives from the public administration, which emphasize an interest in ameliorating teacher training in this field. Examples of these initiatives include digital publications from the Ministry of Education[1], Culture and Sport, such as "Media Literacy at school 2.0" or "Good Practices 2.0 Web"; "Challenges and perspectives of media education in Spain" and "Media literacy and basic competencies", within the *Mediascopio Press Project*, which aim to favor reading of the printed press in classrooms. Other projects from the Ministry offer diverse digital resources for media education, such as "Advertising, industry of desire", "Information on TV", "Reality television: intimacy as entertainment" and "Communication Channel", all of which are available on the Ministry's website.

In February 2013, the "Digital Agenda for Spain"[2] was published, aiming to achieve the objectives set by the European Commission in its Digital Agenda for Europe, 2010[3], which established a series of principles and actions to contribute to facilitating the media literacy of citizens trying to get the most out of digital technologies.

The university also offers prestigious research groups and projects related to training in media competencies. These groups, among which the *Grupo Comunicar* and the *Cabinet of Communication and Education* are prominent, constitute a model of interdisciplinarity and the advancement of the scientific community due to their great contribution to the improvement of media education in the citizenry. A few examples of the scientific meetings organized in Spain, with valuable contributions from experts from abroad, are the first and second International Congress of Media Education and Digital Competence, held in 2011 and 2013, respectively; the first Euro-Iberoamerican Congress ATEI Media literacy an digital cultures, held in 2010; and the first and second International Congress of Video games and Education, held in 2012 and 2013, respectively.

The universities, concerned about the training of competent education professionals in the media, offer postgraduate degrees such as "Masters in Communication and Audio-visual Education" (Huelva University and International University of Andalucia) and "International Masters in Communication and Education" (Autonomous University of Barcelona). Specific university courses, such as "Communication, Education and Society in the digital context" in the Marketing and Public Relations program at the University of Valladolid and the "Education and Communications Media" as part of the "Masters in Ethics and Democracy" at the University of Valencia, have been created. As for the university setting, there are a few prestigious journals, such as *Comunicar*[4], which are eager to contribute to the advancement of scientific knowledge. Other relevant journals include *Pixel Bit*[5], *Icono 14*[6], *Edmetic*[7], *Sphera Publica*[8], and *Revista Mediterranea de Comunicacion Social*[9].

The research projects led by university groups and backed by external financing converge in the common interest of facilitating media education of high quality, where the different protagonists are to be involved. Among these projects, the Grupo Comunicar[10] and Kids & com[11] associations, which include more than 15 research groups, are highlighted. The project that currently has the largest scope is entitled "Competency in audio-visual communication in a digital environment. A diagnostic on the needs of three social environments"[12]. This project, run by more than 30 universities both public and private, investigates the levels of media competency in mandatory education, university education and professional communicators. A subproject, related to mandatory education (EDU201-21395-C03-03), is being replicated in Italy and in various countries in South America such as Colombia, Ecuador, Chile, Argentina and Brazil, with encouraging results in the improvement of Educommunication at the international level. Currently, the results – attained after the application and analysis of diverse tools such as online questionnaires, interviews and group discussions, where the media competency levels of different collectives, such as students ranging from daycare to high school, personnel from every educational stage, families with school-aged children, adults older than 55, and private citizens in jail – are being disseminated.

Media education in other environments

In 2010, the Audio-Visual Communication Law was approved in Spain. This law legislates and regulates all aspects related to communication media, and it is from this, and under the auspices of the Spanish Constitution, that the "Self-regulation code of television content and children" was created, with the intent of making compatible the values that form the current social and democratic rule of law: the freedom of expression, respecting the personal rights of the private citizen; the interdiction of violence; the elimination of discrimination and intolerance; and the protection of children and youth. The code establishes a series of general principles to improve the efficiency of the legal protection of minors with respect to television programming shown from 6pm to 10pm.

Aside from this, the different Spanish Autonomous Communities have established their own competencies in social communication media, creating their own Audio-Visual Councils. Examples include Catalonia, Andalucia, Navarre, Galicia and Madrid; the aim is to safeguard the rights of citizens, guaranteeing that the content shown on television and radio as well as that related to advertising suit the present legislation, as well as to protect freedom of expression. Currently, only two of these Councils are still active, and a national Audio-Visual Council does not yet exist, unlike in other European countries.

There are also other initiatives being developed in Spain that are remarkably contributing to the improvement of the media literacy of the people. Among them, we draw attention to "The Madrid Declaration" (2005)[13], an initiative that tries to link communication and education by asking media and schools to responsibly collaborate in the improvement of media literacy. "Teleduca"[14] is an independent association that tries to improve communication competency. The "European Observatory of Children's Television", the "Deontology code for children's advertisement and advertising conduct", the "Green Book on the protection of minors and human dignity in audio-visual and information services" have also been created.

This growing interest for educommunication also extends to public television, where, for the first time, a program concerned with both environments converging for the education of the citizenry is being aired. "La aventura del saber"[15] gives the general public the opportunity to receive audio-visual material produced by the Comunicar group. Examples of these programs are "Los Bubuskiski" and "El Monosabio", as well as other audio-visual "pills" that try to contribute to the diffusion of education in a media-driven culture, which is regarded as more necessary than ever (Aguaded Gómez, 2014).

Good practices in media education in Spain

In Spain as well as other countries, we have seen how the implementation of communication technology in classrooms (computers, digital blackboards, Internet connections, etc.) was a necessary but not sufficient condition for attaining good practices in media education; the attitude, training and previous beliefs of the teaching staff are also fundamental in making this possible (Sugar, Crawley & Fine, 2004; Tirado & Aguaded Gómez, 2014). In the year 2000, there were an average of 23.7 students per computer in the classroom, which is higher than the European average. However, in 2011 this relation was inverted: the average number of students per computer was three, as compared to five in Europe (Pérez-Tornero & Pi, 2013). Something similar has occurred with Internet connectivity and the addition of digital blackboards at educational centers. Does this mean that the implementation of the ICT (Information and Communication Technologies) has automatically led to good practices in media education?

Obviously not in every case. However, there are many pioneering centers that excel in the use of communication technology according to more collaborative educational methodologies, following the criteria set by CSCL (Computer Supported Collaborative Learning) (Elboj, Puigdellívol, Soler & Valls, 2006; Stahl, Koschamann & Suthers, 2006), as well as the Learning Communities methods. This use leads to what we understand as "good practices" in media education: those that encourage the pedagogic, cooperative and civil use of media and new technologies. For example, since 2003-2004 the rural school of Ariño[16] (Teruel) has made a great effort to re-formulate learning in a cooperative way, with proposals such as the "Sierra de Arcos" school radio, a school television station, the press workshop "Hola de prensa", the creation of blogs, and the use of tablet and notebook computers, etc. Their innovative proposals, which closely link education with communication and collaborative interaction, have received the "Computer World" prize as well as the "Smart-dim" prize for innovative education with digital blackboards (2005-2006).

The María Auxiliadora de Santander (Cantabria)[17] school has become a leader in the application of the so-called Web 2.0, combining educational technology with communication media (radio and television) as a didactic resource that facilitates student learning, thanks to their innovative curricular proposal (Aguaded Gómez & Pérez Rodríguez, 2006). Among other things, it has won first place in the "Apadrina un monumento" (2013) contest and the seal of "Good TIC practices in education" from the Espiral Association (2012), and was a finalist for the "Web Cantabria 2013" and "SIMO, Best work for Projects category" (2013) awards, thanks to projects in which students become "prosumers", meaning not only media and audio-visual consumers but also content creators, defined as those having a critical, creative, responsible and democratic perspective (Sánchez & Contreras, 2012; García-Ruiz, Diego & Berlanga, 2013).

As we understand it, these cases provide clear evidence that good practices in the media education sphere exist; practices that are, in fact, extending to many educational centers in the country (Casanova & Pavón, 2010), and that are a great contribution to the development of media competency in the citizenry (Aguaded Gómez, 2012; Gozálvez, 2013).

Notes

1. Ministerio de Educación (Instituto Nacional de Tecnologías Educativas y de Formación del Profesorado) http://www.ite.educacion.es/
2. Ministerio de Industria, Energía y Turismo (2013). *Agenda Digital para España*. http://www.agendadigital.gob.es/agenda-digital/recursos/Recursos/1.%20Versi%C3%B3n%20definitiva/Agenda_Digital_para_Espana.pdf
3. European Commission (2010). Digital Agenda for Europe. https://ec.europa.eu/digital-agenda/digital-agenda-europe
4. Revista Comunicar http://www.revistacomunicar.com/
5. Revista Pixel Bit http://acdc.sav.us.es/pixelbit/
6. Revista Icono 14 http://www.icono14.net/ojs/index.php/icono14
7. Revista Edmetic http://www.edmetic.es/revistaedmetic/
8. Revista Shera Pública http://sphera.ucam.edu/index.php/sphera-01
9. Revista Mediterránea de Comunicación Social http://mediterranea-comunicacion.org/
10. Grupo Comunicar http://www.grupocomunicar.com/
11. Asociación Kids & com http://www.infanciaycomunicacion.org/
12. Proyecto EDU2010-21395-C03-03 http://www.competenciamediatica.es
13. www.uned.es/ntedu/espanol/novedades/Declaracion_Madrid.doc
14. Teleduca http://www.teleduca.org/
15. http://www.rtve.es/alacarta/videos/la-aventura-del-saber/aventura-del-saber-20130528 -0930-169/1842017/
16. http://e-ducativa.catedu.es/44004720/sitio/
17. www.salesianossantander.org

References

Aguaded Gómez, J.I. (2012). La competencia mediática, una acción educativa inaplazable. *Comunicar, 39*, 7-8.

Aguaded Gómez, J.I. (2014). Desde la infoxicación al derecho a la comunicación. *Comunicar, 42*, 7-8.

Aguaded Gómez, J.I., & Pérez Rodríguez, M.A. (2006). Diseño de programas didácticos para integrar los medios y las tecnologías en el curriculum escolar. In J. Salinas, J.I. Aguaded Gómez & J.

Cabero (Coords.), *Tecnologías para la educación. Diseño, producción y evaluación de medios para la formación docente* (pp. 69-87). Madrid: Alianza Editorial.

Casanova, J., & Pavón, F. (2010). Las TIC en los centros de educación obligatoria: hacia las comunidades de aprendizaje. *Fuentes, 10,* 124-139.

European Commission (2007). *Current trends and approaches to media literacy in europe.*http://ec.europa.eu/culture/media/media-content/medialiteracy/studies/spain.pdf

Elboj, C., Puigdellívol, I., Soler, M., & Valls, R. (2006). *Comunidades de Aprendizaje. Transformar la educación.* Barcelona: Graó.

García-Ruiz, R., Diego, R., & Berlanga, I. (2013). La educación mediática en Educación Mediática y el trabajo por proyectos. *II Congreso Internacional de Educación Mediática y Competencia Digital. Barcelona, 14 y 15 de noviembre.* http://www.uoc.edu/portal/es/symposia/congreso_ludoliteracy2013/programa/ACTAS_EDUMED_2013.pdf.

General Organic Law *n° 7/2010,* March 31st. Boletín Oficial del Estado n° 79 – Jefatura del Estado. Madrid.

General Organic Law *n° 1/1990,* October 3rd. Boletín Oficial del Estado n° 238 – Jefatura del Estado. Madrid.

Gozálvez, V. (2013). *Ciudadanía mediática. Una mirada educativa.* Madrid: Dykinson.

Organic Law of Education n° 2/2006, May 3rd. Boletín Oficial del Estado n° 106 – Jefatura del Estado. Madrid.

Pérez-Tornero, J. M., & Pi, M. (Coords.) (2013). *La integración de las TIC y los libros digitales en la educación.* Barcelona: Editorial Planeta, SAU.

Sánchez, J., & Contreras, P. (2012). De cara al prosumidor. *Icono 14,* 3(10), 62-84.

Stahl, G., Koschmann, T., & Suthers, D. (2006). Computer-supported collaborative learning: An historical perspective. En R. K. Sawyer (Ed.), *Cambridge handbook of the learning sciences* (pp. 409-426). Cambridge, UK: Cambridge University Press.

Sugar, W., Crawley, F., & Fine, B. (2004). Examining Teachers' Decisions to Adopt new Technology. *Educational Technology and Society, 7*(4), 201-213.

Tirado, R., & Aguaded Gómez, J. I. (2014). Influencia de las creencias del profesorado sobre el uso de la tecnología en el aula. *Revista de Educación, 363.* http://www.revistaeducacion.mec.es/doi/363_179.pdf

Media Education as a Failing

Joan Ferrés Prats, Maria-Jose Masanet & Saúl Blanco

Shortcomings in the media competence of citizens

In a social and cultural environment where a high percentage of communication is mediated, media education (ME) is now more necessary than ever to
guarantee the comprehensive training of citizens and the establishment of a
fully democratic society.

Yet this need is only theoretical. In 2008, while the European Parliament
urged the incorporation of ME into formal and non-formal education, a team of
researchers from 17 Spanish universities, one from each autonomous community,
were working on determining the level of media competence among citizens.

This research stemmed from previous work carried out under sponsorship
from the *Catalan Audiovisual Council* (CAC), in which over 60 Ibero-American
ME experts were consulted to define the six dimensions this education should
cover: languages, technology, production and diffusion processes, interaction
processes, ideology and values, and aesthetics (Ferrés Prats, 2006; Ferrés Prats
& Piscitelli, 2012).

A total of 6,626 questionnaires were distributed during the quantitative phase,
while the qualitative phase involved 31 in-depth interviews and 28 focus groups.
In each autonomous community the sample was segmented according to three
variables: age (young people aged 16-24, adults aged -64 and the elderly, over
65), gender, and level of education (people without education, and those with
primary education, secondary education and higher education).

The results are significant. The people surveyed achieved a passing mark
only in topics related to the technology dimension, in which the percentage of
passes exceeded that of fails (61.6% vs 38.4%). The lowest mark was obtained
in questions about the dimensions of languages as well as ideology and values,

with 98.1% and 93% of fails, respectively. The aesthetics dimension questions also saw a very low score (90.2% of fails), as did production and diffusion processes (81.3% of fails) and interaction (76.2% of fails). The overall average test score was 2.45, a long way from a 5, which represents a pass.

Thus, huge gaps were demonstrated in most dimensions of media competence (Ferrés Prats et al. 2011; Aguaded Gómez et al., 2011; Ferrés Prats & Santibáñez, 2011; Ferrés Prats, Aguaded Gómez & García, 2012; Marta & Grandío, 2013; Masanet Jordá, Contreras & Ferrés Prats, 2013).

Shortcomings in university education provision

The revelation of these failings prompted the initiation of the R&D&I project funded by the Ministry of Economy and Competitiveness, *University education in light of media competence in a digital environment*. Its aim was to detect the presence or absence of ME in education and communication degree teaching guides syllabuses. Subjects directly related to ME were analysed, understanding as such those that include at least four of the six aforementioned dimensions (Masanet Jordá & Ferrés Prats, 2013).

Of the 252 degrees offered by Spanish universities in the education area only 53 (21.03%) have a directly related subject, and of the 119 degrees in the communication area, only 14 do (11.76%).

Each topic in these subjects' teaching guides was quantified to detect which ME dimensions were included and which were not. In 21.3% of subjects, the languages dimension is overlooked. In another 21.3% no references are made to technology. In 60% there is no interaction process component. The aesthetics dimension is ignored by 84% of these subjects, that of production and diffusion processes by 40%, and ideology and values by 24%.

It is difficult to guarantee media competence in society if most education and communication professionals themselves do not receive training in the subject: there will be serious failings in this competence if the training provided contains gaps such as a lack of knowledge of the codes that govern new languages, a disregard for the encouragement of critical reflection, insufficient learning to manage the mental processes that come into play when interacting with screens, or poor knowledge of what is hidden behind professional and popular production processes.

Shortcomings in the focus of media education
New approach to teaching guides

A semantic analysis was also carried out on the teaching guides for subjects directly related to ME in order to detect gaps and contradictions in relation to several important indicators in the area of neuroscience. If media experience is the result of interaction between a medium and a person, it is not sufficient to analyse just media or messages; the mental processes of the people interacting with them also need to be ascertained and managed.

Quantitative content analysis methodology was applied to 78 teaching guides. A computer tool was also used, which had been designed ad hoc to enable the systematic discovery of the presence or absence of certain categories selected in a collection[1]. The tool enabled the revelation of the terms selected to be quantified, subsequent to having been distributed in semantic fields in a prior investigation (Ferrés Prats, Masanet Jordá, & Marta-Lazo, 2013):

Table 1. Distribution of terms by semantic fields

Semantic field	Terms linked to the semantic field
Cognitive/Rational	Reason/s, rationale/s, to reason, reflection/s, reflective, to reflect, knowledge, to know, to understand, to find out, information, to inform, comprehension, to comprehend, concept/s, opinion/s, thought/s, to think, analysis, analytical
Emotive	Emotion/s, emotive, emotional, to excite, feeling/s, sentimental, to feel, motivation/s, motivator/s, to motivate, attitude/s, attitudinal, desire/s, to desire, pleasure/s, empathy, taste/s, to like, unaware, subconscious
Information/Knowledge	To inform, information, informations, to know, knowledge
Entertainment	Entertainment, to entertain, leisure
Narrative	Story/ies, narration/s
Unconscious	Unconscious, subconscious
Critique	Critical
Evaluation	Value, evaluation, to evaluate, assessment, to assess, evaluative
Critique linked to knowledge	Critical thought/s, critical comprehension, critical analysis, critical reading/s/ reader, critical interpretation/s
Critique linked to attitude	Critical attitude/s, critical posture/s/position/s, critical behaviour/s, critical evaluation/s, critical use/s

Source: Adaptation of table by Ferrés Prats, Masanet Jordá, & Marta-Lazo (2013)

Analysis and Results

Shortcomings in dealing with emotions

This document analysis revealed a polarization in the cognitive and rational semantic field compared to the emotive one. There are 1,867 references linked to the rational semantic field, and only 161 relating to the emotive one.

A total of 37 references to the emotive semantic field were counted, although two guides monopolized 37.84% of these appearances and in the 18 remaining documents (62.16%) there were only one or two references. In other words, a term from the emotive semantic field appeared in only 20 of the 78 guides, which means that in 74.36% there was no presence.

This disproportion is more significant than it might appear, given the importance neuroscience attributes to the emotional part of the brain for the functioning of the rational part. 'Emotions constitute the basis of everything we do, including reasoning' (Maturana & Bloch, 1998, p. 137). 'Some aspects of the process of emotion and feeling are essential for rationality' (Damasio, 1996, p. 10). Perhaps the most definitive expression comes from Jonah Lehrer: 'Reason without emotion is impotent' (Lehrer, 2009, p. 13).

Shortcomings in dealing with entertainment

The scarce attention paid to entertainment is also significant. The expressions *information society* and *knowledge society* appear 52 and 31 times, respectively. There are also 991 references linked to the field of information and knowledge. If we count the terms linked to information only, the number of appearances is high as well: 498 times.

However, terms in the entertainment semantic field appear only 11 times, concentrated in eight documents, in which there are only one or two references. In short, in 89.74% of documents no reference is made to the field of entertainment. It is referred to in 10.26%, but even then receives only minor attention.

The academic world therefore gives precedence to information competence – the ability to seek, analyse, select, organize, compare, synthesize, use and communicate information – while neuromarketing professionals design their strategies based on the conviction that stories are the most effective way to influence the collection of information (Lehrer, 2010: 188; Heath & Heath, 2008, pp. 165-166). Despite these discoveries, ME continues to devote attention almost exclusively to information. The terms *story* and *narration* appear only 12 times.

Shortcomings in dealing with unconsciousness

In the identification of failings, the relationship between conscious and unconscious is also important. In the collection of guides, there is only one reference to the unconscious. This marginalization contrasts with the importance neuroscience attributes to it: 'Freud was right when he defined consciousness as the tip of the mental iceberg' (LeDoux, 1999, p. 20). In neuromarketing, a message is not considered good if it obliges the receiver to consciously deliberate; and it is still not good even if it incites adhesion. A good message must make the customer 'not deliberate, but be anxious to buy or have the product. It is an instinctive act' (Braidot, 2005, p. 450).

Despite these solid positionings, in ME unconscious mental processes are still not catered for: the fact that 'the conscious can only be understood if the unconscious processes that make it possible are studied' (LeDoux 1999, p. 32) is overlooked.

Shortcomings in the conception of critical reflection

The analysis of the guides reveals the importance teachers concede to critique, with the terms linked to this semantic field appearing 380 times. If terms from the field evaluation are added, the total is 852 references.

Yet there is not as much unanimity regarding the conception of critical reflection. Disproportion was observed between the linking of the critical to the cognitive and its link to the attitudinal. There are 52 expressions corresponding to the first semantic field, and only 11 to the second. A total of 82.54% of expressions relate critique to knowledge, and only 14.46% to attitudes.

To summarize, we are confronted by a media competence based on knowledge, while neuroscience has demonstrated that when there is a disassociation between what is thought and what is felt, what is felt invariably comes out on top. For example: people spend more money when they pay by credit card than when they pay in cash (Prelec & Simester, 2001). The knowledge that the expense is the same is irrelevant; perception carries more weight.

In research on the degree of media competence of citizens of Spain (Ferrés et al., 2011), an insufficient ME limited to the cognitive was demonstrated. For example, in an in-depth interview it was shown that a woman was not bothered by an advertisement making blatant commercial use of a woman's body, despite being aware that a stereotype was being employed.

In the words of the neuroscientist Donald Calne (quoted by Roberts, 2005), while emotions lead to action, thoughts only lead to the drawing of conclusions. As educators, do we aim to mobilize people or is it sufficient for us that they draw conclusions?

Final reflection

The failings in the degree of media competence of citizens of Spain are exacerbated not only by the lack of ME in university teaching guides, but also by shortcomings in the focus applied when it is taught (Ferrés Prats, 2014). In short, ME does not only require empowerment: it also needs an overhaul.

Acknowledgements

This study was approved in the call for R&D Projects by the Ministry for Economy and Competiveness key code number: EDU2010-21395-C03, entitled *Audiovisual communication competence in a digital environment. Diagnosis of needs in three social environments.*

Note

1. The computer tool was developed in Python and Bash, in a Linux-based environment.

References

Aguaded Gómez, J. I., Férres Prats, J., Diáz, M. del R. C., Rodríguez, M. A. P., Carrero, J. S., & Delgado, L. A. (2011). *El grado de competencia mediática en la ciudadanía andaluza*. Grupo Comunicar y Universidad de Huelva: Huelva.

Braidot, N. P. (2005). *Neuromarketing. Neuroeconomía y Negocios*. Madrid: Puerto Norte-Sur.

Damasio, A. R. (1996). *El error de Descartes. La emoción, la razón y el cerebro humano* (Col. Drakontos). Barcelona: Grijalbo Mondadori, S. A.

Ferrés Prats, J. (2014). *Las pantallas y el cerebro emocional*. Gedisa: Barcelona.

Ferrés Prats, J., Masanet Jordá, M.J., & Marta-Lazo, C. (2013). Neurociencia y educación mediática: carencias en el caso español. *Historia y Comunicación Social, 18*, 129-144.

Ferrés Prats, J., & Piscitelli, A. (2012). La competencia mediática: propuesta articulada de dimensiones e indicadores. *Comunicar, 38*, 75-82. doi:10.3916/C38-2012-02-08

Ferrés Prats, J., Aguaded Gómez, J. I., & García, A. (2012). La competencia mediática de la ciudadanía española: dificultades y retos. *Icono ,14,* 10(3), 23-42. doi: 10.7195/ri14.v10i3.201

Ferrés Prats, J., García Matilla, A., Aguaded Gómez, J. I., Cavia, J. F., Figueiras, M., & Blanes, M. (2011). *Competencia mediática. Investigación sobre el grado de competencia de la ciudadanía en España*. Ministerio de Educación (Instituto de Tecnología Educativa), Consell de l'Audiovisual de Catalunya y Grupo Comunicar: España.

Ferrés Prats, J., & Santibáñez, J. (2011). *Informe de investigación Competencia mediática. Investigación sobre el grado de competencia de la ciudadanía en la Comunidad Autónoma de La Rioja.* Grupo Comunicar y Universidad de La Rioja: Huelva.

Ferrés Prats, J. (2006). La competencia en comunicación audiovisual: Propuesta articulada de dimensiones e indicadores. *Quaderns del CAC, 25*, 9-17.

Heath, C. H., & Heath, D. (2008). *Pegar y pegar*. LID Editorial Empresarial: Madrid.

Ledoux, J. (1999) *El cerebro emocional* (Col. Documento). Barcelona: Editorial Ariel y Editorial Planeta.

Lehrer, J. (2009). *How We Decide*. Mariner Books: Boston.

Lehrer, J. (2010). *Proust y la neurociencia*. Ediciones Paidós Ibérica: Barcelona

Marta, C., & Grandío, M. (2013). Análisis de la competencia audiovisual de la ciudadanía española en la dimensión de recepción y audiencia. *Communication & Society, 26*(2), 114-130.

Masanet Jordá, M. J., Contretas, P., & Ferrés Prats, J. (2013). Highly qualified students? Research into the media competence level of Spanish youth. *Communication & Society, 26*(4), 217-234.

Masanet Jordá, M. J., & Ferrés Prats, J. (2013). La enseñanza universitaria española en materia de educación mediática. *Communication papers –Media Literacy & Gender Studies*, II (2), 83-90.

Maturana, H., & Bloch, S. (1998). *Biología del Emocionar y Alba Emoting. Respiración y emoción* (2nd). Dolmen Ediciones: Santiago de Chile.

Prelec, D., & Simester, D. (2001). Always Leave Home Without It. *Marketing Letters, 12*, 5-12.

Roberts, K. (2005). *Lovemarks. El futuro más allá de las marcas*. Ediciones Urano: Barcelona.

Acknowledgement

The I+D Project, funded by the Spanish Ministry of Economy and Competitiveness. Ref.: EDU2010-21395-C03-02. Title: *La competencia en comunicación audiovisual en un entorno digital. Diagnóstico de necesidades en tres ámbitos sociales.*

Methods for the Use of Radio in Pre-schools and Primary Schools as an Inroad Towards Media Literacy[1]

Irene Melgarejo-Moreno & María M Rodríguez-Rosell

Radio and its didactic capabilities

In the multiscreen society the pedagogic role of radio seems to have been forgotten, and the listening culture is being relegated to the background by the visual culture. If we cater to this lack, then the integration of radio in the classroom or school presents itself as an ideal agent for the development of participative, collaborative and cooperative methods with which we can foster the true value of the oral and radio language from earliest childhood. We have to be especially aware that the hearing process is never passive, because "the listener always adopts an active role from the moment they have to deduce, from an exclusively aural source, the conceptual meaning and the iconic characteristics that will allow the understanding of the global sense of the stimulus" (Rodero, 2008, p. 103-104). Thus, the true potential of radio lies in the power of imagination it can awaken in the human mind.

Radio is presented as a conductive media that can be used to awaken a child's critical spirit so that s/he starts to perceive the reality surrounding him/her; we should not forget that radio is a powerful method of communication that informs us, which could be another incentive for understanding its use in the education processes of the children. As such, the possibilities and repercussions of sound in the classroom are varied, and for this, teaching staff should know and keep in mind the different degrees of interpretation of sound, as Rafael Quintana (2001) affirms: "on the edge of the universal value of pre-determined sounds, most of them can stem different attitudes, according to the particular situation s/he finds her/himself" (p. 98). Listening to different radio genres (informative, fiction, opinion, etc., as well as the creation of different programmes in the classroom, will help in training the student in auditory skills and in the uses of oral and written language, and it will arouse his/her expressive, creative, imaginative and critical capacities, as well as allowing for experimentation with the possibilities for teamwork that radio awakens through the different roles involved in radio production, direction and creation. If we examine the school curriculum, we find that from the earliest educational stages, specifically pre-school, learning through communication media is used expressly:

> Audio-visual language and information and communication technologies in a child's life require educational treatment that, through its appropriate and significative use, start the children in the comprehension of audio-visual messages and its balanced and creative use (ORDEN ECI/3960/2007, p. 1027).

In this way, and if the curricula were catered to in a credible way, it would not be strange to start integrating the radio medium – not only in the pre-school classroom but at all educational levels, as this medium presents multiple applications for stimulating the mind, the ear and the child's language.

Applications of radio in the pre-school classroom

In pre-school the use and application of radio is difficult, due to the essential characteristics (cognitive and developmental) the children have at this stage; it is not an impossible task, but the implementation of directed recording must be placed upon the teaching staff so that the application of radio is effective for the child's development. Due to this, support for the teaching staff in using radio at this learning stage will be more of a necessity, as the use of radio in the classroom will have different aspects and will cater more to the use of sound as an element used to bring the world closer to the students, than to the radio medium itself. As such, the activities could be diverse:

1. Listening to fairy tales, fables and stories: stimulates their imagination, shows them a fantasy-filled world and instils values, norms and behaviours through the story morals. But listening alone is not instructive in itself; a period of reflection or a forum where simple questions are asked should be planned afterwards, helping the children retain in their memory the essential parts of the story they have just heard, so that what was learned and comprehended by each child is commonly known as well.

2. Designing tales: a child's imagination is infinite, and one of the activities we can plan in the classroom is the creation of tales and stories along with the children. With their help we can create characters, unheard-of places, and incredible events. This will awaken their imagination and allow them to share the moments of creation with their classmates in a storytelling session afterwards, where the students can add sound effects to identify the events they just imagined.

3. Recording tales, fables and stories: allows the improvement of oral expression, and broadens their vocabulary. We have to keep in mind that this stage, as the children start school not knowing how to read, is where they take their first steps in the reading processes. The fact that they cannot read is not an impediment to their recitation of stories that, in most cases, will emerge from their imagination or will be told "in their own way" from those already-known stories, with their spontaneity greatly enriching this activity. In this way, we can add music and sound effects to the stories, so they can learn the value of silence when telling a story.

4. Identifying sounds: sound effects can have many functions in the classroom. Different games and contests can be thought up with the children to identify sounds with real elements (animals, instruments, vehicles, machinery, sounds of nature, sounds of the city, etc.). This could result in the improvement of listening, and put a "face" on the sounds they hear.

5. Music as mood: the great influence of music not only for creating moods but also for describing surroundings and situations is well known. Therefore, another exercise that could be performed in the classroom is using music as a relaxing element, or as an element that can be used to evoke places in the children's minds; this could allow them to learn to identify places through music. An ideal place for the enjoyment of music could be the carpet in the corner, where they routinely assemble for educational purposes.

6. Songs and other languages: the use of foreign languages is important, and an increasing number of schools have begun to adopt a bilingual curriculum. For this, using songs, listening to stories, and identifying words in another language besides increasing their listening skills – will contribute to improving their pronunciation and ability to work in phonetic and writing aspects.

The ideal situation would be that all these activities would be adapted to the content to be worked on in the classroom, basing them on the pre-school curriculum. The objective of the use of sound in the classroom with pre-school children would be justified, as we have seen, as with the activities that we have planned we are able not only to reinforce aural and oral aspects, but also to encourage the acquisition of knowledge and teamwork through the use of radio as pedagogic content.

Application of radio in primary education

The possibilities the radio medium presents us with in primary school are greater than those in pre-school. Here we can include the radio medium as it is, not only at the classroom level, but at the education centre level, when we believe the children's capacities and development are greater. In this sense, from the ages of 7 to 12, we find a "phase of influential cognitive evolution that is apt for the final appearance of filmic intelligence" that can be characterized by the conscious and reflexive imitation of models found especially in the audio-visual field (Andrés Tripero, 2006). During the primary school stage a logical memory, and a visual, aural or kinaesthetic memory manifests in a more meaningful manner; therefore, "the school-aged child…possesses intellectual and cognitive functions that make him/her especially apt in articulating his/her audio-visual learning experiences within an intelligent, structured system of perceptions, concepts and experiences: cognitive, affective and of learning" (Andrés Tripero, 2006). With the use of radio in primary education, the importance of community work in radio programme production, the dialogue, the debate and information will be encouraged, the most important aspect being the awakening and encouraging of the creative capacity. In this way, radio presents itself as a fortuitous medium, as the content and competencies the curriculum treats at this stage are ideal for its application. Throughout primary school, "the use of radio will serve as an attempt to make students able to acquire determined knowledge on the basis of their personal development and well-being through the acquisition of different social, work and study habits related to cultural, artistic, creative, affective and expression, reading, writing and calculation abilities" (Melgarejo & Rodríguez, 2011). In this sense, we present a series of activities at the classroom level as well as the centre level:

1. In the radio medium: In primary school, we can start to introduce those aspects that are purely radio and technical language, the aim being that the students start recognizing the peculiarities of the medium and start becoming accustomed to its use. For this, it will be necessary for teaching staff to have prior knowledge of the material used (language, radio techniques and scripts), the latter being essential so that they are able to create their own works.

2. Creating, producing and directing the podcast: radio is so versatile that any subject can form part of a radio programme; it would be ideal if the topics could be associated with the courses currently being taught at this educational stage. This activity can be used to allow students work as a team; the importance and fundamental characteristics of this method of communication will be taught as their imagination is encouraged, among other aspects. Also, it allows us to work with them on a pre-determined subject, to conduct research on it to produce the radio show. Its documentation could be used to reinforce the theory presented in class; or, alternatively, the students themselves could generate subjects that interest them.

3. Types of programmes: active listening presents itself as ideal for these ages, as the variety of radio programmes allows us to work on the critical reading of messages, allowing dialogue with the younger ones. We could simply start

differentiating the information with pure opinion or entertainment pieces, to be able to then generate debate and dialogue through listening to pre-determined radio spaces (cultural, sport, informative, educational, musical, etc.).

4. Recording fairy tales, fables and stories: the subject of language and literature in school is ideal for the development of this activity; besides creating a reading habit, diction can be improved, and it allows the children to become the characters in the stories they themselves adapt or create. With this activity we can also work on intonation, and on how to transmit emotions through the spoken word, music, special effects and silence.

5. The school radio station: the creation of a radio station can become a useful service for informing on the novelties that arise in the school setting, as well as allowing the students participants in the academic day-to-day. It is not necessary to broadcast through electromagnetic waves, as every school has an internal public address system that could be used to create a small radio station with primary school children, as well as to broadcast the radio productions created in class. The time of day reserved for recess is the ideal time for broadcasting these works, which could be included in a radio programme conducted and directed by the children regularly, governed by a pre-determined block of time just like in professional radio.

6. Collaborations in radio: local broadcasters are usually the most accessible and closest; schools could collaborate with them in creating a radio space where the children could be the authentic protagonists. Genres such as the interview, debate or reportage are the most adequate for students to work in through professional radio. The simple act of being broadcasted is very motivating for children, and this becomes a gratifying experience as they experience first-hand the rhythm and social function of local radio.

Other types of initiatives exist, arising from more professional settings such as universities, which are looking for collaboration in school settings. This is the case of the initiative being carried out by the Research Group 'Communications and Minors' at the UCAM (Catholic University San Antonio of Murcia), offering communication media workshops for minors and teaching staff. For example, "Radio, a practical workshop" stands out, having materialized as the "Radiofonica83" podcast (http://blip.tv/radiofonica83), allowing the children to discover all the peculiarities of the radio medium and showing them how to produce small, community-created works.

Note

1. The following chapter is an extract from the "La radio como recurso didáctico en el aula de infantil y primaria: los *podcast* y su naturaleza educativa" (2013) article, published by both authors in Scientific Journal *Tendencias Pedagógicas* Nº 21, 29-46.

References

Boletín Oficial del Estado, ORDEN ECI/3960/2007, de 19th December. Ministerio de Educación y Ciencia. Currículum de Educación Infantil. BOE, saturday 5th January 2008.

Ándres Tripero, T. de (2006). *El desarrollo de la inteligencia fílmica. La comprensión audiovisual y su evolución en la infancia y adolescencia*. Madrid: CNICE. http://ares.cnice.mec.es/informes/15/documentos/34.htm

Melgarejo, I., & Rodríguez, M.M. (2013). La radio como recurso didáctico en el aula de infantil y primaria: los *podcast* y su naturaleza educativa. *Tendencias Pedagógicas, 21*, 29-46.

Melgarejo, I., & Rodríguez, M.M. (2011). Educación Mediática y Competencia Digital: la segmentación de edades y el currículum escolar en los canales infantiles politemáticos de televisión. In R. Aparici, A. G. Matilla & A. Gutiérrez (Coords.), *Educación Mediática & Competencia Digital. La cultura de la participación*. Segovia: E.U de Magisterio de Segovia (UVA).

Quintana, R. (2011). El lenguaje de la radio y sus posibilidades educativas. *Comunicar, 17*, 97-101.

Rodero, E. (2008). Educar a través de la radio. *Signo y pensamiento, 52*(27), 97-109.